INTRODUCTION TO CLASSICAL NAHUATL
WORKBOOK

 Introduction to

Classical Nahuatl

WORKBOOK

by J. Richard Andrews

UNIVERSITY OF TEXAS PRESS, AUSTIN & LONDON

The publication of this book was assisted by a grant from the Andrew W. Mellon Foundation.

Library of Congress Cataloging in Publication Data

Andrews, James Richard, 1924–
    Introduction to classical Nahuatl.

    Bibliography: v. 1, p.
    Includes index.
    1. Aztec language–Grammar.   I. Title.
PM4063.A66   1975   497'.4   74-30370

Complete Set: International Standard Book Number 0-292-73802-1
Workbook: International Standard Book Number 0-292-73805-6

CONTENTS

Part Four. Modification. Complementation. Conjunction

Supplementary Readings

Key to the Exercises and Supplementary Readings

PREFACE

This support volume for the *Introduction to Classical Nahuatl* consists of an exercise section and a key. Remarks concerning the key will preface that section; so here comment is limited to the exercises.

The exercise section consists of two parts; the first offers the main body of exercise material, and the second, much shorter, presents ten selections for supplementary reading.

The main body of exercises follows the forty-eight lessons of the *Introduction* and presents to the student materials with which he can become proficient in the principles and structures presented there. For the most part, this exercise material consists of unconnected sentences so that the patterns of the language can be thrown into clear focus. This presentation, which is frowned on by many modern writers of grammars, seeks to get the student to attend to the grammatical (morphological or syntactical) point at issue without the distracting "help" of a context. It is precisely the reliance on this kind of "help" and a concomitant disregard for grammatical principles and facts that have generated so much questionable translation of Nahuatl material. Translation must be made from grammatical strength, not from weakness that guesses its way along with the help of contextual highpoints.

Another aspect of this presentation that goes against the current of much modern grammar-writing theory is that the exercises are almost entirely of a "recognition" type—addressed, that is, toward analysis of items and translation from Nahuatl to English. Only on rare occasions (as, for example, in Exercise 11D) is a "production" type of effort required. The decision to contradict modern theory was not made lightly but came in answer to a careful consideration of the purposes and peculiar nature of the language-learning problem faced in this particular instance, as is explained in the preface to the main text.

Returning to the organization of the exercises, connected material is not introduced until Exercise 42E. With only one exception (Exercise 46D), this material is a reworking (respelling, repunctuation) of selections taken from the A. J. O. Anderson and C. E. Dibble edition of Bernardino de Sahagún's

Florentine Codex: General History of the Things of New Spain (Santa Fe: The School of American Research and the University of Utah, 1950–1969).

The supplementary readings that make up the second part of the exercise section were also taken, with the exception of the first selection, from the same source. It is not intended that this supplementary reading material be covered in class. It is meant as a bridge between the earlier grammatically centered exercises and later reading. After having worked through this material and after having studied Appendix F of the main text (Spelling Conventions in Older Texts), the student should become acquainted with the textual problem posed by older spelling by comparing these versions with the Anderson and Dibble sources (see references given in the key). He should then be in a position to proceed with further reading of the *Florentine Codex.*

It is hoped that the student will not find the reading of the connected material (nineteen short passages beginning with Exercise 42E and ten longer passages in the supplementary readings) too difficult, since these passages have served as the source for the vocabulary items and many of the sentences used in the earlier exercises. So one will have read most of this material before—most, but not all, however, since an effort was made to limit vocabulary items to around twenty per exercise set; consequently, not all the words used in the connected passages are found in the earlier material. Incidentally, with regard to the twenty-odd new items per exercise set, it should be noted that on occasion considerably more than that number will be found, but this extravagance was considered legitimate in that in these instances derivational items exploiting the derivational principles of the text are being used.

The exercises have been designed to facilitate the acquisition of a comprehension competence of Nahuatl. For them to accomplish this purpose, they must be approached with the right attitude. They should not be treated as one would treat a crossword puzzle. They are not to be "solved" and then set aside. Internalizing a language depends on activating a knowledge of grammatical principles through the formation of habitual responses to forms and constructions structured by those principles. A one-time performance of an exercise item will obviously not accomplish this—such hit-and-run tactics, in fact, accomplish very little. One must drill oneself, do the same exercise over and over, practice with the persistence with which one practices a football play or a musical composition—preferably with spaced training periods. Do not, therefore, write English glosses over the Nahuatl words. Leave the item as something to challenge your analytical and recognitive abilities again and again until you acquire ease and skill in performance.

While on the subject of attitude, it might be well to mention two other points. One concerns the willingness to exert effort. Part of the frustration in language learning arises from the desire to possess the language immediately without taking the time and energy that drilling and review require. One must accept the fact that a patient, unhurried, persistent effort is the way to accomplishment.

The other point concerning attitude involves open-mindedness. A foreign language is foreign. One must be willing to allow it to be so. Try, therefore, to be on guard against being annoyed with Nahuatl ways of doing things. Do not rebel, for example, at having to accept the existence of sentence-words or at having to recognize the important difference between a stem and a word. Each language is a valid symbol system—valid simply because its existence depends on success—that is, on whether or not it actually works in the symbolic organization of human living. As you become more and more involved in Nahuatl you will, I believe, realize that it goes beyond mere validity, mere effectiveness, and is a truly magnificent human accomplishment.

J. R. A.

ABBREVIATIONS AND SYMBOLS USED

abs: absolutive
admon: admonitive
fut: future
H: honorific
lit: literally
nonspec: nonspecific
obj: object
opt: optative
P: pejorative
pl: plural
poss: possessor
pred: predicate
pres: present
pret: preterit
R: reverential
reflex: reflexive
sg: singular
s.o.: someone
s.th.: something
subj: subject
suppl: supplementary
1st: first person
2nd: second person
3rd: third person
~ or
> changes to; is represented as
< derives from
∅ zero element (silently present element)
* a reconstructed, hypothetical, or unattested form
/ / phonemic representation of sounds
[ ] phonetic representation of sounds
( ) major stem boundaries
 - other boundaries

PART ONE

Basic Verb Words

EXERCISE 1. Pronunciation

1A. *The Correlation of Sound Symbols and Spelling Symbols.* Pronounce
and spell the following words.

1. /weːi/	8. /teːmaːkiːštiaːni/	15. /kiyawiλ/
2. /ahko/	9. /aːškaːiλ/	16. /miːmikkeh/
3. /kiːsa/	10. /kʷeλaːčλi/	17. /šikmoːλa/
4. /kʷeːiλ/	11. /nekʷλi/	18. /teːkʷλi/
5. /ahwiːk/	12. /nosiwaːw/	19. /keːškič/
6. /¢ah¢i/	13. /kikʷaːs/	20. /nehwaːλ/
7. /kʷaːwtemok¢in/	14. /oːničoːkak/	21. /toːkwah/

1B. *The Importance of Vowel Length.* Pronounce. (Do not confuse *length*
and *stress.*)

1. quipatla = he changes it   quipātla = he dissolves it
2. momatia = he was pondering   momātia = it puts out branches
3. nocuauh = it is my tree   nocuāuh = it is my eagle
4. quitlatia = he burns it   quitlātia = he hides it
5. chichi = it is a dog   chīchi = it suckles
6. quipiloa = he hangs it up   quipīloa = he makes it thinner
7. piltic = it is noble   pīltic = it is thin
8. teco = it is cut   tēco = it is laid down
9. notex = it is my flour   notēx = he is my brother-in-law
10. motema = he takes a steam   motēma = it is put into a con-
    bath   tainer
11. quipoloa = he loses it   quipōloa = he kneads it (clay, etc.)
12. quiyecoa = he tastes it   quiyēcoa = he finishes it

1C. *The Variant Sounds ([o] and [u]) Represented by the Letter o.* Pronounce.

1. ōmpa	9. xōpantli	17. āmoxtli
2. nōchtli	10. cōztic	18. huīlōtl
3. tozcatl	11. quitzopa	19. cotztli
4. ōquitzauc	12. yōli	20. mochi
5. tōtolin	13. quitoca	21 tepoztli
6. conētl	14. tozan	22. tzopqui
7. quiyecoa	15. xocotl	23. coyōtl
8. quihtzoma	16. tlaōcoya	24. ītepotzco

1D. *Sound Changes Resulting from the Juxtaposition of Certain Consonants.*
Join the indicated items, making any necessary changes in spelling. Pronounce the result.

Example: am- + -ceah = azceah /asseah/

1. am- + -cihuah
2. teuh- + -yoh
3. am- + -huih
4. tlāl- + -tli
5. ītech + -tzinco
6. am- + -tzīnquīzah
7. mitz- + -chōctia
8. quim- + -xiccāhua
9. am- + -yezqueh

10. tēuc- + -yōtl
11. quim- + -zāzaca
12. oh- + -pitzactli
13. xāl- + -yoh
14. tepoz- + -chicōlli
15. nimitz- + -tzonhuilāna
16. tepoz- + -xomahtli
17. petlān- + -qui
18. am- + -tlaczah

EXERCISE 2. Intransitive Verb Forms: Imperfective Stem

2A. *Number Differences in Verb Forms Built on the Imperfective Stem.*
Separate the constituent parts, identify them, and translate the word. Be
sure to take zero elements into account.

Example: oncholōz; oncholōzqueh
$\emptyset$-on(cholō)z-$\emptyset$ = 3rd-thither(flee)fut-sg = he will flee thither
$\emptyset$-on(cholō)z-queh = 3rd-thither(flee)fut-pl = they will flee
thither

1.	nontemo, tontemoh	10.	anhuālcholoah, tihuālcholoa
2.	amāhuiazqueh, tāhuiaz	11.	tixhuiz, amixhuizqueh
3.	huetzca, huetzcah	12.	cēhuia, cēhuiah
4.	nixhui, tixhuih	13.	nitomāhuaz, titomāhuazqueh
5.	timiquizqueh, nimiquiz	14.	nemih, nemi
6.	nāhuiani, tāhuianih	15.	nihuālquīzaya, tihuālquīzayah
7.	nāltiāni, tāltiānih	16.	anchōcanih, tichōcani
8.	amāltiāyah, tāltiāya	17.	huāltemoz, huāltemozqueh
9.	ōtihuetzcaya, ōanhuetzcayah	18.	tixōtla, axxōtlah

2B. *The Cooperation of Person-Number Affixes with the Future Theme.*
Combine the indicated person-number affixes with the following future
themes: *-(āhuia)z-; -(āltī)z-; -(yā)z-; -(chicāhua)z-*. Translate the resulting
verb words.

1.	ni- . . . -$\emptyset$	3.	ti- . . . -queh	5.	$\emptyset$- . . . -queh
2.	ti- . . . -$\emptyset$	4.	am- . . . -queh	6.	$\emptyset$- . . . -$\emptyset$

2C. *The Cooperation of Person-Number Affixes with the Present and Customary Present Themes.* Combine the indicated person-number affixes
with the following present and customary present themes: *-(temo)$\emptyset$-;
-(quīza)$\emptyset$-; -(choloa)$\emptyset$-; -(temo)ni-; -(quīza)ni-; -(āltiā)ni-; -(yā)ni-*. Translate the resulting verb words.

1.	$\emptyset$- . . . -$\emptyset$	3.	ti- . . . -h	5.	ni- . . . -$\emptyset$
2.	$\emptyset$- . . . -h	4.	ti- . . . -$\emptyset$	6.	am- . . . -h

2D. *Competence with Person-Number Signals Associated with Future
Themes.* Convert the following future themes into future-tense verb
words by affixing the person-number information contained in the English pronouns. Translate the results.

1.	-(cēhui)z- [he; you (pl)]	4.	-(temo)z- [he; we]
2.	-(huetzca)z- [you; we]	5.	-(cholō)z- [they; I]
3.	-(yā)z- [I; they]	6.	-(ixhui)z- [you (pl); you]

2E. *Competence with Person-Number Signals Associated with Imperfect Themes.* Convert the following imperfect themes into imperfect-tense verb words by affixing the person-number information contained in the English pronouns. Translate the results.

1. -(āhuia)ya- [I; they]
2. -(āltiā)ya- [you (pl); she]
3. -(miqui)a- [he; they]
4. -(temo)ya- [I; you (pl)]
5. -(choloā)ya- [they; I]
6. -(xōtla)ya- [we; you]

2F. *Automatic Response to Tense Difference in Indicative Verb Forms Built on the Imperfective Stem.* Pronounce and translate.

1. tāhuiaya, tāhuiani, tāhuiaz
2. tāltiāya, tāltiāni, tāltīz
3. miquia, miquini, miquiz
4. ancholoāyah, ancholoānih, ancholōzqueh
5. xōtlayah, xōtlanih, xōtlazqueh
6. tichōcayah, tichōcanih, tichōcazqueh
7. tihuetzcaya, tihuetzcani, tihuetzcaz
8. nitemoya, nitemoni, nitemoz
9. anquīzayah, anquīzanih, anquīzazqueh
10. ninemia, ninemini, ninemiz

2G. *Automatic Response to the Various Affixes in Indicative Verb Forms Built on the Imperfective Stem.* Pronounce and translate.

1. miquiah, ammiquinih, timiquizqueh
2. tāltiāyah, amāltiānih, āltīzqueh
3. āhuiayah, amāhuianih, tāhuiazqueh
4. ticholoāya, nicholoāni, cholōz
5. titemoyah, antemonih, temozqueh
6. nixōtlaya, xōtlani, tixōtlaz

2H. *Competence with Person-Number Signals.* Translate and then change to the singular form.

1. anchōcah
2. tihuetzcazqueh
3. amontemoyah
4. ixhuizqueh
5. timiquiah
6. anhuāltemozqueh
7. ōonquīzayah
8. tāhuiah

2I. *The Significance of Direction Prefixes.* Translate and then insert first one and then the other direction prefix in the following. Translate the results.

1. ōticholoāya
2. temoni
3. anquīzazqueh
4. ōtiquīzayah
5. cholōz
6. nitemoz

EXERCISE 3. Intransitive Verb Forms: Perfective Stem

3A. *Number Differences in Verb Forms Built on the Perfective Stem.* Separate the constituent parts, identify them, and translate the word.

Example: tonquīzqueh; nonquīz
t-on(quīz)∅-queh = 1st-thither(exit)pret-pl = we went out
n-on(quīz)∅-∅ = 1st-thither(exit)pret-sg = I went out

1. ōnontemoc, ōtontemoqueh
2. ōamāhuixcah, ōtāhuixca
3. ōchōcaqueh, ōchōcac
4. toncholoh, amoncholohqueh
5. ōtihuetzcaqueh, ōnihuetzcac
6. ōixhuica, ōixhuicah
7. ōtihuālquīzqueh, ōnihuālquīz
8. ōmiccah, ōmicca
9. ōnāhuix, ōtāhuixqueh
10. ōamixhuiqueh, ōtixhuic
11. nēz, nēzqueh
12. ōnencah, ōnenca
13. nāltih, tāltihqueh
14. ōazcēuhqueh, ōticēuh
15. ōhuetzcah, ōhuetzca
16. yōl, yōlqueh

3B. *The Cooperation of Person-Number Affixes with the Preterit Theme.* Combine the indicated person-number affixes with the following preterit themes: -(cez)∅-; -(chōca)∅-; -(āltih)∅-; -(yah)∅-. Translate the results.

1. am- . . . -queh
2. ni- . . . -c ~ -∅
3. ti- . . . -queh
4. ti- . . . -c ~ -∅
5. ∅- . . . -c ~ -∅
6. ∅- . . . -queh

3C. *The Cooperation of Person-Number Affixes with the Pluperfect Theme.* Combine the indicated person-number affixes with the following pluperfect themes: -(huetzca)ca-; -(huetz)ca-; -(āltih)ca-; -(yah)ca-. Translate the results.

1. ti- . . . -h
2. ∅- . . . -h
3. ni- . . . -∅
4. ∅ - . . . -∅
5. am- . . . -h
6. ti- . . . -∅

3D. *Competence with Person-Number Signals Associated with Preterit Themes.* Convert the following preterit themes into preterit verb words by affixing the person-number information contained in the English pronouns. Translate the results.

1. -(temo)∅- [I, they]
2. -(choloh)∅- [they; you]
3. -(ixhui)∅- [I; we]
4. -(āhuix)∅- [we; you]
5. -(āltih)∅- [we; you]
6. -(tlācat)∅- [I; you (pl)]
7. -(tlatziuh)∅- [we; he]
8. -(cez)∅- [you (pl); I]

3E. *Competence with Person-Number Signals Associated with Pluperfect Themes.* Convert the following pluperfect themes into pluperfect-tense

verb words by affixing the person-number information contained in the
English pronouns. Translate the results.

1. -(huetz)ca- [you (pl); she]
2. -(tōloh)ca- [I; they]
3. -(chōca)ca- [they; he]
4. -(mic)ca- [we; she]
5. -(cēuh)ca- [I; you (pl)]
6. -(huetzca)ca- [we; you]
7. -(pāc)ca- [she; I]
8. -(xōtla)ca- [you (pl); he]

3F. *Tense Themes Built on Perfective and Imperfective Stems.* Pronounce.
Identify the tense theme (recognizing the presence of a zero tense suffix
when necessary). Translate.

1. ōticezca, ōticez, ticea, ticeaz
2. ōnēzca, ōnēz, nēci, nēciz
3. ōnipācca, ōnipāc, nipāqui, nipāquiz
4. ōtlācatca, ōtlācat, tlācati, tlācatiz
5. ōnencah, ōnenqueh, nemih, nemizqueh
6. ōampachiuhcah, ōampachiuhqueh, ampachihuih, ampachihuizqueh
7. ōchicāhuacah, ōchicāhuaqueh, chicāhuah, chicāhuazqueh
8. ōyōlca, ōyōl, yōli, yōliz
9. ōamixhuicah, ōamixhuiqueh, amixhuih, amixhuizqueh
10. ōcochcah, ōcochqueh, cochih, cochizqueh
11. ōnāltihca, ōnāltih, nāltia, nāltīz
12. ōnāhuixca, ōnāhuix, nāhuia, nāhuiaz
13. ōticholohcah, ōticholohqueh, ticholoah, ticholōzqueh
14. ōtitemocah, ōtitemoqueh, titemoh, titemozqueh
15. ōtepēuhca, ōtepēuh, tepēhui, tepēhuiz

3G. *Competence with Person-Number Signals.* Translate. Change to plural
forms and translate.

1. ōnāltih
2. ōticezca
3. ōcoch
4. ōnīlōtca
5. ōnichōcac
6. ōtitlaōcox

3H. *Competence with Preterit-, Present-, and Future-Tense Forms in the Various Person-Number Combinations.* Pronounce and translate.

1. ōcezqueh, ticeah, azceazqueh
2. ōtīlōtqueh, amīlōtih, īlōtizqueh
3. ōnitemoc, titemo, temoz
4. ōtinen, nemi, ninemiz
5. ōticholoh, nicholoa, cholōz
6. ōtipachiuhqueh, ampachihuih, pachihuizqueh
7. tāltih, nāltia, āltīz
8. ōtlaōcoxqueh, antlaōcoyah, titlaōcoyazqueh

EXERCISE 4. The Intransitive Sentence

4A. *Review of the Indicative Tense Formations.* Pronounce and translate.
1. naquia, naquini, naquiz
2. ōcocōx, cocōya, cocōyaz
3. ōticuīcac, ticuīca, ticuīcaz
4. melāhuaya, melāhuani, melāhuaz
5. ōtlehcoqueh, tlehcoh, tlehcozqueh
6. ammahuiah, ammahuinih, ammahuizqueh
7. ōticualānqueh, ticualānih, ticualānizqueh
8. ōnihcihuia, nihcihuini, nihcihuiz
9. ōtipanoqueh, tipanoh, tipanozqueh
10. ōtitzahtzic, titzahtzi, titzahtziz

4B. *The Nuclear Functions of Intransitive Sentences.* Identify the subject and the predicate of each of the following sentences. Translate.

Examples: Nicochiz. *Subj:* ni- . . . -∅; *pred:* -(cochi)z-; I shall sleep.
Ōtihuāltlehcoc. *Subj:* ti- . . . -c; *pred:* ō- . . . -huāl(tlehco)∅-;
You came up.

1. Amāltīzqueh.
2. Cochia.
3. Pāquih.
4. Tihuālcholōz.
5. Ōmicca.
6. Axxōtlanih.
7. Ōnihuetzca.
8. Tīlōtqueh.
9. Anyōlcah.
10. Melāhua.
11. Nicea.
12. Ōhuālacqueh.

4C. *The Negative Transformation.* Translate the following sentences and then transform them into their negative counterparts (two versions). Translate the results.

Example: Nihcihuiz. = I shall hurry.
Ahnihcihuiz. = I shall not hurry.
Ahmō nihcihuiz. = I shall not hurry.

1. Ōnicualān.
2. Cuīcaz.
3. Cuix tonpanozqueh?
4. Timahuia?
5. Ōpoliuh.
6. Cuix ōticocōx?

4D. *The Emphatic-Assertion Transformation.* Translate the following assertions and then transform them into their emphatic counterparts. Translate the results.

Example: Ōchihchac. = He spat.
Ca ōchihchac. = He did spit. He indeed spat.

1. Ōompēuh.
2. Ahtontlehcozqueh.
3. Ahmō huālacqueh.
4. Nihcihuiz.
5. Ahonaqui.
6. Titzahtzic.

4E. *The Yes/No-Question Transformation.* Translate the following sentences
     and then transform them into *yes/no* questions (two versions). Translate
     the results.

    Example: Ōcualān. = He became angry.
                Ōcualān? = Did he become angry?
                Cuix ōcualān? = Did he become angry?

1. Ōamacqueh.	3. Ōnitzahtzic.	5. Timahuini.
2. Ahihcihuih.	4. Ahmō ticocōyaya.	6. Ahōontlehcoc.

4F. *The Relationship between Questions and Answers.* Pronounce and trans-
     late.

    1. Cuix ōticocox? —Ahmō, ahnicocōx.
    2. Cualāniz? —Quēmahca, cualāniz.
    3. Cuix timahui? —Quēmah, nimahui.
    4. Cuix ampēhuazqueh? —Ahmō, ahtipēhuazqueh.
    5. Ōpanoc? —Ahmō, ahmō ōpanoc.
    6. Cuix ticea? —Ca quēmahca, ca nicea.

4G. *Review of Certain Single-Base Transformations.* Pronounce and trans-
     late.

1. Cuix amonaquizqueh?	9. Cuix quīzazqueh?
2. Ahōancocōxqueh?	10. Ahōtipanoqueh.
3. Ca nicualāni.	11. Cuīca?
4. Quēmah, ca ōmauh.	12. Ca ticualānia.
5. Ca ahōpanoc.	13. Quēmahca, ōnitzahtzic.
6. Ahmō ancuīcayah?	14. Cuix tlehcozqueh?
7. Ahmō, ahōtontlehcocah.	15. Ahmō nixōtla.
8. Ōtzahtzic?	16. Cuix onaquiz?

EXERCISE 5. Adverbs and Adverbials

5A. *Free and Bound Adverbial Modifiers.* Identify the subject and predicate of each of the following sentences. Translate.

> *Example:* Nichipāhuacānemi. *Subj:* ni- ...-∅; *pred:* -(chipāhuacā-nemi)∅-;
> I live chastely.
> Chipāhuacā ninemi. *Subj:* ni- ....-∅; *pred:* chipāhuacā -(nemi)∅-;
> I live chastely.

1. Mauhcā tiquīzayah. Timauhcāquīzayah.
2. Anhuelcochizqueh? Huel ancochizqueh?
3. Cualāncā ōtzahtzic. Ōcualāncātzahtzic.
4. Nahcopaihcihuiz. Ahcopa nihcihuiz.
5. Nōncuah nemi? Nōncuahnemi?

5B. *Notional Contrasts Expressed by Adverbial Modifiers.* Pronounce and translate.

1. Mochipa huetzca. Icah tihuetzca.
2. Ye ōpanoc. Ayamō nipano.
3. Oc ticuīcani? −Aocmō nicuīcani.
4. Cecni cochih. Nōhuiān cochih.
5. Oncān annemizqueh? −Ahmō, nicān tinemizqueh.
6. Cencah ihciuh? −Ahmō, ayāxcān ihciuh.
7. Huel tlehco. Ahhuel temoz.

5C. *The Difference between Negative Head and Negative Adverbial Modifiers.* Pronounce and translate.

1. Temo. Ahtemo. Oncān ahtemo.
2. Temo. Ohuihcā temo. Ayohuihcā temo.
3. Ticeah. Ahticeah. Oc ahticeah.
4. Ticeah. Oc ticeah. Ayocmō ticeah.
5. Ticuīca. Ahticuīca. Āxcān ahticuīca.
6. Ticuīca. Ye ticuīca. Ayamō ticuīca.

5D. *Review of the Yes/No-Question Transformation.* Translate the following assertions and then transform them into *yes/no* questions. Translate the results.

1. Cencah tipāquini.
2. Ahhuel ompēuh.
3. Ahmō ticemmahuizqueh.
4. Ōmpa anchipāhuacānemih.
5. Nō cea.
6. Ye ōpoliuh.

5E. *Further Practice with Adverbial Modifiers.* Pronounce and translate.

1. Necoc huālhuetzih.
2. Niman ōtlanihuetzqueh.
3. Huīptla pāccā cuīcaz.
4. Mochipa ōchipāhuacānencah.
5. Huel ōtontlehcoqueh.
6. Ca cualāncā ōnonquīz.
7. Cuix mōztla tonīlōtiz?
8. Aocmō huālaquizqueh.
9. Cuix īyōlic huāltemoh?
10. Quin ōnicēuh.
11. Ihciuhcā ōmic.
12. Cuix icah ōtimauh?

13. Achtopa niquīz.
14. In oncān panoz.
15. Tlahcah nēcini.
16. Tlacuāuh chōcayah.
17. Cuix oc ancocōyah?
18. Nohmah nāhuia.
19. Ahzo mōztla tlācatiz.
20. Ayāxcān ōtipachiuhqueh.
21. Ticennemiah.
22. Yēhua ōxōtlac.
23. Mōztla nāltīz.
24. In yohuac ahhuel cochi.

EXERCISE 6. Adverbial Phrases. Information Questions

6A. *Hierarchical Levels within Adverbial Phrases.* Pronounce and translate.
1. Temo. Iz temo. Zan iz temo.
2. Quīzah. Āxcān quīzah. Yeāxcān quīzah.
3. Nihciuh. Tlapīc nihciuh. Zantlapīc nihciuh.
4. Tlehcoz. Miecpa tlehcoz. Huelmiecpa tlehcoz.
5. Ōmic. Yohuac ōmic. Yālhua yohuac ōmic.
6. Titlaōcoyazqueh. Mochipa titlaōcoyazqueh. Zan mochipa titlaōco-yazqueh.
7. Huetzi. Āxcān huetzi. Huel āxcān huetzi. Quin huel āxcān ōhuetz.
8. Tipanoz. Huel tipanoz. Ahhuel tipanoz. Niman ahhuel tipanoz.

6B. *Sentences with Adverbial Phrases.* Pronounce and translate.
1. Huīptla teōtlāc miquiz.
2. Cencah mauhcā ōtihciuhqueh.
3. Cuix zan quēmman ancocōyah?
4. Ayamō cencah chicāhuacā tlehco.
5. Ahzozan huehca nemi.
6. Huel zanicah tihuetzcaya.
7. Ca cencah īyōlic pano.
8. Niman ahmō nicea.
9. Āxcān occencah huel cochi.
10. Huelāxcān āltia.
11. Zanniman ōquīzqueh.
12. Quintēpan ōoncholoh.
13. Niman ahhuel cuīcah.
14. Yecuēl ōīlōt.
15. Cuix ye ōpachiuh? —Ahzo-quēmah.
16. Occeppa nixōtla.

6C. *The Information-Question Transformation.* Translate the following *yes/no* questions and then transform them into information questions. Translate the results.

Examples: Īyōlic ōnēz? = Did it appear slowly?
Quēnin ōnēz? = How did it appear?

Cuix ōmpa nemi? = Does he live there?
Cāmpa cuix nemi? = Where does he live?

1. Cuix miecpa ōhuetzcac?
2. Oncān titlatzihuizqueh?
3. Cuix huīptla panoz?
4. Nicān ticochiz?

6D. *The Relation between Interrogative and Noninterrogative Adverbs.* Translate the following questions. Answer each with an adverb.

1. Cān cuix nemih?
2. Īquin nēciz?
3. Quēnin cuīca?
4. Quēxquich cuix tichicāhua?
5. Quēzquipa ōhuetz?
6. Īccuix ōtitlācat?

6E. *The Function of Interrogative Adverbs in Sentences.* Pronounce and
translate.

1. Cānin ōtipanoc?
2. Quēzquicān ōnēz?
3. Quēn cuix tontemozqueh?
4. Quēmman ōquīz?
5. Cān amontlehcozqueh?
6. Quēzquipa ōāltih?
7. Īccuix ticholōz?

8. Cāmpa ōhuetz?
9. Īquin tiquīzaz?
10. Cānin ōcochqueh?
11. Quēnin ōtlehcoc?
12. Quēmman cuix tāltīz?
13. Ahcān niquīza.
14. Cānin mach tinemi?

EXERCISE 7. Transitive Verb Forms. The Transitive Sentence

7A. *The Correspondence of Specific- and Nonspecific-Object Prefixes.* Analyze and translate. (Remember that the specification of "inanimate *tla-*" permits only a common-number form, while that of "animate *tla-*" permits singular and plural forms.)

1. nitlatēmoa, nictēmoa
2. titlama, ticma, tiquimma
3. tētlamaca, quitēmaca
4. tētlamaca, quitēmaca, quintēmaca
5. tētlamaca, nēchtlamaca, mitztlamaca, motlamaca, quitlamaca, tēchtlamaca, amēchtlamaca, quintlamaca
6. nitlatta, niquitta, niquimitta
7. nitlatta, niquitta
8. nitēitta, ninotta, nimitzitta, niquitta, nitēchitta, namēchitta, niquimitta
9. titlahtoa, tiquihtoa
10. tlacua, quicua
11. tlacua, quicua, quincua
12. titlachīhua, ticchīhua
13. tēchīhua, mitzchīhua

7B. *The Category of Number in Object Prefixes.* Analyze and translate.

1. niquitta, niquimitta
2. tinēchnōtza, titēchnōtza
3. ninozōma, titozōmah
4. mitzcaqui, amēchcaqui
5. ōquichix, ōquinchix
6. ōtimottac, ōammottaqueh
7. ōtinēchcac, ōtitēchcac
8. ōnimitznōtz, ōnamēchnōtz
9. mozōmāz, mozōmāzqueh
10. ticchiazqueh, tiquinchiazqueh
11. nēchihuāzqueh, tēchihuāzqueh
12. anquitlalhuīzqueh, anquintlalhuīzqueh
13. timitzittayah, tamēchittayah
14. anquicuāyah, anquincuāyah
15. nēchtlalhuiāyah, tēchtlalhuiāyah
16. mottaya, mottayah

7C. *The Category of Person in Object Prefixes.* Analyze and translate.

1. ōticchix, nimichchia, nēchchiaz
2. ōninottac, timotta, mottaz
3. ōtitēchittac, namēchitta, quimittaz
4. ōniquincac, amēchcaqui, titēchcaquiz
5. ōmozōmahqueh, titozōmah, ammozōmāzqueh
6. ōtamēchihuahqueh, tēchihuah, anquimihuāzqueh

7. ōtiquittaqueh, annēchittah, mitzittazqueh
8. ōanquicacqueh, timitzcaquih, nēchcaquizqueh

7D. *The Silently Present Object Prefix.* Analyze and translate.

1. mitznōtza, mitzmaca
2. nēchilhuia, nēchchia
3. niquihtoa, niquilhuia
4. ticcui, ticmaca

5. amēchilhuiah, amēchittah
6. quihuah, quilhuiah
7. quimacah, quimah
8. quimilhuīz, quimihuāz

7E. *The Difference between Single-Object and Double-Object Verbs.* Change the specific objects in the following words to their nonspecific counterparts. Translate.

1. tēchnōtzazqueh
2. ōnēchmacac
3. ōniquihtoāya
4. mitzilhuīz

5. ōquimittac
6. ticmacazqueh
7. ōnicchīuh
8. ōniquilhuih

7F. *The Constituent Functions of a Transitive Sentence.* Identify the functions of each sentence (subject, predicate) and the subfunctions of the predicate (predicator, direct object, indirect object, adverbial modifier). Translate.

Examples:

Toconcaquizqueh. *Subj:* to- . . . -queh (*for* ti- . . . -queh); *pred:* -c-on-(caqui)z-; *predicator:* -(caqui)z-; *direct obj:* -c-; *adverbial modifier:* -on-; We shall go and hear it.

Annēchilhuihqueh. *Subj:* an- . . . -queh; *pred:* -nēch-∅(ilhuih)∅-; *predicator:* -(ilhuih)∅-; *direct obj:* -∅-; *indirect obj:* -nēch-; You (pl) said it to me.

1. Ahquitēmōz. Ahtemoz.
2. Tamēchmacah.
3. Ōnichuālnōtzca.
4. Tiquintlalhuīz.
5. Noconihuāz.
6. Titēchia. Titēchchia.

7. Titētlalhuīzqueh.
8. Tēchihua. Tlachīhua.
9. Ōquicuic. Ōconcuic.
10. Ōtiquimonnōtz.
11. Quihuālmacazqueh.
12. Ticmāmah.

7G. *Transitive Sentences.* Pronounce and translate.

1. Īquin ōanquihuahqueh?
2. Cualāncā ōnēchilhuih.
3. Cuix mōztla tocottaz?
4. Cān cuix ōticcac?
5. Ahmō tictēmoa? —Quēmahcatzin, nictēmoa.
6. Ōtlacuāuhtlahtoh.

7. Ahhuel nicmāma.
8. Quēzquipa ōtinēchchix?
9. Cāmpa ōtocommēmeh?
10. Ahhuel tlahtoa. Cencah cocōya.
11. Āxcān titlacuah. Cuix ye ōtitlacuah?
12. Cuix tichuelcaqui?
13. Quinēnchīhuaya.
14. Quin ōnimitzilhuih.
15. Ayoquīc ticchīhuah.
16. Ahmō nichuelitta.
17. Ōnahcopatlachix.
18. Cuix yālhua ahōnimitzimmacac?
19. Ōchicotlahtoh. Ca miquiz.
20. Zātēpan ōtitozōmahqueh.
21. Nicān ōquiman.
22. Cuix ahōmahcoman?

EXERCISE 8. The Optative Mode. Wish Sentences. Command/Exhortation
Sentences

8A. *Past and Present Optative Forms.* Analyze and translate.

1. mā āltiāni, mā ālti
2. mā quipiani, mā quipia
3. mā nicpōhuani, mā nicpōhua
4. mā titotlāliānih, mā titotlālīcān
5. mā xictōcani, mā xictōca
6. mā motlaloānih, mā motlalōcān
7. mā xiccōhuanih, mā xiccōhuacān
8. mā xicmāmānih, mā xicmāmācān
9. mā quihtlanini, mā quihtlani
10. mā quizahuiāni, mā quizahui

8B. *The Property of Number on Past and Present Optative Forms.* Analyze
and translate.

1. mā niquiczani, mā tiquiczanih; mā niquicza, mā tiquiczacān
2. mā ximotlāliāni, mā ximotlāliānih; mā ximotlāli, mā ximotlālīcān
3. mā quitquini, mā quitquinih; mā quitqui, mā quitquicān
4. mā ticpītzanih, mā nicpītzani; mā ticpītzacān, mā nicpītza
5. mā xitlacuānih, mā xitlacuāni; mā xitlacuācān, mā xitlacua
6. mā quitocanih, mā quitocani; mā quitocacān, mā quitoca
7. mā xiczaloāni, mā xiczaloānih; mā xiczalo, mā xiczalōcān
8. mā quinhuītequini, mā quinhuītequinih; mā quinhuītequi, mā
quinhuītequicān

8C. *The Wish-Sentence Transformation (Affirmative and Negative).* Translate the following assertions and then transform them into wish sentences.
Translate the results.

Examples: Titlapixqueh. = We guarded things.
Source: — ti-tla(pix)∅-queh
Transform: mā ti-tla(pia)ni-h
Mā titlapianih. = If only we had guarded things.

Ahmō tiquihtlani. = You do not request it.
Source: — ahmō ti-qu(ihtlani)∅-∅
Transform: mā-camō xi-qu(ihtlani)∅-∅
Mācamō xiquihtlani. = If only you don't request it. I hope
you don't request it.

1. Nitlanamacaya.
2. Ōtictōcac.
3. Quintlālīz.
4. Ninopia.
5. Ahtitlapōhuazqueh.

6. Anquitquih.
7. Ōniquintocac.
8. Ahmō ōmotlaloh.
9. Quicōhuaz.
10. Ahōtitotlālihqueh.

8D. *The Command/Exhortation-Sentence Transformation.* Translate the following assertions and then transform them into command/exhortation sentences. Translate the results.

Examples: Anquipītzah. = You (pl) smelt it.
Source: — an-qui(pītza)∅-h
Transform: mā xi-c(pītza)∅-cān
            Mā xicpītzacān! = Smelt (pl) it!

Ahmō tinēchizahuia. = You don't amaze me.
Source: — ahmō ti-nēch(izahuia)∅-∅
Transform: mā-camō xi-nēch(izahui)∅-∅
            Mācamō xinēchizahui! = Don't shock me! Don't surprise me!

1. Ticcōhua.
2. Ahmō titlapītzazqueh.
3. Quihtlani.
4. Ahanquiczah.
5. Timotlaloa.
6. Ahninocuepa.

7. Tictlāliah.
8. Ahmō quinamacazqueh.
9. Timopia.
10. Ahmō anquīzazqueh.
11. Quintocah.
12. Ticcuepa.

8E. *Review of Wish Sentences and Command/Exhortation Sentences.* Pronounce and translate.

1. Mā xiquimilhui.
2. Mā tiquihtlanizqueh.
3. Māca īc nipolihui. Māca īc nimiqui.
4. Mācamō quihuāltepēhua.
5. Mā āxcān xicnamaca.
6. Tlā nicchīhuani.
7. Māyecuēleh xiquitta!
8. Mā ōticpixqueh.
9. Mācamō titlapītzaz.
10. Tlā xiccaqui!

11. Mācamō tiquīzaz.
12. Mātēl tiquihtōcān!
13. Mā quin ticpōhuaz.
14. Māca xiccuācān!
15. Māca xonquīza.
16. Mā quitocacān. Mā quitōcacān.
17. Māca xiccōhuacān. — Ye ōticcōuhqueh.
18. Oc xicchia.
19. Mā xonāhuiacān.
20. Mācamō ninizahui.

EXERCISE 9. The Admonitive Mode. Admonition Sentences

9A. *The Property of Number in Admonitive Forms.* Analyze and translate.

1. mā niccāuh, mā ticcāuhtin
2. mā timotēcah, mā ammotēcahtin
3. mā mozōmah, mā mozōmahtin
4. mā ticahmantin, mā nicahman
5. mā tlanelohtin, mā tlaneloh
6. mā anquipoztectin, mā ticpoztec
7. mā nicpātzcah, mā ticpātzcahtin
8. mā ticquēn, mā anquiquēntin
9. mā quitzauc, mā quitzauctin
10. mā titlachinohtin, mā nitlachinoh
11. mā anquixcahtin, mā tiquixcah
12. mā moquetztin, mā moquetz

9B. *Recognizing Admonitive Forms.* Identify the tense form and translate the sentence.

Example: Mā mahman. Mā ōmahman. = *Admon:* Let him beware of becoming upset. *Pret opt:* If only he had become upset!

1. Mā ticchīuh. Mā ōticchīuh.
2. Māca ōtimoquetz. Mānēn ahtimoquetz.
3. Mā titocāuhtin. Mā titocāhuacān.
4. Mā tichihchah. Mā xichihcha.
5. Mānēn tlachinoh. Mā ōtlachinoh.
6. Mā quixcah. Mā quixca.
7. Mā ninizahuih. Mā ninizahui. Mā ōninizahuih.
8. Mānēn anquiquetztin. Mā ōanquiquetzqueh.
9. Mā titotēcahtin. Mā titotēcacān.
10. Ximocāhua. Mā timocāuh.
11. Mānēn ahquimāyauhtin. Māca ōquimāyauhqueh.
12. Mā xictēca. Mānēn tictēcah.

9C. *The Admonition-Sentence Transformation.* Translate the following assertions and then transform them into admonition sentences. Translate the results.

Examples: Anquichīhuah. = You (pl) are making it.
Source: — an-qui (chīhua)∅-h
Transform: mā an-qui (chīuh)∅-tin
Mā anquichīuhtin. = Beware (pl) of making it.

Ahmō quicāhua. = He does not leave it.

Source: —ꞁ ahmō Ø-qui(cāhua)Ø-Ø

Transform: mānēn ah-Ø-qui(cāuh)Ø-Ø

 Mānēn ahquicāuh. = Let him beware of not leaving it. Let
 him be sure to leave it. ⹂

1. Ticquetza.	7. Tlama.
2. Ahmō antlaneloah.	8. Ninotēca.
3. Nipēhua.	9. Ticmāyahuih.
4. Ahmō ticahmanah.	10. Anquipoztequih.
5. Tlaxcah.	11. Nicquēmi.
6. Quichinoa.	12. Tictzacua.

9D. *Review of Admonitive Sentences.* Pronounce and translate.

 1. Mā canah tihuetz.
 2. Mā annēchtzauctin.
 3. Mānēn nicān quixcahtin.
 4. Mā mōztla tiquīz.
 5. Mānēn ahquineloh.
 6. Mānēn ammahmantin.
 7. Mānēn ihuiān ahpanohtin.
 8. Mācamō xicpoztequi. Mā ticpoztec.
 9. Mā tiquimahcomantin.
 10. Mā ihciuhcā timoquetz.

22

EXERCISE 10. Irregular Verbs

10A. *The Property of Number in the Indicative Forms of Irregular Verbs.*
Analyze and translate.

1. nicah, ticateh
2. ōtihuītzah, ōnihuītza
3. onoc, onoqueh
4. niauh, tihuih
5. ōanquimatqueh, ōticmah

6. nonoca, tonocah
7. tihuītz, anhuītzeh
8. nihuia, tihuiah
9. āc, āqueh
10. ninahcoc, titahcocqueh

10B. *The Properties of Person and Tense in the Indicative Forms of Irregular Verbs.* Analyze and translate. (Remember that the majority of forms in an irregular verb's paradigm are perfectly regular.)

1. ōnicatca, ticah, yez
2. ōcatca, nieni, tiez
3. ōniahca, ōhuia, ōyah, tiauh, niāz
4. ōniāya, tiāni, yāz
5. ōihcaca, nihcac, tihcaz
6. ōnihcaya, tihcani, ihcaz
7. ōtonoca, onoc, nonoz
8. ōnonoya, tononi, onoz
9. ōhuāllahca, tihuālhuia, ōtihuāllah, nihuāllauh, huāllāz
10. ōhuāllāya, nihuāllāni, tihuāllāz
11. ōnicahcocca, ōticahcoc, cahcocui, nicahcocuiz
12. ōnicahcocuia, cahcocuini, ticahcocuiz
13. ōmanca, mani, maniz
14. ōmania, manini, maniz

10C. *The Properties of Person and Tense in the Indicative Forms of Irregular Verbs.* Analyze and translate.

1. ōticatcah, ancateh, yezqueh
2. ōtiahcah, ōhuiah, ōyahqueh, anhuih, tiāzqueh
3. ōtiāyah, anyānih, yāzqueh
4. ōihcacah, tihcaqueh, amihcazqueh
5. ōamonocah, onoqueh, tonozqueh
_ 6. ōhuāllahcah, anhuālhuiah, ōanhuāllahqueh, tihuālhuih, huāllāzqueh
7. ōhuāllāyah, tihuāllānih, anhuāllāzqueh
8. ōticahcoccah, ōancahcocqueh, cahcocuih, ticahcocuizqueh

10D. *The Property of Number in Optative Forms of Irregular Verbs.* Analyze and translate.

1. Mā nono. Mā tonocān.
2. Mā pilcani. Mā pilcanih.
3. Mā tiecān. Mā nie.
4. Mā xihuāllauh. Mā xihuālhuiān.
5. Mā yenih. Mā yeni.
6. Mā xonocān. Mā xono.
7. Mā yāni. Mā yānih.
8. Mā tonhuiān. Mā nonyauh.
9. Mā xihca. Mā xihcacān.
10. Mā cahcocuicān. Mā cahcocui.
11. Mā tiānih. Mā niāni.
12. Mā xiauh. Mā xihuiān.

10E. *The Property of Number in Admonitive Forms of Irregular Verbs.* Analyze and translate.

1. Mā tiahtin. Mā niah.
2. Mā pilcah. Mā pilcahtin.
3. Mā nēn ahquimattin. Mā nēn ahquimah.
4. Mā nicahcoc. Mā ticahcoctin.
5. Mā onohtin. Mā onoh.
6. Mā nēn ahtiah! Mā nēn ahanyahtin.
7. Mā cah. Mā cattin.
8. Mā nihcah. Mā tihcahtin.

10F. *Further Practice with Irregular Verbs.* Pronounce and translate.

1. Cāmpa cah? —Oncān cah.
   Cāmpa mani? —Nicān mani.
2. Ayocmō ōhuītzah.
3. Cānin ōyah? —Ach cānin.
4. Yālhua ōnihuāllah.
5. Mā nicān huāllauh.
6. Tlā teōtlāc xonyauh.
7. Cuix huel ōmahcoc?
8. Mā nēpa xihca.
9. Cuix mōztla nicān pilcaz?
10. Ahmō huehcapa huāllah.
11. Achto niāz.
12. Āxcān ayāc.
13. Cānnelpa tiāz?
14. Quin huāllāz.
15. Zan tinēnyez.
16. Ahquēn ōcommah.
17. Quin huel āxcān ōyah.
18. Ahcān huel niauh.
19. Ayoc oncah.
20. Ye nō ceppa huāllahqueh.
21. Zan quēmmach ōcahcoc.
22. Īxtlapal onoc.

PART TWO

Derived Verb Words

EXERCISE 11. The Nonactive Stem. The Passive Voice

11A. *The Difference between Active and Passive Forms.* Analyze and translate.

1. nicāna, āno, ānalo
2. tichuīca, huīco
3. qui, īhua
4. niquimihcali, ihcalīhuah, ihcalīloh
5. titēchīmacaci, tīmacaxoh
6. amēchtītlani, antītlanoh, antītlanīloh
7. ticnequih, neco
8. anquipoloah, polōlo
9. quitlatiah, tlatīlo
10. tiquintlātiah, tlātiloh
11. antēchtlāzah, titlāxoh, titlāzaloh
12. amēchtocah, antocoh
13. ticnāmiqui, nāmico
14. quinamaca, namaco

11B. *The Relation of the Passive Subject Affixes to the Active Object Prefix.* Translate the following passive forms. For each form, name the subject affixes (person, number) and identify the object prefix that served as their source.

Example: nitto = I am being seen; n- . . . -∅ = I < -nēch- = me.

1. neco
2. tāno
3. huīcoh
4. ninetlātilo
5. amihcalīhuah
6. nīmacaxo
7. tipolōloh
8. annetlāxoh

11C. *The Relation of the Active Object Prefix to the Passive Subject Affixes.* Translate the following active forms. For each form, name the object prefix and tell what passive subject affixes would be generated by it.

Example: tēchīmacaci = he fears and respects us; -tēch- = us > ti- . . . -h = we.

1. namēchhuīcaz
2. ōtiquic
3. ōnēchihcal
4. tiquimpolōzqueh
5. titotlātihqueh
6. cānaz
7. mitztītlan
8. motlāzani

11D. *The Passive Transformation.* (*a*) Translate the active form; (*b*) then use the nonactive stem to transform it into its passive counterpart; and (*c*) translate the result.

   Example: annēchīmacacih; (īmacax-o)

   a. annēchīmacacih = you (pl) fear and respect me
   b. (1) an-nēch(īmacaci)∅-h   [analyze active verb word]
       (2) ↓ -nēch(īmacaci)∅- ↘   [delete person-number affixes]
       (3) — -nēch(īmacax-o)∅- —   [replace active stem with nonactive
                                          counterpart]
       (4) n̄(īmacax-o)∅-∅   [split person-number of object pre-
                                          fix into person prefix and number
                                          suffix to create subject of passive]
   c. nīmacaxo = I am feared and respected

   1. tēchhuīcah; (huīc-o)
   2. niquinnāmiqui; (nāmic-o)
   3. ticchīhua; (chīhua-lo)
   4. tiquih; (ī-hua)
   5. nichuīca; (huīc-o)
   6. amēchihcalih; (ihcalī-hua) ~ (ihcalī-lo)
   7. quinequi; (nec-o)
   8. tēchpoloa; (polō-lo)
   9. nēchilhuiah; (ilhuī-lo)
   10. tictotequitiah; (tequitī-lo)
   11. anquinequih; (nec-o)
   12. timitzmacah; (mac-o)
   13. nicpoloa; (polō-lo)
   14. quitlāza; (tlāx-o) ~ (tlāza-lo)
   15. motlāzah; (tlāx-o) ~ (tlāza-lo)
   16. tictlatia; (tlatī-lo)

11E. *Tense Differences in Passive Forms.* Analyze and translate.
   1. ōtlatīlōca, ōtlatīlōc, tlatīlōya, tlatīlo, tlatīlōni, tlatīlōz
   2. ōnihuīcōca, ōnihuīcōc, nihuīcōya, nihuīco, nihuīcōni, nihuīcōz
   3. ōnecōca, ōnecōc, necōya, neco, necōni, necōz
   4. ōtitītlanīlōcah, ōtitītlanīlōqueh, ōtitītlanīlōyah, titītlanīloh,
       titītlanīlōnih, titītlanīlōzqueh
   5. mā polōlōnih, mā polōlōcān, mā polōlōzqueh
   6. mā tihuīcohtin
   7. ōīhuaca, ōīhuac, īhuaya, īhua, īhuani, īhuaz
   8. mā nimacōni, mā nimaco, mā nimacōz
   9. ōtlāxōca, ōtlāxōc, tlāxōya, tlāxo, tlāxōni, tlāxōz
   10. mā tinetlātiloh

11F. *Expanded Sentences Manifesting a Passive Focus.* Pronounce and translate.

1. Quēnin ōmalōc?
2. Ye ōantlamacōqueh?
3. Aocmō necōz. Aocmō monequiz.
4. Īquin ōonānōc?
5. At īyōlic chīhualōz.
6. Cencah īmacaxōyah.
7. Ihcuāc ōcacōc.
8. Cuix ōmpa mochīhua?
9. Ye oncān ittōqueh.
10. Nōhuiān huālmotepēhua.
11. Cuix ye mīnalōqueh?
12. Cencah mihtoa.

30

EXERCISE 12. The Impersonal Voice

12A. *The Difference between Inherently Impersonal Verbs and Inanimate Verbs.* Analyze and translate.

1. Cēhua.	9. Mani.
2. Pixahuia.	10. Quiahui.
3. Tilāhua. [as impers]	11. Tlamiz.
4. Tilāhua. [as inan]	12. Tecihuia.
5. Ōtēn.	13. Tōnaya.
6. Moyāhuac.	14. Mochīhuaz.
7. Yohuaya.	15. Tlathuiz.
8. Chipīni.	16. Ōchalān.

12B. *The Difference between Forms in the Active and Impersonal Voices.* Analyze and translate.

1. Tahcih. Ahxīhua.
2. Azciahuih. Ciaōhua.
3. Ēhuah. Ēōhua.
4. Titeciz. Texohuaz.
5. Pēhuah. Peōhua. Pēhualo.
6. Titlacaquih. Tlacaco.
7. Antēchiah. Tēchialo.
8. Tlachīhuah. Tlachīhualo.
9. Mozōmah. Nezōmalo.
10. Antlacuih. Tlacuīhua. Tlacuīhualo.

12C. *The Impersonal Transformation.* Translate the active form, and then use the nonactive stem to transform it into its impersonal counterpart.

Example: titēnōtzah; (nōtza-lo)

   a. titēnōtzah = we are calling people

   b. (1) ti-tē(nōtza)∅-h   [analyze active verb word]
       (2) ⊥ -tē(nōtza)∅- ⊥   [delete person-number affixes]
       (3) — -tē(nōtza-lo)∅- — [replace active stem with nonactive counterpart]
       (4) ∅-tē(nōtza-lo)∅-∅ [import impersonal (nonspecific) person prefix and number suffix to serve as subject of impersonal form]

   c. tēnōtzalo = s.o. is calling people; people are being called

1. antlatēmoah; (tēmo-lo)
2. tlahtoah; (ihtō-lo)
3. titozōmah; (zōma-lo)
4. antlaczah; (icx-o) ~ (icza-lo)
5. titlahtlanih; (ihtlan-o) ~ (ihtlanī-lo)
6. tlanamacah; (namac-o)
7. ammizahuiah; (izahuī-lo)
8. titlatquih; (it-co) ~ (itquī-hua)
9. tlapiah; (pia-lo)
10. titētocah; (toc-o)

12D. *The Difference between the Passive and the Impersonal.* Analyze and translate. (Remember: the passive has a specific subject and the impersonal a nonspecific subject.)

1. cōhualo; tlacōhualo
2. tlālilo; tlatlālilo
3. tōcoh; tētōco
4. pītzalo; tlapītzalo
5. izahuīloh; tēizahuīlo
6. titzacualoh; tētzacualo
7. nineahmanalo; neahmanalo
8. neahmanalo; neahmanalo
9. ——; ciaōhua ⎫ [passive form impos-
10. ——; yelohua ⎬ sible from intransi-
⎭ tive source]

12E. *Tense Differences in Forms in the Impersonal Voice.* Analyze and translate.

1. peōhuaca, peōhuac, peōhuaya, peōhua, peōhuani, peōhuaz
2. mā peōhuani, mā peōhua, mā peōhuaz
3. mā peōhuah
4. tlacāhualōca, tlacāhualōc, tlacāhualōya, tlacāhualo, tlacāhualōni, tlacāhualōz
5. mā tlacāhualōni, mā tlacāhualo, mā tlacāhualōz
6. mā tlacāhualoh
7. tlaxcōca, tlaxcōc, tlaxcōya, tlaxco, tlaxcōni, tlaxcōz
8. mā tlaxcōni, mā tlaxco, mā tlaxcōz
9. mā tlaxcoh

12F. *The Difference between the Active and the tla- Impersonal.* Analyze and translate.

1. nēci; tlanēci
2. polihui; tlapolihui
3. yohua; tlayohua
4. onoc; tlaonoc
5. comōni; tlacomōni

12G. *Expanded Sentences Manifesting the Impersonal Focus.* Pronounce and translate.

1. Nēpa pāccā nemohua.
2. Cuix oncān panohua?
3. Ihciuhcā huālhuechohuac.
4. Ayamō ōtlathuica.
5. Mauhcā netlalōlōc.
6. Mā huel īlōcho.
7. Nicān pachiōhua.
8. Yālhua ōtōnac.
9. Mānēn quīxohuah.
10. Mōztla ahmō cēhuaz.

32

EXERCISE 13. Causative Verbs (First Type). Thematic Verbs

13A. *The Transitivization of Intransitive Stems.* Analyze and translate.

1. nahci, nicahci
2. ac, caquih
3. ixtlāhuiz, tiquixtlāhuaz
4. mani, quimana
5. cuepi, mocuepa
6. ōnitotōnix, ōnictotōnih
7. ciahui, quiciahui
8. aqui, maquia
9. chihcha, quichihcha

10. ōtlān, ōquitlamih
11. tēmi, quitēma
12. ōmīn, ōquimīn
13. poztequiz, nicpoztequiz
14. tāltiah, titāltiah
15. cēhuih, mocēhuiah
16. huītequia, quihuītequia
17. ōnīhuintic, ōtinēchīhuintih
18. āltia, cāltia

13B. *Intransitive and Transitive Stems of Thematic Verbs.* Analyze and translate.

1. chipīni, quichipīnia
2. ōchitōn, ōnicchitōnih
3. tomāhuah, quintomāhua
4. comōnia, mocomōniāyah

5. ōchalān, ōtitochalānihqueh
6. zalihui, niczaloa
7. ōmelāhuac, ōticmelāuhqueh
8. pixahui, anquipixoah

13C. *Transitivized Verb Words in Expanded Sentences.* Pronounce and translate.

1. Mānēn ancaquihtin. Mānēn amaquihtin.
2. Yālhua tlapixoāyah. Yālhua pixahuia.
3. Cuix oc tēmi? Cuix oc quitēma?
4. Mānēn ahtiquimahcihtin. Mānēn ahtahcihtin.
5. Mochipa chipīnia. Mochipa quichipīniāya.
6. Cuix huel ōtiquixtlāuh? Cuix ye ōixtlāuh?
7. Mā ihciuhcā tlami. Mā ihciuhcā xictlami.
8. Cāmpa ōquiman? Cāmpa ōmanca?
9. Mā xinēchcēhui. Tlā nicēhui.
10. Ōmpa mochipa ninocēhuiāya. Ōmpa mochipa nicēhuia.
11. Ahmō huel nictotōniāya. Ahmō huel nitotōniaya.
12. Niman ōzaliōhuac. Niman ōzalōlōc.
13. Zan ōmpa ōnahcic. Zan ōmpa ōnicahcic.
14. Ayamō aqui. Ayamō caquiah.
15. Mōztla nāltīz. Mōztla nināltīz. Mōztla niquimāltīz.

EXERCISE 14. Causative Verbs (Second Type)

14A. *The Correspondence between Intransitive Verbs and Their Causative Derivatives.* Analyze and translate.

1. temo, nictemohuia
2. tipano, mitzpanahuia
3. pēhua, nicpēhualtia
4. timahui, nimitzmauhtia
5. ninēci, ninonēxtia
6. tiquīzah, tēchquīxtia

7. quīxohua, nitlaquīxtia
8. ammiquih, amēchmictia
9. chōcah, niquinchōctia
10. panohua, nitēpanahuia
11. amahcih, tamēchahxītiah
12. nihuetzca, tinēchhuetzquītia

14B. *The Correspondence between Transitive Verbs and Their Causative Derivatives.* Analyze and translate.

1. niquitta, tinēchittītia
2. ticcaqui, nimitzcaquītia
3. ninopia, nicnepialtia
4. titlattah, tēchtlattītia
5. ninomati, ninonemachtia

6. quimatih, niquimmachīltia
7. nicnāmiqui, nicnonāmictia
8. ticcāhuah, tictocāhualtiah
9. nictepēhua, nēchtepēhualtiah
10. anquipoloah, namēchpolōltia

14C. *The Causative Transformation Carried Out on an Intransitive Source.* Translate the source form and then transform it into a causative version, using the stem provided and the imported subject indicated. Translate the result.

Example: ninemi; tē-(nemī-tia); 3rd pl

ninemi = I am living

ni(nemi)∅-∅   [analyze the source verb word]
. . . -nēch-. . .   [convert the subject affixes into an object prefix]

. . . -nēch(nemī-tia)∅- . . .   [replace the source stem with a causative stem]

∅-nēch(nemī-tia)∅-h   [import new subject affixes (here, 3rd pl)]

nēchnemītiah = they are causing me to live; i.e., they are sustaining me

1. nimahui; tē-(mauh-tia); 3rd sg
2. pēhua; tla-(pēhua-l-tia); 2nd sg
3. tahci; tē-(ahxī-tia); 1st pl
4. temohua; tla-(temo-huia); 3rd sg
5. tinēci; mo-(nēx-tia); 2nd sg
6. temo; tla-(temo-huia); 2nd pl

14D. *The Causative Transformation from a Transitive Source.* Translate the
following forms and then transform each into a causative version, using
the stem provided and the imported subject indicated.

Example: nitlatta; tē-tla(ittī-tia); 2nd pl

nitlatta = I see s.th.

    ṇi-tla(tta)∅-∅   [analyze the source verb word]
. . . -nēch-⤎. . .   [convert subject affixes into an object
                           prefix]
. . . -nēch-tla(ttī-tia)∅- . . . [replace source stem with causative stem]
an-nēch-tla(ttī-tia)∅-h   [import new subject affixes(here, 2nd pl)]

annēchtlattītiah = you (pl) are causing me to see s.th., you are show-
ing me s.th.

1. ticpoloah; tē-tla-(polō-l-tia); 2nd sg
2. niquincaqui; tē-tla-(caquī-tia); 2nd pl
3. tlatepēhualo; tē-tla-(tepēhua-l-tia); 1st sg
4. titomatih; mo-ne-(mach-tia); 1st pl
5. anquimatih; mo-tla-(mach-tia); 2nd pl
6. tlacuah; tē-tla-(cua-l-tia); 3rd pl

14E. *Causative Verb Words in Expanded Sentences.* Pronounce and translate.

1. Mā xicchīhualtiāni.
2. Yālhua ōtlachīhualtīlōc.
3. Ahhuel nictemohuia.
4. Cuix monemachtih?
5. Ahzo canah quimottītīz.
6. Ayamō tēmachtīlo.
7. Niman quittītihqueh.
8. Oncān ahmō quimonāmictīz.
9. Zan tētlapolōltia.
10. Mā nēn tēhuetzquītih.
11. Oc achto quicualtīz.
12. Niman oncān ōquimahxītihqueh.
13. Nicān monēxtihqueh.
14. Ahmō quincua. Zā quinmictia.
15. Cencah quimauhtih.

EXERCISE 15. Applicative Verbs

15A. *The Difference between Nonapplicative and Applicative Forms.* Analyze and translate.

1. conitta, quimonittilia
2. nināhuati, nimitznāhuatia, nicnāhuatilia
3. titlatzeloa, tinēchtlatzelhuia
4. ticcuih, timitzcuīliah
5. nicchīhua, nimitzchīhuilia
6. nitlachīhua, nimitztlachīhuia
7. titlahtlani, tinēchtlahtlania
8. titlahtlani, tinēchtlahtlanilia
9. niquihtoa, nimitzilhuia [an instance of suppletion. The applicative is *not derived* from the nonapplicative.]
10. nicnamaca, nimitznamaquīltia
11. cocōyah, mococōliah
12. tlaquetza, quintlaquechilia
13. quitlāza, quitlāxilia
14. nictequi, nictequilia
15. tinemi, ticnemilia

15B. *The Applicative Transformation.* Translate the following forms and then transform each into an applicative, using the stem provided and the imported indirect object indicated.

Example: nicpōhua; tētla-(pōhui-lia); 2nd sg

nicpōhua = I am recounting it

ni-c(pōhua)∅-∅   [analyze the source verb word]
. . . -mitz-(. .|. -lia)   [import the indirect object sponsored by *-lia*]
ni-mitz-c(pōhui-lia)∅-∅ [replace nonapplicative stem with applicative counterpart]
ni-mitz-∅(pōhui-lia)∅-∅ [replace direct object with silent variant because of incompatibility of specific objects]

nimitzpōhuilia = I recount it to you

1. tictzacua; tētla-(tzacui-lia); 1st sg
2. niquihtoa; motla-(ilhuia); 1st sg (reflex)
3. tzahtzih; tē-(tzahtzi-lia); 3rd pl
4. antlapiah; tētla-(pia-lia); 1st pl
5. ticcaquih; tētla-(caqui-lia); nonspec human

   6. conitta; motla-(iʔti-lia); 3rd sg (reflex)
   7. quinōtza; tētla-(nōchi-lia); 2nd pl
   8. tecihui; tla-(tecihu-ia); 3rd sg

15C. *Applicative Verb Words in Expanded Sentences.* Pronounce and translate.

   1. Cuix ahmō tecihuīloz?
   2. Niman quinānquiliah.
   3. Mā xicnemili.
   4. Yālhua teōtlāc ōnēchcaquilihqueh.
   5. Yēppa mococōliāyah.
   6. Īquin ōtiquinchīhuilih?
   7. Mācamō xictzelhui.
   8. Oncān ōconmottilih.
   9. Mānēn tiquincuīlih.
   10. Quihuālmacaya.
   11. Mā tiquixtlāhuihtin.
   12. Niman tētzahtzilīlōc.

15D. *The Importance of Recognizing the Boundary between Stems and Affixes (Review Exercise).* Analyze and translate.

   1. quīzqueh; quizqueh
   2. quimāna; quimana
   3. ōmanca; ōmānca
   4. tēchilhuih; tēchix
   5. tēchihua; tēchīhua
   6. ticcuah; ōticcuah

EXERCISE 16. Honorific Verb Forms. Pejorative Verb Forms

16A. *The Contrast between Neutral and Honorific Forms of Intransitive and Projective Verbs.* Analyze and translate.

1. quitlātia, quimotlātilia
2. tinēchtlapialia, tinēchmotlapialilia
3. tlamauhtia, motlamauhtilia
4. huapāhuah, mohuapāhuiltiah
5. niccelia, nicnocelilia
6. nēchpalēhuia, nēchmopalēhuilia
7. amēchihxilih, amēchmihxililiah
8. tinēchilpia, tinēchmolpilia
9. tiquicnēliah, tictocnēliliah
10. tlamōtla, motlamōchilia
11. quipetlāhua, quimopetlāhuilia
12. nēchxōxa, nēchmoxōxilia

16B. *The Contrast between Neutral and Honorific Forms of Reflexive Verbs.* Analyze and translate.

1. molpia, molpihtzinoa
2. mopia, mopixtzinoa
3. ammotolīniah, ammotolīnihtzinoah
4. mozōma, mozōmahtzinoa
5. timozcalia, timozcalihtzinoa
6. timotēca, timotēcatzinoa

16C. *The Contrast between Neutral and Pejorative Verb Forms.* Analyze and translate.

1. nipolōni, nipolōnpōloa
2. quipolōnia, quipolōnihpōloa
3. timitzmōtlah, timitzmōtlapōloah
4. titlacua, titlacuahpōloa
5. quimihxili, quimihxilpōloa
6. nictzomōnia, nictzomōnihpōloa

16D. *Honorific, Reverential, and Pejorative Forms in Expanded Sentences.* Pronounce and translate.

1. Mā xinēchmotlātili.
2. Nicān nitlapixpōloa.
3. Cuix ticmolhuilīz?

4. Mā ximocēhuihtzinōcān!
5. Huel ōnēchmopalēhuilihtzinoh.
6. Cāmpa namēchnohuīquilīz?
7. Yālhua teōtlāc ōquimihxililihqueh.
8. Oc xicmopielīcān.
9. Mā xinēchonmotlaōcolili.
10. Aīc ōtēchmocnēlilih.

EXERCISE 17. Frequentative Forms

17A. *The Difference between Neutral and Frequentative Forms.* Analyze and translate.

1. tzelihui, tzetzelihui
2. tlacua, tlacuacua
3. polōni, popoloca
4. quihxili, quixxihxili
5. chihcha, chihchihcha
6. petlāni, pepetlaca
7. mocēhuia, mocehcēhuiah
8. quipetlāhuah, quimpehpetlāhuah
9. quitlauhtia, quitlātlauhtia
10. nimitznōtza, nimitznohnōtza
11. nimitznōchilia, nimitznōnōchilia
12. mochīhua, mochihchīhua
13. tlama, tlahtlama
14. ninemi, ninehnemi
15. calāni, cacalaca

17B. *Frequentative Forms in Expanded Sentences.* Pronounce and translate.

1. Mā xitēchmotlahtlātili.
2. Oncān huihhuītec.
3. Huāllatōtocah.
4. Xihuālnehnemicān!
5. Oncān tēhuihhuīteco.
6. Niman quihuāltzahtzaucqueh.
7. Cencah quihuihuixoāya.
8. At canah tzotzonalōz.
9. Yālhua ōcontotōtz.
10. Zātēpan quintēnahnāhuatilihqueh.
11. Niman tēxihxilīhuac.
12. Yohuac oc popōcaya.
13. Niman ye tlahcahuaca.
14. Niman ye quimihcahuatz.
15. Mochipa quiquinaca.
16. Ca cencah quitotōtzayah.
17. Ceppa tlahtlamāyah.
18. Cuix huālnehnenqueh?
19. Ye titocehcēhuihqueh.
20. Zātēpan quimmahmacaqueh.

EXERCISE 18. Purposive Forms

18A. *The Relation between the Future-Tense Theme and the Purposive Forms Derived from It.* Analyze and translate.

1. quittītīz, quittītīto
2. quittaz, quittato
3. niccomōlōz, niccomōlōtīuh
4. titocuiltōnōzqueh, titocuiltōnōcoh
5. ticōyaz, ticōyaquīuh
6. anquihuītōlōzqueh, anquihuītōlōtoh
7. nictatacaz, nictatacaco
8. tamēchpachōzqueh, tamēchpachōquīhuih
9. quimpēhuaz, quimpēhuatīuh
10. titlahtlamāz, titlahtlamātīuh
11. nictlapōz, nictlapōto
12. nimitztlapōlhuīz, nimitztlapōlhuīto

18B. *The Tense Differences of Purposive Forms.* Analyze and translate.

1. nimitztlaxīmato, nimitztlaxīmatīuh
2. timopachōco, timopachōquīuh
3. tlaihmatito, tlaihmatitīuh
4. mihtōtīto, mihtōtītīuh
5. titlanechicōcoh, titlanechicōquīhuih
6. monechicōcoh, monechicōquīhuih
7. anquimotzolōtoh, anquimotzolōtīhuih
8. tlacihuicoh, tlacihuiquīhuih

18C. *The Optative of the Purposive Forms.* Analyze and translate.

1. mā tēihpītzati, mā tēihpītzatīn
2. mā nēchtlahpalōqui, mā nēchtlahpalōquih
3. mā xicmecanīti, mā xicmecanītih
4. mā nitlacomōlōti, mā titlacomōlōtīn
5. mā nitlapachōqui, mā titlapachōquih

18D. *Purposive Forms in Expanded Sentences.* Pronounce and translate.

1. Mā xoconilhuītīn!
2. Ahzo ōnōhuiān mitzonmohottītihtzinōco.
3. At nimitzoncuīlītīuh.
4. Mā xinēchmopalēhuilīquih.
5. Tlahcah tlaōyaquīhuih.

6. Achto ōmpa tiquimpēhuaquīhuih.
7. Niman ahōnimitzihtlacōco.
8. Mā yohuan tocontatacatīn.
9. Ca huehca ōmohuālihtōtīcoh.
10. Mācamō quimecanītih.
11. Ahzo ōmpa miquitīuh.
12. Huehca huehhuetzito.
13. Niman quinohnōtzato.
14. Oncān quinnāmiquico.
15. Ichtacā nimitzilhuīco.

42

EXERCISE 19. Compound Verbs: Verbal Embed

19A. *The "Connective -cā-" Compound.* Analyze and translate.

   Example: tihciuhcāquīzaz = t(ihciuh-∅-cā-quīza)z-∅ = you will leave
   hurriedly

   1. timotlamelāuhcāquetzaz
   2. yōcoxcātlahtoa
   3. ōnēchpāccātlahpalohqueh

   4. ichtacāmictīlōqueh
   5. amēchmauhcāittayah
   6. ihciuhcāmiquiz

19B. *The Preterit Form as the Source of the Embed in a "Connective -ti-"
   Compound.* Analyze and translate.

   Example: ōquichīuhqueh; quichīuhtinemih
      ō-∅-qui(chīuh)∅-queh = they made it ~ they have begun making it
      ∅-qui(chīuh-∅-ti-nemi)∅-h = they go along making it

   1. ōmomimiloh; momimilohtiuh
   2. ōquiquinacac; quiquinacatiuh
   3. ōtehtēn; tehtēntiuh
   4. ōtlamah; tlamahtiuh
   5. ōtlamah; tlamattiuh
   6. ōmīn; mīntoc
   7. ihcac; ihcatiuh
   8. huālcateh; huālyetihuih
      [Exception! See § 19.4.1.]

   9. ōquiauh; quiauhtimani
   10. ōmopixqueh; mopixtoqueh
   11. ōchōcac; chōcaticah
   12. ōquicuic; quicuītihuetzi
   13. ōxapot, xapottihcac
   14. ōquiquetzqueh;
       quiquetztihuītzeh

19C. *The Property of Tense in "Connective -ti-" Compounds.* Analyze and
   translate.

   1. māntiahca, māntiah, māntiuh, māntiāz
   2. ninoquetztihcaca, ninoquetztihcac, ninoquetztihcaz
   3. ihihcīcatihuītzah, ihihcīcatihuītzeh
   4. xitīntocah, xitīntoqueh, xitīntozqueh
   5. tlanēztimanca, tlanēztimani, tlanēztimaniz
   6. ōtlamattinenca, ōtlamattinen, tlamattinemi, tlamattinemiz

19D. *Compounds Whose Matrix Is an Intransitivized Reflexive.* Analyze and
   translate.

   Example: tōlohtimotlālīz = ∅(tōloh-∅-ti-mo-tlālī)z-∅ = he will settle
      down to nodding, he will begin nodding

   1. xapottimotlālia
   2. tlīliuhtimoquetzaz

   3. xeliuhtimocāhua
   4. ōihyāyatimotēcac

5. tlanēztimoquetza
6. ōtlamattimoman

7. tomāhuatimoquetza
8. tlayohuatimomana

19E. *The "Future-Embed" Compound.* Analyze and translate.

Example: quihtōz; quihtōznequi
Ø-qu(ihtō)z-Ø = it will say it
Ø-qu(ihtō-z-nequi)Ø-Ø = it wishes to say it; i.e., it means it

1. ticchīhuazqueh; ticchīhuaznequih
2. nihuelitiz; nihuelitizquia
3. mihtōtīzqueh; mihtōtīzquiah
4. tihcopiz; tihcopiznequia
5. quinecuilōz; quinecuilōznequiz
6. huetztoz; ōhuetztoznec
7. nicyōcoyaz; nicyōcoyazquia
8. motztiezqueh; motztieznequih

19F. *The Various Compound Verbs (of the Verbal-Embed Type) in Expanded Sentences.* Pronounce and translate.

1. Zan quipāccānāmiquito.
2. Necoc micohuatiuh.
3. Niman huālmocueptihuetzqueh.
4. Aoc quēmman cactoc.
5. Cencah huālmotlamauhtilihtiahqueh.
6. Ye quinānquilīzquia.
7. Zā oncān huāltōlohtimotlāliah.
8. Cencah ahmō tlatlamatcāchīhuah.
9. Yēppa mochalānihticatcah.
10. Yālhua quimpāccātlahpalōtoh.
11. Zā mahcomantinemi.
12. Cencah mauhcāittōyah.
13. Oc achto tictēmōzquia.
14. Nōhuiān quitohtocatinemi.
15. Ōmpa huihhuītectoc.
16. Mochipa mocualāncāitzticatcah.
17. Huel yacattihuiah.
18. Ye tlathuiznequi.
19. Oncān quinhuālitztoqueh.
20. Zan itztiahqueh.

PART THREE

Noun Words
Supplementation

EXERCISE 20. Absolutive-State Nouns. The Equational Sentence

20A. *The Property of Person in Absolutive-State Noun Words.* Analyze and translate.

> *Example:* niteōtl, titeōtl, teōtl
> ni-∅(teō)tl = I am a god; ti-∅(teō)tl = you are a god; ∅-∅(teō)tl = he is a god

1. noquichtli, toquichtli, oquichtli
2. nipilli, tipilli, pilli
3. tipōchtēcah, ampōchtēcah, pōchtēcah
4. titlācah, antlācah, tlācah
5. nicihuātl, ticihuātl, cihuātl
6. titahtin, antahtin, tahtin
7. titētēuctin, antētēuctin, tētēuctin
8. nitlācohtli, titlācohtli, tlācohtli

20B. *The Property of Number in Absolutive-State Noun Words.* Analyze and translate.

> *Example:* niteōtl, titēteoh
> ni-∅(teō)tl = I am a god; ti-∅(tē-teo)h = we are gods

1. tepētl, tētepeh	6. cōātl, cōcōah
2. tipilli, ampīpiltin	7. chichi, chichimeh
3. nipōchtēcatl, tipōchtēcah	8. cītlalin, cīcītlaltin
4. mītl	9. tepoztli
5. ticihuātl, azcihuah	10. tlācatl, tlācah

20C. *The Nuclear Functions of Equational Sentences Manifested by Absolutive-State Nouns.* Identify the subject and predicate of each of the following sentences. Translate.

> *Examples:* Nitēuctli. *Subj:* ni- . . . -tli; *pred:* -∅(tēuc)-; I am a lord.
> Tipīpiltin. *Subj:* ti- . . . -tin; *pred:* -∅(pī-pil)-; We are noblemen.

1. Mētztli.	5. Titlācatl.
2. Cīcītlaltin.	6. Tōtolmeh.
3. Nipōchtēcatl.	7. Tlatl.
4. Antēteoh.	8. Toquichtin.

20D. *The Negative Transformation.* Translate the following sentences and then transform them into their negative counterparts (two variants). Translate the results.

Example: Nitōchin. = I am a rabbit.
        Ahnitōchin. Ahmō nitōchin. = I am not a rabbit.

1. Titōtoltin.   4. Ancōcoyoh.
2. Cōātl.   5. Ahtlatl.
3. Tichichi.   6. Toquichtli.

20E. *The Yes/No-Question Transformation.* Translate the following asser-
     tions and then transform them into *yes/no* questions (two variants).
     Translate the results.

Example: Ticoyōtl. = You are a coyote.
        Ticoyōtl? = Are you a coyote?
        Cuix tıcoyōtl? = Are you a coyote?

1. Tōtolmeh.   4. Ahtlatl.
2. Titeōtl.   5. Tzīntli.
3. Azcihuah.   6. Ampōchtēcah.

20F. *The Emphatic-Assertion Transformation.* Translate the following asser-
     tions and then transform them into emphatic counterparts.

Example: Tepoztli. = It is copper.
        Ca tepoztli. = It is indeed copper.

1. Mītl.   4. Cōcōah.
2. Tipīpiltin.   5. Antētēuctin.
3. Ahtlatl.   6. Ahmō tlātlācohtin.

20G. *The Relationship between Questions and Answers.* Pronounce and
     translate.

1. Cuix titēuctli? —Quēmah, nitēuctli.
2. Cuix antlātlācohtin? —Ahmō, ahtitlātlācohtin.
3. Mītl? —Ahmō, ahmō mītl.
4. Tēteoh? —Ca quēmahca, ca tēteoh.
5. Cuix tiPetoloh? —Ahmōtzin, ahniPetoloh.

20H. *Further Practice with Equational Sentences.* Pronounce and translate.

1. Ahocmō titlātlācohtin.
2. Ahmō chichimeh. Coyōmeh.
3. Ahzo tētēuctin.
4. Zan nicihuātl.
5. Niman ahmō cīcītlaltin.
6. Cuix zā huel tipōchtēcatl?
7. Ca ahtlācatl.
8. Ahcazomō pīpiltin.

EXERCISE 21. Possessive-State Nouns

21A. *The Property of Number in Possessive-State Noun Words.* Analyze and translate.

Example: tinocōl, annocōlhuān
ti-no(cōl)∅ = you are my grandfather
an-no(cōl)huān = you are my grandfathers

1. nimocnīuh, timocnīhuān
2. nomā
3. īnnān, īnnāhuān
4. motōch, motōchhuān
5. īohhui
6. īteōuh, īteōhuān
7. nocuāuh, nocuāhuān
8. nocuauh
9. amotēucyo, amotēucyōhuān
10. totlācauh, totlācahuān

21B. *The Property of State in Possessive-State Noun Words.* Analyze and translate.

Examples: nīnān, nīnnān
n-ī(nān)∅ = I am his mother; n-īn(nān)∅ = I am their mother

nocuauh, tocuauh
∅-no(cuauh)∅ = it is my tree, they are my trees; ∅-to(cuauh)∅ = it is our tree; they are our trees

1. nocal, tocal
2. īchīmal, īnchīmal
3. nāuh, tāuh
4. īmā, īmmā
5. mohhui, amohhui
6. nopetl, topetl
7. motecon, amotecon
8. īteuh, īnteuh
9. noyac, toyac
10. ītōcā, īntōcā
11. noyāōuh, toyāōuh
12. motenān, amotenān
13. īmāx
14. nochān, tochān

21C. *The Properties of Number and State in Possessive-State Nouns.* Analyze and translate.

1. annocnīhuān, namocnīuh
2. īncōl, īcōlhuān
3. notah, totah, totahhuān
4. motōtolhuān, amotōtol

     5. nīcihuāuh, tīcihuāhuān, tīzcihuāhuān
     6. tinonān, titonān, antonāhuān
     7. tīyāōhuān, toyāōuh

21D. *The Nuclear Functions of Equational Sentences Manifested by Posses-sive-State Nouns.* Identify the subject and predicate of each of the following sentences. Translate.

    Examples: Amichhui. *Subj:* ∅- . . . -hui; *pred:* -am(ich)-; It is your (pl)
            maguey thread. ~ They are your (pl) maguey threads.

    Nimoyāōuh. *Subj:* ni- . . . -uh; *pred:* -mo(yāō)-; I am your enemy.

    1. Īxxo.   5. Īneuc.
    2. Nīcnīuh.   6. Tīmoquichhuān.
    3. Totlācahuān.   7. Tinocōl.
    4. Amocxi.   8. Īnteuh.

21E. *The Negative, the Emphatic, and the Yes/No-Question Transformations from Sources Containing Possessive-State Noun Words.* Translate the following single-base transformations and give the source sentence for each.

    1. Ahmō nonān.   6. Cuix ahnomīuh?
    2. Ca toyāōhuān.   7. Ahmō topetl.
    3. Cuix tīcihuāuh?   8. Ahmō motōtol.
    4. Īchichi?   9. Mocal?
    5. Ca ahnimocnīuh.   10. Ahmō amochān?

21F. *Further Practice with Equational Sentences.* Pronounce and translate.

     1. Ahzo īāuh.
     2. Ca īteuh.
     3. Cuix ahtinocnīuh?
     4. Ca īnchichihuān.
     5. Cuix motēucyo? —Ahmō, ahnotēucyo.
     6. Ahmō tomā. Toxo.
     7. Zan totecon.
     8. Ahmō ītah. Īcōl.
     9. Niman ahmō īohhui.
    10. Cuix oc īcnīhuān?

EXERCISE 22. Compound Noun Stems. Affective Noun Stems

22A. *The Compounding of Noun Stems.* Analyze and translate.

Example: tetl: cuāitl, cuātetl

Ø-Ø(te)tl = it is a rock; Ø-Ø(cuāi)tl = it is a head; Ø-Ø(cuā-te)tl = it is a rock like a head, i.e., it is a hard head. [Notice that English reverses the perspective: "a head like a rock," as in "He has a head like a rock." Train yourself to see such differences in perspective when they occur. Remember that the same principle of *order* (embed precedes matrix) that occurs in English compounds (contrast, for example, *guesthouse* and *house-guest*) occurs in Nahuatl.]

1. tlatl: māitl, mātlatl; māxatl, māxtlatl [note irregularity]
2. calli: teōtl, teōcalli; petlatl, petlacalli; ātl, ācalli
3. tēntli: ātl, ātēntli; calli, caltēntli; īxtli, īxtēntli
4. tetl: īxtli, īxtetl; tōtolin, tōtoltetl; tēntli, tēntetl
5. cuahuitl: māitl, mācuahuitl; cuāitl, cuācuahuitl
6. ātl: ilhuicatl, ilhuicaātl; teōtl, teōātl
7. cuitlatl: teōtl, teōcuitlatl; mētztli, mētzcuitlatl
8. conētl: tōtōtl, tōtōconētl; mazātl, mazāconētl
9. pilli: tletl, tlepilli; cuitlatl, cuitlapilli
10. tlācotl: tetl, tetlācotl; ōlli, ōllācotl

22B. *The Role of Matrix in Compound Nouns.* (a) Translate the word that serves as the source for the matrix; (b) identify and translate the embed stem; (c) translate the compound.

Example: tecomatl: tzontecomatl

  a. tecomatl = it is a pot
  b. (tzon)-tli = hair
  c. tzontecomatl = it is a pot for hair; i.e., it is a head

1. tōcāitl: piltōcāitl
2. tzontli: tēntzontli
3. tenāmitl: cuauhtenāmitl
4. tepētl: āltepētl
5. mītl: tepozmītl
6. omitl: huitzomitl
7. mīlli: xōchimīlli
8. ātl: nexātl

22C. *Recursion in Compounding.* (a) Identify the elements of the compound; (b) state whether the compound is built on the formula $a+(b+c)$ (i.e., with a compound matrix) or $(a+b)+c$ (i.e., with a compound embed); (c) analyze and translate the compound.

Example: ācalchīmalli

    a. (ā)-tl = water; (cal)-li = house; (chīmal)-li = protective shelter, shield

    b. formula: (*a+b*)+*c* ; (ā-cal)-li + (chīmal)-li

    c. ∅-∅(*ā-cal*-chīmal)li = it is a shield in the form of a boat; i.e., it is a war canoe

1. ācalohtli
2. temātlatl
3. ācalyacatl

4. ilhuicaātēntli
5. āltepētenāmitl

22D. *Affective Noun Stems.* Analyze and translate.

Example: momāxtli, momāxtlazol
    ∅-mo(māx-tli)∅ = it is your breechcloth
    ∅-mo(māx-tla-zol)∅ = it is your old breechcloth

1. āltepētl, āltepētōntli
2. nonān, nonantzin
3. tochichiconēhuān, tochichiconēpipīlhuān
4. ācalli, ācalzolli
5. notah, notahtzin
6. cuācuahuitl, cuācuahuitōntli
7. noconēuh, noconētzin
8. tōtolin, tōtolpōl
9. cuitlapilli, cuitlapiltōntli
10. tēlpōchtli, tēlpōtzintli

22E. *Compound and Affective Forms in Wider Sentence Contexts.* Pronounce and translate.

1. Ahmō totōtōconēhuān.
2. Cuix motahtzin? —Ca quēmahca, ca notahtzin.
3. Ahzo īmācalchīmal.
4. Zan niman ahmō īpiltōcā.
5. Cuix amoteōcuitl?
6. Ahzozan nexātl.
7. Āxcān teōcalli.
8. At mētzcuitlatl.
9. Cuix tepozmītl? —Ahmō, zan cuauhmītl.
10. Huel nāltepēuh.

EXERCISE 23. Compound Verbs: Substantival Embed

23A. *The Incorporated-Noun-as-Object Compound.* Analyze and translate. Some of these compounds require a novel way of thinking about the action signified.

> *Example:* tlālli, niccua; nitlālcua
> Ø-Ø(tlāl)li = it is the ground
> ni-c(cua)Ø-Ø = I eat it
> ni(tlāl-cua)Ø-Ø = I eat the ground; i.e., I kiss the earth (a solemn, reverent form of greeting or vowing)

1. ilhuitl, quiquīxtiah; ilhuiquīxtiah, quilhuiquīxtiliah
2. ohtli, anquitlāza; amohtlāzah, anquimohtlāxiliah
3. tlācatl, ticmictia; titlācamictia
4. tequitl, niccāhua; nitequicāhua
5. ātl, niqui; nātli
6. tlahuēlli, quicui; tlahuēlcui
7. ohtli, quiquetzah; ohquetzah, tēchohquechiliah
8. ātl, quicui; ātlacui

23B. *The Incorporated-Noun-as-Adverb Compound.* Analyze and translate.

> *Example:* tetl, quipachoah; quitepachoah
> Ø-Ø(te)tl = it is a rock, they are rocks
> Ø-qui(pachoa)Ø-h = they are pressing her down
> Ø-qui(te-pachoa)Ø-h = they are pressing her down with rocks, i.e., they are stoning her

1. mecatl, nicpātzca; nicmecapātzca
2. ātl, panoh; āpanoh
3. ōlli, ticchipīnia; ticōlchipīnia
4. ācalli, mohuītequih; mācalhuītequih
5. ahhuachtli, pixahui; ahhuachpixahui
6. tequitl, timopachoa; timotequipachoa
7. nāhuatl, titlahtoah; tināhuatlahtoah
8. īnyac, niquimāna; niquinyacāna
9. calli, taqui; ticalaqui
10. ītzīn, tlacza; tzīntlacza
11. tēntli, anquēhuah; anquitēnēhuah
12. īīx, miqui; īxmihmiqui
13. camatl, niccāhua; niccamacāhua

23C. *The Incorporated-Noun-as-Complement Compound.* Analyze and translate.

> *Example:* nitlācatl, nēchmati; nēchtlācamati
> ni-∅(tlāca)tl = I am a person, I am a master
> ∅-nēch(mati)∅-∅ = he knows me
> ∅-nēch(tlāca-mati)∅-∅ = he knows me to be master, i.e., he obeys me

1. ticōātl, nimitzchīhua; nimitzcōāchīhua
2. teōtl, ticmatih; ticteōmatih
3. cōzcacuāuhtli, monehnequi; mocōzcacuāuhnehnequi
4. pilli, quīza; pilquīza, quipilquīxtia
5. tixōlopihtli, timocuepa; timoxōlopihcuepa
6. tlātlācohtin, tiquinmatih; tiquintlācohmatih
7. annocnīhuān, namēchtoca; namēchicnīuhtoca
8. tētzāhuitl, anquimatih; anquitētzāmmatih

23D. *Recognizing the Function of the Embed.* (a) Analyze; (b) identify the function (direct object, adverb, complement) of the embed; (c) "explain" the translation of the compound by means of a more literal version.

> *Example:* Oquichēhuah. = They are attacking manfully.
> (a) ∅(oquich-ēhua)∅-h; (b) embed = adverb of compared manner; (c) "They are arising like men."

1. Niquimīximati. = I am acquainted with them.
2. Mācalaquia. = It is being loaded on a boat.
3. Titequitlaneloa. = You are rowing diligently.
4. Īxtehtēnmotzoloah. = They are squeezing their eyes shut.
5. Tlālpolihui. = It is being laid waste.
6. Ninoquichquetza. = I am standing up bravely.
7. Mocuācuauhtlāza. = It is discarding its horns.
8. Ticcōānōtzah. = We are inviting him.
9. Tēchyacatzacuiliah. = They are heading us off. They are blocking our path.
10. Tāmiqui. = You are thirsty.
11. Ammocuitlacuepah. = You (pl) are fleeing to the rear.
12. Quitēnquīxtiah. = They are pronouncing it. They are uttering it. They are mentioning it.
13. Ticteōtocah. = We are worshipping him.
14. Moquechmecania. = He is hanging himself.
15. Nimitztlahuēlchīhua. = I am becoming angry at you. I am becoming annoyed with you.
16. Tēīxcuepa. = He is deceiving people.

17. Yāōtēca. = He is commanding troups in battle.
18. Yāōtlahtoah. = They are preparing for war.

23E. *Compound Formations in Wider Sentence Structures.* Pronounce and translate.

1. Cuix ōilac? —Ahmō, ōquilactihqueh.
2. Ahzo ilaquīlōz.
3. Zan mochipa ōēlcihciuhtinenca.
4. Yēppa motlahuēlitzticatcah.
5. Niman tzīnquīza. Quitzīnquīxtihqueh.
6. Zan quitequicua.
7. Ihcuāc ahhuachtzetzeliuhtimani.
8. Cencah ōquinyāōchīuhqueh.
9. Niman quiyāōnāmiquitoh.
10. Zan mocuitlacueptinemi.
11. Cencah motzonteconhuihuixoah.
12. Zan huālmoyāōchihchīuhtiah. [caution: not a causative]

EXERCISE 24. Pronouns and Pronominals

24A. *Pronoun and Pronominal Forms.* Analyze and translate.

1. tacah	9. amehhuāntin
2. antlehmeh	10. cātlein?
3. quēxquichtōn	11. ixachin
4. ammiequintin	12. yehhuāmpopōl
5. nitlah	13. ammochin
6. izquin	14. anquēxquichtin
7. yehyehhuātl	15. azcequintin
8. achitōn	16. nitleimpōl

24B. *Pronoun and Pronominal Forms in Wider Sentence Contexts.* Pronounce and translate.

1. Ahmō itlahmeh.	7. Ahmō zan tiquēzquintin.
2. Huel yehhuātl.	8. Ahtleitin.
3. Oc nō ixquichtin.	9. Ye amixquichtin.
4. Ahzo amacahmeh.	10. Quēmmach huel tehhuāntin!
5. Cuix yehhuāntin?	11. Cuix amitlahmeh?
6. Huel izquitetl.	12. Zan achitōn.

EXERCISE 25. Cardinal Numbers

25A. *Number Words.* Analyze and translate.
1. caxtōltetl omōme
2. ōmpōhualli onchiucnāhui
3. mahtlācpantli ocē
4. chiucnāuhōlōtl
5. yēpōhualtetl omēi
6. chicuacentlamantli
7. tlamic ommahtlāctli omōme
8. mahtlācpōhualli oncaxtōlli omēi
9. cempōhualli ommahtlāctli onnāhui
10. nāuhpōhualtetl ommācuīlli

25B. *Number Words in Wider Sentence Contexts.* Pronounce and translate.
1. Zan mahtlāctli omōme.
2. Cuix oc yēi?
3. Quēmmaniān nāhui.
4. Ye caxtōltetl.
5. Anquēxquichtin? —Tināhuintin.
6. Āxcān zan caxtōltin. Yālhua caxtōltin omēi.
7. Ahocmō chicuacē.
8. Cuix timācuīltin? —Ahmō, zan tēintin.
9. Zan tlamic ommahtlāctli omēi.
10. Cuix ētēcpantli?
11. Niman ōmocentlālihqueh.
12. Nel centēcpantli.
13. Cuix ētetl? —Ahmō, zan ōntetl.
14. Zan quicencua.

58

EXERCISE 26. Supplementation (Part One)

26A. *The Supplementary Subject Function.* Analyze and translate.

> *Examples:* Ōnicoch. Ōnicoch nehhuātl.
> ō-ni(coch)∅-∅ = I slept.
> ō-ni(coch)∅-∅ n-∅(eh-huā)tl = I-slept I-am-the-one; i.e., *I* slept.

Ahtleh. Ahtleh īmāxtli.
> ∅-∅(ah-tleh)∅ = It is nothing.
> ∅-∅(ah-tleh)∅ ∅-ī(māx-tli)∅ = It-is-nothing it-is-his-breechcloth; i.e.,
> His breechcloth is nothing; i.e., He has no breechcloth. ~ He wears
> no breechcloth.

1. Chōca. Chōca centetl.
2. Tzahtzih. Tzahtzih mochintin.
3. Ōittōqueh. Ōittōqueh yehhuāntin.
4. Ca ahtleh. Ca ahtleh īpatiuh.
5. Nicān ōtonocah. Nicān ōtonocah timiequintin.
6. Ōme. Ōme ītēn.
7. Ōmpa mochīhua. Ōmpa mochīhua chīlli.
8. Tēihtlacoa. Tēihtlacoa peyōtl.
9. Monamaca. Monamaca ocōtl.
10. Ōmotlālih. Ōmotlālih tletl.

26B. *The Supplementary Object Function.* Analyze and translate.

> *Example:* Ōquic. Ōquic octli.
> ō-∅-qu(i)∅-c = He drank it.
> ō-∅-qu(i)∅-c ∅-∅(oc)tli = He-drank-it it-is-pulque; i.e., He drank pul-
> que.

1. Cōyah. Cōyah cintli.
2. Quimittac. Quimittac cīcītlaltin.
3. Cahciqueh. Cahciqueh centetl.
4. Quimihua. Quimihua mochehhuāntin.
5. Quichīuhqueh. Quichīuhqueh īn.
6. Quinhuīcac. Quinhuīcac oc cequintin.
7. Quimmacatoh. Quimmacatoh tilmahtli.
8. Quihuāllāzah. Quihuāllāzah tepozmītl.
9. Quinhuālitztoc. Quinhuālitztoc māmazah.
10. Nicchīhua. Nicchīhua cactli.
11. Quinhuālmacaqueh. Quinhuālmacaqueh cōzcatl.
12. Quitzomōnih. Quitzomōnih ocōtl.

26C. *The Supplementary-Possessor Function.* Analyze and translate.

> *Example:* Īncuen. Īncuen nāhuintin.
> Ø-īn(cuen)Ø = It is their spaded land. ~ They are their spaded lands.
> Ø-īn(cuen)Ø Ø-Ø(nāhui-n)tin = It-is-their-spaded-land they-are-four-in-number; i.e., It is the spaded land of the four. ~ They-are-their-spaded-lands they-are-four-in-number; i.e., They are the spaded lands of the four.

1. Notōpīl. Notōpīl nehhuātl.
2. Māmauh. Māmauh tehhuātl.
3. Īntilmah. Īntilmah ēintin.
4. Īocuilhuān. Īocuilhuān cuahuitl.
5. Īmācal. Īmācal yehhuāntin.
6. Īxāl. Īxāl ātoyatl.
7. Tohhui. Tohhui tehhuāntin.
8. Īteuh. Īteuh michin.
9. Īnhuīpīl. Īnhuīpīl cihuah.
10. Amocnīhuān. Amocnīhuān amoquichtin.

26D. *Multiple Supplements.* Identify the supplementary functions of the adjuncts and translate the sentences.

1. Nēchcocōlia nehhuātl īoquichhui.
2. Quimmictih notōtolhuān mochichi.
3. Cuix nēchnamaquīltīz ocōtl mocnīuh?
4. Mochipa qui ītah octli.
5. Quitēmoa nocac nonān.
6. Ye ōmācalaquih mochhui tehhuātl.
7. Ahtleh ītōcā īmpiltōn nocnīhuān.
8. Ahniquimpalēhuīz īyāōhuān nāltepēuh.

26E. *The Topicalization Transformation.* Identify the function of the supplement and translate.

1. Cualo peyōtl. Peyōtl cualo.
2. Ticpia ētetl. Ētetl ticpia.
3. Quīzah mochintin. Mochintin quīzah.
4. Tepēhui miec. Miec tepēhui.
5. Yetiuh nochīmal. Nochīmal yetiuh.
6. Mā moquetz yehhuātl. Yehhuātl mā moquetz.
7. Ca īmicnīuh notah. Notah ca īmicnīuh.
8. Mā xictlati āmatl. Āmatl mā xictlati.

26F. *Supplements in Information Questions.* Identify the function of the supplement and translate.

    1. Monequi mācuilli. Quēxquich monequi?
    2. Ticcōhuaz cactli. Tleh ticcōhuaz?
    3. Mitzahman nopiltzin. Āc mitzahman?
    4. Quinechicōz ocōtl. Tleh quinechicōz?
    5. Cuix ītilmah mocōl? Āquin ītilmah?
    6. Cāna nāuhtetl. Quēzquitetl cāna?

26G. *Further Practice with Sentences Involving Supplementation.* Pronounce and translate.

    1. Mānēn calac mochichi.
    2. Ca ēintin īpilhuān.
    3. Tlein tinēchmacaz?
    4. Mānēn tiquihtlacoh nocōzqui.
    5. Ōmpa huetzticah īohhui teōcuitlatl.
    6. Īmācal mā tiquilactīcān.
    7. Ōmpa onhuetzqueh mochintin.
    8. Tleh nicchīhuaz?
    9. Tetl ītzontecon.
   10. Ahtleh nimitzcelilīz.
   11. Mā zan tehhuāntin tihuiān.
   12. Ōmpa ahmō tleh mochīhua.
   13. Āc tehhuātl?
   14. Aoc tleh huel quihtohqueh.
   15. Ayāc tleh contēnquīxtīz.
   16. Occeppa mochintin huālyetiahqueh.
   17. Ye acah cholōz.
   18. Moch quincuīlihqueh.
   19. Ahmō monān monān. Ahmō motah motah.
   20. Mochipa īntemātl yetinemi.

EXERCISE 27. Supplementation (Part Two)

27A. *Marked Supplementation.* Identify the function of the supplement and translate.

> *Example:* Quināmiquitoh. Quināmiquitoh in pīpiltin. = They went in order to meet him. The nobles went in order to meet him. [*in pīpiltin* = suppl subj]

1. Quixihxīpēuhtinemi. Quixihxīpēuhtinemi in cuahuitl.
2. Oncān quimāna. Oncān quimāna in cuauhocuiltin.
3. Huālpoztequi. Huālpoztequi in metlatl.
4. Miquizqueh. Miquizqueh in ītlācahuān.
5. Ahmō quitatacayah. Ahmō quitatacayah in teōcuitlatl.
6. Ye quīzah! Ye quīzah in amoyāōhuān!
7. Ahmō tecihuīlōz. Ahmō tecihuīlōz in īmīl.
8. Ca ōtiquimittatoh. Ca ōtiquimittatoh in totēucyōhuān.
9. Companahuihqueh. Companahuihqueh in ātoyatōntli.
10. Yacattihuītzeh. Yacattihuītzeh in īmitzcuinhuān.
11. Ca zā cē. Ca zā cē in īnteōuh.
12. Huel ōmpa mochīhua. Huel ōmpa mochīhua in momochitl.
13. Ahhuel ticcōhuaz. Ahhuel ticcōhuaz inīn.
14. Māntiāz. Māntiāz in āltepētl.
15. Ca nāxcā. Ca nāxcā inōn.

27B. *Marked Supplements in the Topicalized Transformation.* Identify the function of the supplement serving as the sentence topic and translate.

> *Example:* Ōmpa cah. Ōmpa cah īchān. In Petoloh ōmpa cah īchan. = It is there. His home is there. Peter's home is there. [*in Petoloh* = suppl poss of *īchān,* which is the suppl subj]

1. Ca nocōltzin. In yehhuātl, ca nocōltzin.
2. Mānēn ticahmantih. Inīn, mānēn ticahmantih.
3. Quitqui. Quitqui teōcuitlatl. In ātoyatl quitqui teōcuitlatl.
4. Huehca huehhuetzito. In tetl huehca huehhuetzito.
5. Nontlehcoz. In nehhuātl nontlehcoz.
6. Ca Cōltzin. Ītōcā ca Cōltzin. In īnteōuh ītōcā, ca Cōltzin.
7. Ahmō mihtōtiah. In yehhuāntin ahmō mihtōtiah.
8. Niccuāznequi. In nacatl niccuāznequi.
9. Quihuāllāzah. Quihuāllāzah in tepozmītl. In yehhuāntin quihuāllāzah in tepozmītl.
10. Cencah ōquihuelcac. Cencah ōquihuelcac in piltōntli. In zazanīlli cencah ōquihuelcac in piltōntli.

11. Oncān mocēhuihqueh. In yehhuāntin oncān mocēhuihqueh.
12. Huālmotepēhua. In eztli huālmotepēhua.
13. Yetinemi. Īntēnteuh yetinemi. Īntēnteuh yetinemi in oquichtin.
14. Cencah momauhtihqueh. In ixquichtin cencah momauhtihqueh.

27C. *Ambiguity in Supplements.* Translate each supplement in as many functions as possible.

> *Example:* In Petoloh quilhuih in ītah. = Peter said it to his father. His father said it to Peter. Peter's father said it to him. Peter's father said it to her. He said it to Peter's father.

1. In tocuilcoyōtl quitta in cueyatl.
2. In oquichtli in cihuātl ōquimictih.
3. Quimacac in nocnīuh in piltōntli.
4. In tzinācan ōquimauhtih in tecolōtl.
5. In xōlo quicocōliāya in tlācatl.
6. Yehhuātlīn conihua yehhuātlōn.

27D. *Peculiarities in the Use of Supplements.* Point out the peculiarity and translate.

> *Example:* Mōztla ōmpa tiāzquez in notēlpōch. = My son and I shall go there tomorrow. ["named-partner" construction]

1. Tleh ōamāxqueh?
2. Cān īchān?
3. Tilmahtli contlāliliāyah in toquichtin.
4. Tichtec? Tiquichtec in cōzcatl?
5. Cuix ōanquimolhuihqueh in pōchtēcatl?
6. Moch oncān ōāpanoqueh.
7. Tētzāhuitl catca.
8. Ōtitonohnōtzqueh in nocnīuh.

27E. *The Vocative Construction.* Pronounce and translate.

1. Āc tehhuātl, in nocné?
2. Mācamō ximotequipacho, nocnīhué.
3. Ca nicān anmonoltihtoqueh, nopilhuāné.
4. Huel ximopia, nopiltzé.
5. In tinopiltzin, tlā xiccaqui.
6. Tlācatl, mā xicmocuīli.
7. Ca nicān ticah, in tinotēlpōchtzin.
8. Nopilhuāntzitziné, mā nicān ximohuetzitīcān!
9. In Tēteoh TīnNān, mā xicmomaquili!
10. In antēnānhuān, āc oc nel anquimottiliah?

27F. *Further Practice on Shared-Referent Supplementation.* Pronounce and translate.

1. Quimīximatiah in cīcītlaltin.
2. Īmācal quitzīnquīxtihqueh in toyāōhuān.
3. Ye tlālpolihuiz in īchān.
4. Quinhuālitztoqueh in īmicnīhuān.
5. Zan niman ahhuelitqueh in nānāhualtin.
6. Cencah popōca in cuahuitl.
7. Ye contocaz in tōchtli īohhui.
8. Zan quimpāccānāmiquito in notah īcnīuh.
9. Ca in ōmpa mitzonmotlapieliliah in mocōlhuān.
10. Huāllāzqueh in pīpiltin īmpilhuān.
11. Ahzo huel quinxōxazqueh in tlācatecoloh.
12. Cuix ītleuh yetinemi in coyōtl? [Note: *coyōtl* is not the supple-
    mentary subject of *yetinemi*.]
13. Cencah ōmpa mochīhua in tōlin.
14. Zan ye quimitzticateh in cihuah.
15. In cihuah ahtleh in īnhuīpīl catca.

64

EXERCISE 28. Supplementation (Part Three)

28A. *Verbal Sentences as Shared-Referent Supplements.* Identify the function of the supplement and translate.

Example: Ontlatotōnih. Ontlatotōnih in tēcōānōtza. = He warmed something. The one who calls people as guests warmed something; i.e., The host offered up incense. [*tēcōānōtza,* "he calls people as guests" = suppl subj]

1. Huālquīzah. Huālquīzah in mihtōtīzqueh.
2. Oncateh. Oncateh in nāhuatlahtoah.
3. Ōniquimihuah. Ōniquimihuah in ōyahqueh.
4. Ōittōqueh. Ōittōqueh in āquihqueh ōhuāllahqueh.
5. Quimittazqueh. Quimittazqueh in quēnamihqueh.
6. Huāllāzqueh. Huāllāzqueh in tēyacānah.
7. Oc ceppa huālmonechicohqueh. Oc ceppa huālmonechicohqueh in moyāhuacah.
8. Ye calaquiz. Ye calaquiz in tōnatiuh.
9. Ye miquiz. Ye miquiz in ōtecia.
10. Caxtōltin. Caxtōltin in ōānōqueh.
11. Ōquimīxcuep. In īntēucyo ōquimīxcuep. Inihqueh īn, in īntēucyo ōquimīxcuep.
12. Iz catqui. Iz catqui anquimacazqueh.
13. Ca popolocah. Inihqueh ōn, ca popolocah.
14. Ōniquittac. Ōniquittac in ōticchīuh.

28B. *The Quotative Construction.* Identify the function of the supplement and translate.

Example: Quimilhuihqueh, "Āc amihqueh?" = They said to them, "Who are you?" [The embed *Āc amihqueh* is the supplementary direct object of the silently present object prefix of *quimilhuihqueh.* It serves as the referent of that nuclear direct object.]

1. Quilhuih, "Mācamō ximotequipacho."
2. "Cuātatl," quihtōznequi "tetl ītzontecon."
3. Mihtoa, "Huel cuātatl īn!"
4. Quilhuia, "Xinēchcāhua."
5. Quihtoah, "Mā ihciuhcā ontlamih."
6. Nōhuiān ilhuīlōqueh, "Āc amehhuān? Cāmpa anhuītzeh?"

28C. *The Factive Construction.* Identify the function of the supplement and translate.

> *Example:* Cuix nelli ōmpa ōhuāllahqueh? = Is it true that they came there? [*Ōmpa ōhuāllahqueh* is functioning as the supplementary subject of the matrix sentence *nelli* and serves as the referent of its subject affixes $\emptyset$- . . . -$\emptyset$.]

1. Mā xicnemili in quēnamih ōtinen.
2. Quilmach mochi quitlātilih.
3. Monequi in tiquimtlaīxtlātiah.
4. Quilmach ahmō tecihuīlōz in īmīl.
5. Huel quittaya in cāmpa ye itztiāz. [Translate future as future-in-the-past: "he will go (going)" = "he would go (going)."]
6. Oncān mihtoa in quēnin quixīnqueh īmācal.
7. Ahmō ticmatih cuix mōztla mochīhuaz.
8. In quēnin tzonquīz ahmō huel macho.
9. Nicnequi nictemanaz.
10. In acah conmottilia tēcuātepachōz.
11. Quimolhuiah in tlein ōconmottilihqueh.
12. Quil quinnōtztiuh in īnteōuh.

28D. *Further Practice with Sentences Containing Supplements.* Pronounce and translate.

1. Nicān cah in tictēmoa.
2. Monequi anquimatizqueh in ītōcā.
3. Inihqueh ōn mocuiltōnoah.
4. Quimilhuīco, "Mā xicmopalēhuilīcān in āltepētl!"
5. Iz catqui ōticchīuhqueh.
6. Quimilhuih, "Tlā xihuālhuiān!"
7. Nēcia, quilmach, ye miquiz in ōtecia. [Translate future as future-in-the-past, "she would die."]
8. Quinhuālnānquilihqueh, "Tleh ītōcā?" [not a supplement; see § 28.7]
9. Inihqueh īn mozcaliah.
10. Nicnequi niccuāz in etl.
11. Cuix ticmati in quēn titco?
12. Nicān motēnēhua in āquihqueh Otomih.

66

EXERCISE 29. Nominalization of Verbs (Part One)

29A. *Preterit Agentive Nouns.* Analyze and translate each of the following pairs as preterit verb words and preterit agentive noun words.

Example: ōtitlahtoh, titlahtohqui
ō-ti(tla-htoh)∅-∅ = you spoke, you have spoken [example of *tla-*fusion]
ti-∅(tla-htoh-∅)qui = you are one who has spoken, you are a speaker, you are a king

1. ōnicalpix, nicalpixqui
2. ōtitemoc, titemoc
3. ōtitlanamacaqueh, titlanamacaqueh
4. ōtlan, tlanqui
5. ōnitlatquic, nitlatquic
6. ōmicqueh, mīmicqueh
7. ōtitlahuēlilōc, titlahuēlilōc
8. ōancualānqueh, ancualānqueh
9. ōnitlachix, nitlachixqui
10. ōtipācqueh, tipācqueh
11. ōnimauh, nimauhqui
12. ōtitlaxcac, titlaxcac
13. ōyah, yahqui
14. ōtitlaneloh, titlaneloh

29B. *The Difference between Absolutive and Possessive Forms of Preterit Agentive Nouns.* Analyze and translate.

Example: nitlamīnqui, nimotlamīncāuh
ni-∅(tla-mīn-∅)qui = I am an archer
ni-mo(tla-mīn-∅-cā)uh = I am your archer

1. ticalpixqueh, tīcalpixcāhuān
2. niyahqui, nitiyahcāuh
3. titlahtohqui, tinotlahtohcāuh
4. ninomachtihqui, nīnemachtihcāuh
5. mozcalihqueh, īneizcalihcāhuān
6. ihciuhqui, īmihciuhcāuh
7. titēyacānqui, titotēyacāncāuh
8. nitlamelāuhqui, nimotlamelāuhcāuh
9. tlaciuhqueh, ītlaciuhcāhuān
10. ammihtōtihqueh, amīnneihtōtihcāhuān

29C. *The Three Kinds of Agentive Nouns of Possession.* Analyze and translate.

> *Example:* tzitzilin, tzitzileh
> Ø-Ø(tzi-tzil)in = it is a bell, they are bells
> Ø-Ø(tzi-tzil-eh-Ø)Ø = he is a bell owner

1. nacochtli, tinacocheh
2. oyōhualli, oyōhualehqueh
3. neuctli, neucyoh
4. cuācuahuitl, cuācuahueh
5. eztli, ezzoh
6. cicuilli, nicicuileh
7. popōtl, popōhuah
8. malacatl, malaquehqueh
9. xocotl, xocohuah
10. xāyacatl, xāyaqueh
11. mixtli, mixxoh
12. teōtl, titeōhuahqueh
13. tequitl, tequihuahqueh
14. temātlatl, temātleh
15. āmalacatl, āmalacayoh

29D. *Affective Forms of Preterit Agentive Nouns.* Analyze and translate.

> *Example:* mihtōtihqui, mihtōtihcātzintli
> Ø-Ø(m-ihtōtih-Ø)qui = he is a dancer
> Ø-Ø(m-ihtōtih-Ø-cā-tzin)tli = he is a dancer (H)

1. titlahuēlilōc, titlahuēlilōcāpōl
2. micqui, miccātōntli
3. anteōpixqueh, anteōpixcātzitzin
4. nimīleh, nimīlehcātōntli
5. īnemachtihcāhuān, īnemachtihcāpipīlhuān

29E. *The Preterit Agentive Noun as Embed.* Analyze and translate.

> *Example:* mauhqui, nimauhcātlācatl
> Ø-Ø(mauh-Ø)qui = he is a coward
> ni-Ø(mauh-Ø-cā-tlāca)tl = I am a cowardly person, I am a coward

1. tlamelāuhqui, timotlamelāuhcāquetzaz
2. tlahtohqui, antlahtohcātlahtoah
3. pācqui, quimpāccātlahpalōtoh
4. mauhqui, quimmauhcāittah
5. tlahuēlilōc, tinēchtlahuēlilōcāmati

29F. *Preterit Agentive Nouns in Expanded Sentence Contexts.* Pronounce
and translate.

1. Tleh ītlahtohcātōcā?
2. In huēhuētqueh ahmō mihtōtiah.
3. Yahqueh in teōmāmahqueh.
4. In ācalchīmalehqueh totōcah.
5. In tilmahtli cōāxāyacayoh.
6. Tōtolnamacac tōtoleh.
7. Quinhuīcac in calpixqueh.
8. In pōchtēcahuēhuētqueh tēnāmicqueh.
9. In īntēnteuh in tlahtohqueh teōcuitlatēntetl.
10. Cencah mauhcāittōyah.
11. Inihqueh īn, mīlehqueh.
12. In tēntzoneh nōhuiāmpa tlahtlachia.
13. In piltōntli nāneh.
14. In acah conmottilia tlācahuah yez.
15. Cuauhtenāmehtoc. Cuauhtenānyohtoc. [Explain why the embeds
are not preterit-agentive-noun constructions.]

EXERCISE 30. Nominalization of Verbs (Part Two)

30A. *Customary-Present Agentive Nouns.* Analyze and translate the following pairs as customary-present verb words and customary-present agentive noun words.

Example: nitlacuāni, nitlacuāni
ni-tla(cuā)ni-∅ = I customarily eat things
ni-∅(tla-cuā-ni)∅ = I am one who customarily eats things, I am an
eater

1. nitlahtoāni, nitlahtoāni
2. itzcuincuāni, itzcuincuāni
3. antlamatinih, antlamatinih
4. tēcuānih, tēcuānimeh
5. ninotlātiāni, ninotlātiāni
6. tichōcani, tichōcani
7. tlaini, tlaini
8. titozcaliānih, titozcaliānih
9. nipanoni, nipanoni
10. neminih, neminimeh
11. titlamatini, titlamatinitōn
12. tlāhuānani, tlāhuānanipōl

30B. *Absolutive-State Instrumentive Nouns.* Analyze and translate the following pairs (verb word and derived noun).

Example: panohuani, panohuani
∅(pano-hua)ni-∅ = all customarily cross a river
∅-∅(pano-hua-ni)∅ = it is the means by which people cross a river, it
is passage on a boat, it is a bridge

1. tlālpōhualōni, tlālpōhualōni
2. texōni, texōni
3. tlacōhualōni, tlacōhualōni
4. nemachtilōni, nemachtilōni
5. nelpilōni, nelpilōni
6. tlatlapōlōni, tlatlapōlōnitōn
7. netlālilōni, netlālilōni
8. tlapātzcōni, tlapātzcōni
9. tlapātzcalōni, tlapātzcalōni
10. tlatlāxōni, tlatlāxōni

30C. *Possessive-State Instrumentive Nouns.* Analyze and translate the following pairs (verb words and derived nouns).

Example: tētlahpaloāya, ītētlahpaloāya
Ø-tē(tlahpaloā)ya-Ø = he used to greet people
Ø-ī(tē-tlahpaloā-ya)Ø = it is the means by which he greeted people, it is his salutation, they are his words of greeting, it is his gift of greeting

1. nitlanequia, notlanequia
2. titlacuāya, motlacuāya
3. ceaya, īceaya
4. titlamātocayah, totlamātocaya
5. temīnaya, ītemīnaya
6. ammomānāhuiāyah, amonemānāhuiāya

30D. *Passive Action Nouns.* Analyze and translate the following pairs (verb words and derived nouns).

Example: ōnecōca, īnecōca
ō-Ø(nec-ō)ca-Ø = it had been needed
Ø-ī(nec-ō-ca)Ø = it is its being needed; i.e., it is its usefulness, it is their usefulness; it is useful, they are useful; there is a need for it, there is a need for them

1. ōpalēhuilōca, īpalēhuilōca
2. ōnitlapōlōca, notlapōlōca
3. ōtīximachōcah, tīximachōca
4. ōmictīlōca, īmictīlōca
5. ōnemictīlōca, īnemictīlōca

30E. *The First Type of Active Action Nouns.* Analyze and translate the following pairs (verb words and derived nouns).

Example: ōyacaceliaca [for *ōyacaceliyaca*], īyacacelica
ō-Ø(yaca-celi-ya)ca-Ø = it had become fresh at the tips [(yaca)-tl = nose, point, tip; (celi-ya) = to sprout]
Ø-ī(yaca-celi-ca)Ø = it is its freshness at the tips; i.e., it is its new growth [Notice the use of the archaic pluperfect: *ōyacacelica.*]

1. ōihtlacauhcah, īmihtlacauhca
2. ōmocuepca, īnecuepca
3. ōniyōlca, noyōlca
4. ōtinēzcah, tonēzca
5. ōtihuelnēzca, mohuelnēzca

30F. *Customary-Present Agentive Nouns, Instrumentive Nouns, Passive Action Nouns and the First Type of Active Action Nouns in Wider Sentence Contexts.* Pronounce and translate.

1. Ca nō miec in īnnēzca. Nōhuiān cah in īnnēzca.
2. In cihuātl ōquicelih in nepahtīlōni.
3. Ahquēmman ommocāhua in tepoztlatecōni.
4. Cuix amītēyāōchīhuanih ayeznequih in tlahtoāni? [*Ayeznequih* is a variant spelling of *anyeznequih.*]
5. Ahmō tleh īnecōca.
6. Quintēcuāncua.
7. Iz catqui in īmihtlacauhca in Otomih.
8. Quicua in cuahuitl īyacacelica.
9. Yāōtēcani in teōtl.
10. Īxmihmiquini in tlahcah.

EXERCISE 31. Deverbative Nouns (Part One)

31A. *The Second Type of Active Action Nouns.* Analyze and translate the following triplets (verb words and derived nouns in the possessive and absolutive states).

Example: nicocōya, nococōliz, cocōliztli
ni(cocōya)∅-∅ = I become sick, I am sick
∅-no(cocō-liz)∅ = it is my becoming sick, it is my sickness
∅-∅(cocō-liz)tli = it is the act of becoming sick, it is sickness

1. tzahtzi, ītzahtziliz, tzahtziliztli
2. titētlahpaloa, motētlahpalōliz, tētlahpalōliztli
3. titonēxtiah, tonenēxtīliz, nenēxtīliztli
4. antēxōxah, amotēxōxaliz, tēxōxaliztli
5. mocuepa, īnecuepaliz, necuepaliztli
6. nimahui, nomahuiz, mahuiztli

31B. *Passive Patientive Nouns.* Analyze and translate the following pairs (verb words and derived nouns).

Example: ticmah, malo, malli
ti-c(ma)∅-h = we take him prisoner
∅(ma-lo)∅-∅ = he is taken prisoner
∅-∅(ma-l)li = he is one who has been taken prisoner; he is a prisoner

1. annēchtītlanih, nitītlano, nitīlantli
2. quicuah, cualo, cualli
3. ticnāhuatiah, nāhuatīlo, tonāhuatīl
4. quitzacua, tzacuīlo, tzacuīlli
5. quitta, ithualo, ithualli
6. ticpozōnah, pozōnalo, pozōnalli
7. nicpa, palo, palli
8. quināmiquih, nāmico, nāmictli
9. quiquetzah, quetzalo, quetzalli
10. nictēmaca, tēmaco, notēmac

31C. *Passive Patientives and the Second Type of Active Action Nouns in Wider Sentence Contexts.* Pronounce and translate.

1. Cuauhtenāmehtoc in ithualli.
2. Quichīuhqueh īn in tītlantin.
3. Quimihua in nānāhualtin.
4. Malmiquih in pōchtēcah. Malmicohua.

5. Quimotequitiah in tēihpītzaliztli.
6. Quihtlanilīz in ītēicnēlīliz.
7. Ahzo cocōlizcuizqueh.
8. Ye nāhualquīzah in amoyāōhuān!
9. Nō quimāhuīltiah in tēxōxaliztli.
10. Ahmō titēnāmichuān.

74

EXERCISE 32. Deverbative Nouns (Part Two)

32A. *Impersonal Patientive Nouns.* Analyze and translate the following pairs (verb words and derived nouns).

> *Example:* titlachinoah, tlachinōlo, tlachinōlli
> ti-tla(chinoa)Ø-h = we burn fields
> Ø-tla(chinō-lo)Ø-Ø = fields are burnt
> Ø-Ø(tla-chinō-l)li = it is a burnt field

1. nichihcha, chihchīhua, chihchītl
2. antlatatacah, tlatataco, tlatatactli
3. titlamanah, tlamano, tlamantli
4. tlalpiah, tlalpīlo, tlalpīlli
5. titlacuah, tlacualo, tlacualli
6. amāhuiah [for *amāhuiyah*], āhuilo, āhuīlli
7. titlaōyah, tlaōlo, tlaōlli
8. tōna, tōnalli
9. titlahtoah, tlahtōlo, tlahtōlli
10. antlaih, tlaīlo, tlaīlli
11. tlachipīniah, tlachipīnilo, tlachipīnīlli
12. cāltiah, āltīlo, tlaāltīlli
13. titlaxcah, tlaxcalo, tlaxcalli
14. yohua, yohualli
15. titocuiltōnoah, necuiltōnolo, necuiltōnōlli

32B. *Compound Patientive (Passive or Impersonal) Nouns.* Analyze and translate.

> *Example:* quicuāchiquih, cuāchico, cuāchictli
> Ø-qui(cuā-chiqui)Ø-h = they are scraping him at the head; i.e., they are shaving his head [*cuā-* is embedded as an incorporated noun as adverb.]
> Ø(cuā-chic-o)Ø-Ø = he is being scraped at the head; i.e., his head is being shaved
> Ø-Ø(cuā-chic)tli = he is one whose head is shaved, he is a high-ranking warrior

1. quincuāchiquih, cuāchicoh, cuācuāchictin
2. āpozōnah, āpozōnalo, āpozōnalli
3. ninīxcāhuia, neīxcāhuilo, neīxcāhuīlli
4. tochpānah, ochpāno, ochpāntli
5. teōtl, nāhuatīlli, teōnāhuatīlli
6. ammācēhuah, mācēhualo, ammācēhualtin

32C. *Impersonal Patientive Nouns and Compound Patientives (Passive and Impersonal) in Wider Sentence Structures.* Pronounce and translate.

1. Neteōithualtēmalōc.
2. Māpozōnalnehnequi.
3. Āquin tlaxcalixcac?
4. Cuix titlaxcalchīhuaz?
5. Tlaāltīlmicohuaya. Tēāltiāyah in pōchtēcah.
6. Quihua tlahtōlitquic.
7. Quihuālcaquītiāyah in ītlahtōl.
8. Niman huālquīzah in cuācuāchictin.
9. Quinmacah izquitlamantli.
10. Zan huel īneīxcāhuīl.
11. Inihqueh īn, cencah īntlacual in etl.
12. Zan quimātlatēmah in tlaōlli.

76

EXERCISE 33. Deverbative Nouns (Part Three)

33A. *The Past Patientive.* Analyze and translate the following pairs (verb words and derived nouns).

Example: ōnen, īnen
ō-∅(nen)∅-∅ = he has lived
∅-ī(nen)∅ = it is what he has lived; i.e., it is his life

1. ōtlaquēn, tlaquēntli
2. ōtlequiquiz, tlequiquiztli
3. ōtēnōtz, tlanōtzli
4. ōtlaquetz, tlaquetztli

5. ōnitlachīuh, notlachīuh
6. ōyōl, yōlli
7. *ōyōlloh, yōllohtli, īyōlloh
8. *ōtlazoh, tlazohtli

33B. *Contrast between Preterit Agentive Nouns and Past Patientive Nouns.* Analyze and translate.

Example: tezqui, textli
∅-∅(tez-∅)qui = she is one who grinds [e.g., corn on a metate]
∅-∅(tex)tli = it is what is ground [e.g., it is corn meal]

1. tlanamacac, tlanamactli
2. tlamelāuhqui, tlamelāuhtli
3. tlachīuhqui, tlachīuhtli

4. nenqui, nentli
5. tlaquetzqui, tlaquetztli
6. cualānqui, cualāntli

33C. *The Present Patientive Noun.* Analyze and translate the following pairs (verb words and derived nouns).

Example: quiahui, quiahuitl
∅(quiahui)∅-∅ = it is raining
∅-∅(quiahui)tl = it is rain

1. nitlatqui, notlatqui, tlatquitl
2. ehca, ehcatl
3. tecihui, tecihuitl
4. tlatzopiloa, tzopilōtl

5. tlatechaloa, techalōtl
6. tlacui, tlacuitl
7. tlaquēmi, tlaquēmitl
8. tlacua, tlacuatl

33.D. *Present Patientive Nouns Formed from Compound Verbs Having *tla-(yoa) as Matrix.* Analyze and translate.

Example: yāōtl, yāōyōtl
∅-∅(yāō)tl = he is an enemy
∅-∅(yāō-yō)tl = it is war, it is enmity

1. tlahtōlli, tlahtōllōtl
2. tlācatl, tlācayōtl
3. oquichtli, oquichchōtl

4. nāntli, nānyōtl
5. mahuiztli, mahuizzōtl
6. tēntli, tēnyōtl

7. tlahtohqui, tlahtohcāyōtl
8. xōlopihtli, xōlopihyōtl

9. ichcatl, ichcayōtl
10. tahtli, tahyōtl

33E. *The Difference between Alien and Organic Possession.* Analyze and translate.

Example: īxōchihcual, īxōchihcuallō
$\emptyset$-ī(xōchih-cual)$\emptyset$ = it is his fruit
$\emptyset$-ī(xōchih-cual-lo)$\emptyset$ = it is its fruit (part of the tree)

1. īmez, īmezzo
2. iihhuiuh, iihhuiyo

3. momiuh, momiyo
4. monac, monacayo

33F. *Root Patientive Nouns.* Analyze and translate the following pairs (verb words and derived nouns).

Example: olōlihui, olōlli
$\emptyset$(olōl-ihui)$\emptyset$-$\emptyset$ = it becomes spherical
$\emptyset$-$\emptyset$(olōl)li = it is something that has become spherical; it is a ball

1. pepeyoca, pepeyoctli
2. tīzatl, tīcēhua, tīcectli
3. xoxōhui, xoxoctli
4. cualāni, cualactli
5. catzāhua, catzactli
6. yēcahui, yēctli
7. tlapechoa, tlapechtli

8. pechahui, pechtli
9. tlahuītōloa, tlahuītōlli
10. tlacomōloa, tlacomōlli
11. malacachihui, malacachtli
12. tzōlihui, tzōlli
13. tlahpalihui, tlahpalli
14. ilacachihui, ilacachtli

33G. *Past Patientives, Present Patientives, and Root Patientives in Wider Sentence Contexts.* Pronounce and translate.

1. Cocōya in īnacayo.
2. Ihciuhcā quipoloa in ītlatqui.
3. Huel quīximatih xihuitl in iihiyo.
4. Quimatiah in īmihiyo cīcītlaltin.
5. Conquēntia in quetzalquēmitl.
6. Tepoztli in īntlahuītōl.
7. In īmezzo in miquiah huel ōmpa huālahcia.
8. Ōmpa quitēcah tlapechtli.
9. Huel monequi amotlahpal.
10. In ahmō yōllōtlahpalihui zan motlaloa.
11. Oncān ihiyōcuiqueh. In īmihiyo quicuiqueh.
12. Quihuīcatiahqueh cuauhtlapechtli.
13. In īntlaquēn catca ichtli.

PART FOUR

Modification
Complementation
Conjunction

EXERCISE 34. Adjectives (Part One)

34A. *Patientive Nouns as Adjectives.* Analyze and translate the following pairs (verb words and patientive nouns). Translate each noun as (*a*) a noun and (*b*) an adjective.

Example: tlīlihui, tlīlli
$\emptyset$(tlīl-ihui)$\emptyset$-$\emptyset$ = it becomes inky
$\emptyset$-$\emptyset$(tlīl)li = (*a*) it is ink; (*b*) it is black

1. cōzahui, cōztli
2. ilacachihui, ilacachtli
3. tzōlihui, tzōlli
4. yēcahui, yēctli
5. catzāhua, catzactli
6. tīcēhua, tīcectli   [The source contains the incorporated noun *(tīza)-tl.*]
7. tlacua, cualli
8. tlalpia, tlalpīlli
9. tlachinoa, tlachinōlli
10. ninīxcāhuia, neīxcāhuīlli   [The source contains the incorporated noun *(īx)-tli.*]

34B. *Nominalized Verbs as Adjectives.* Analyze and translate the following pairs (verb words and derived agentive nouns). Translate each noun as (*a*) a noun and (*b*) an adjective.

Example: ōhuāc, huācqui
ō-$\emptyset$(huāc)$\emptyset$-$\emptyset$ = it has become dry
$\emptyset$-$\emptyset$(huāc-$\emptyset$)qui = (*a*) it is a dry thing; (*b*) it is dry

1. ōtlīliuh, tlīliuhqui
2. ōcatzāhuac, catzāhuac
3. ōichtic, ichtic
4. ōxoxōuh, xoxōuhqui
5. ōhuēiyac, huēiyac
6. ōchicāhuac, chicāhuac
7. cemihcac, cemihcac [The stem incorporates *(cem)-$\emptyset$* as an adverb. Remember that the verb word is a preterit-as-present–tense form.]
8. ōxoxoctic, xoxoctic
9. ōtilāhuac, tilāhuac
10. *ōihiyoh, ihiyoh [The stem incorporates the obsolete noun *(ihi)-

tl as direct object. The source stem **(ihi-yoa)* no longer occurs in a freestanding *verb* word, and for that reason the preterit form is here marked with an asterisk.]

34C. *Nominalized Obsolete Preterit Forms as Adjectives.* Analyze and translate the following pairs (current preterit forms and obsolete preterit forms used as adjectives). Analyze each obsolete preterit form as a preterit form, and then reanalyze it as a derived agentive noun.

Example: ōiztayac, iztac
ō-∅(izta-ya)∅-c = it has become white
*∅(izta)∅-c > ∅-∅(izta-∅)c = it is white

1. ōihyāyac, ihyāc
2. ōātix, ātic
3. ōcocōx, cocōc
4. ōyancuix, yancuic
5. ōitztiac, itztic
6. ōtlīltiac, tlīltic
7. ōcōztiac, cōztic
8. ōcecēyac, cecēc

34D. *The Nominalized Customary-Present Passive Form as an Adjective.* Analyze and translate the following pairs (verb words and derived adjectives).

Example: cualōni, cualōni
∅(cua-lō)ni-∅ = it is customarily eaten
∅-∅(cua-lō-ni)∅ = it is edible

1. chialōni, chialōni
2. pōhualōni, pōhualōni
3. necōni, necōni
4. chōquilīlōni, chōquilīlōni
5. namacōni, namacōni
6. ichtecōni, ichtecōni

34E. *The Predicate-Adjective Sentence with Supplements and Adverbial Adjuncts.* Pronounce and translate.

1. Tenāmeh in āltepētl.
2. Miec in tlamantli.
3. Zan tiyohqueh in tihuēhuētqueh.
4. In īmitzcuinhuān huehhuēintin.
5. Yehhuāntin ahīmel. Tlatziuhqueh.
6. Cencah iztac in īnxāyac.
7. In tlālchīuhqui chicāhuac.

8. In īpōcyo cencah ihyāc.
9. Cequintin tlīltic in īntzon.
10. Ahmō huēyac in īncuē.
11. Ēintin cencah chicāhuaqueh.
12. In oquichtin huellazohtli in īncac.
13. Nehhuātl ezzoh noxāyac.
14. Nepāpan in cōlōtl.
15. In ītēntzon cencah huīac.
16. Inīn cualōni.
17. Cencah īmacaxōni.
18. Cencah huēi in ācalli.

EXERCISE 35. Adjectives (Part Two)

35A. *Intensified Adjective Stems.* Analyze and translate the following pairs.

Example: huehhuēintin, huehhuēipopōl
    Ø-Ø(hueh-huēi-n)tin = they are big
    Ø-Ø(hueh-huēi-po-pōl)Ø = they are very big

1. chichic, chichipahtic
2. huitztli, huitztōntli
3. cōztli, cōzpōl
4. huapactli, huapacpahtic
5. huehhuēi, huehhuēipōl
6. itztic, itzticāpahtic
7. tapayōltic, tapayōlticātōntli
8. tlahpaltic, tlahpalticāpōl

35B. *Adjectives Involving Various Kinds of Compound Formations.* Analyze and translate the following pairs.

Example: tecontic, cuātecontic
    Ø-Ø(tecon-ti-Ø)c = it is pot-shaped
    Ø-Ø(cuā-tecon-ti-Ø)c = it is pot-shaped at the head; i.e., it is pot-headed

1. niztac, nicuāiztac
2. tlahuēlilōc, tēntlahuēlilōc
3. huitztic, tzīnhuitztic
4. tichicāhuac, tiyōllōchicāhuac
5. titlahuēlilōqueh, tiyāōtlahuēlilōqueh
6. niztalli, nicuāiztalli
7. huāctli, tlālhuāctli
8. huācqui, tlālhuācqui
9. huīac, tlācahuīac
10. ihyāc, xoquihyāc
11. tilāhuac, ihhuitilāhuac
12. tilāhuac, ihhuiyōtilāhuac
13. olōltic, cuitlaolōltic
14. ancatzactin, anteōcatzactin

35C. *Adjectives as Embeds in Compound Nouns.* Analyze and translate the following pairs.

Example: mauhqui, mauhcātlācatl
    Ø-Ø(mauh-Ø)qui = he is afraid
    Ø-Ø(mauh-Ø-cā-tlāca)tl = he is a cowardly person

1. tlazohtli, tlazohtilmahtli
2. tepoztli, īntepoztōpīl
3. tlahuēlilōc, tlahuēlilōcātlahtōlli
4. ichtli, īmichtilmahtli
5. cocōxqui, mococōxcānān

35D. *Intensified Adjectives and Adjectives in Compounds (Either as Matrix or as Embed) in Wider Sentence Contexts.* Pronounce and translate.

1. Ahmō yōllōchicāhuac in īcnīuh.
2. Īmichmāxtli catca.
3. Tlazohtlanqui in tilmahtli.
4. In īmitzcuinhuān huehhuēipopōl.
5. Huālquīza in īhuēitlatqui. [Here *(huēi-)* has the meaning of "important."]
6. Yōllōtlahuēlilōc in tēlpōchtli.
7. Quinmacaya in tlazohtilmahtli.
8. Ōtlālhuāccāquīzacoh.
9. Ye nicuāiztaleh.
10. In tlanōtztli tlahtōlhuēlic.

EXERCISE 36. Adjectival Modification (Part One)

36A. *The Adjectival-Modification Transformation.* In each of the following pairs the first sentence serves as the source for the second. Translate the first as a structure of supplementation and the second as a structure of adjectival modification.

> *Example:* Huēi in calli. Calli huēi.
> > The house is big. [The adjective word is matrix.]
> > It is a house that is big. [The noun word is matrix.]

> 1. Huēyac in īncuē. Īncuē huēyac.
> 2. Neucyoh in tlaxcalli. Tlaxcalli in neucyoh.
> 3. Ihyāc in pōctli. Pōctli ihyāc.
> 4. Itztic in ehcatl. Ehcatl in itztic.
> 5. Cualli in petlatl. Petlatl cualli.
> 6. Yēctli in ātl. Ātl yēctli.
> 7. Chicāhuac in tlālchīuhqui. Tlālchīuhqui chicāhuac.
> 8. Tlatziuhqui in notlācauh. Notlācauh in tlatziuhqui.

36B. *The Problem of Ambiguity in Structures of Supplementation and Structures of Adjectival Modification.* Translate the embed first as a supplement and second as an adjectival modifier.

> *Example:* Tohmitl in huēyac.
> > That which is long is fur.
> > It is fur which is long.

> 1. Titlācatl in timozcalih.
> 2. Tletl in tictlālihqueh.
> 3. Nimopil in nicualli.
> 4. Calli in quichīuhqueh.
> 5. Tlālli in huācqui.

36C. *The Preposing Transformation.* Translate (source and transform).

> *Example:* Quih in octli in cualli. Quih in cualli octli. = They drink the pulque that is good. They drink the good pulque.

> 1. Yah in calpixqui in huēi. Yah in huēi calpixqui.
> 2. Monequi in tlaxcalli iztac. Monequi in iztac tlaxcalli.
> 3. Nicān cocōliztli in huēi mochīuh. Nicān huēi cocōliztli mochīuh.
> 4. Quitataca in teōcuitlatl in cōztic. Quitataca in cōztic teōcuitlatl.
> 5. Quinamaca in tilmahtli in tlazohtli. Quinamaca in tlazohtli tilmahtli.

36D. *Further Practice with Sentences Involving Adjectival Modification.* Pronounce and translate.

1. Zan mocenchīhuaya in tlacualli in quicuāyah.
2. Quinamaca in nepāpan ihhuitl.
3. In cōātl quimitta in onoqueh mācēhualtin.
4. In īāuh itztic ātl.
5. Quimīximatiah in ōmpa onoqueh cīcītlaltin.
6. Ca nō miec in īnnēzca in quichīuhqueh.
7. Quinhuīcac oc cequintin calpixqueh.
8. Izcah in tlahtōlli in quihtohtihuih in huēhuētqueh.
9. Yehhuāntin īntlaīximach in ōmpa mochīhua peyōtl.
10. Cencah tomāhuac in cuahuitl ihcaca.
11. Quimittītih in quihuālcuiqueh cōzcatl.
12. Ōntetl in ācalli in concalaquihqueh.
13. Ixquich tlācatl quicac.
14. Quimmacah in izquitlamantli quitquiqueh.

EXERCISE 37. Adjectival Modification (Part Two)

37A. *Constructions Involving the Nonpreposed Adjectival Modifier.* Translate.

1. Huel nehhuātl in niquimahman.
2. In cihuah, cencah tlazohtli in huīpīlli in quichīuhqueh.
3. Ca yehhuātl in quitlālih in zazanīlli.
4. Cencah momauhtihqueh in nānāhualtin in quimictihqueh in pōchtēcatl.
5. Tlatziuhqueh in mācēhualtin in ōmpa cah īmmīl.
6. In tamalli quinamaca, yehhuātl in tōtoltetamalli.
7. Quicuiqueh in ixquich in quittaqueh.

37B. *Sentences Containing Both Preposed and Nonpreposed Adjectival Modifiers.* Translate.

1. Cē ātlacuic cihuātl in quimittac.
2. Inīn tlatquitl in monec quipiayah in pīpiltin.
3. Quinamaca in nepāpan ihhuitl in tlazohtli.
4. Conānqueh cē huēi tiahcāuh in cencah chicāhuac.
5. Quipia cē tezcatl in malacachtic.

37C. *The Topicalization of the Head of a Structure of Modification.* Translate the source and the transform.

1. Nimitzmaca mochi in necuiltōnōlli. Mochi nimitzmaca in necuiltōnōlli.
2. Cencah ihiyoh in octli in quiah. In octli cencah ihiyoh in quiah.
3. Quinhuālhuīcac miequintin Españoles. Miequintin quinhuālhuīcac Españoles.
4. Oncah ixquich in tōnacayōtl. Ixquich oncah in tōnacayōtl.
5. Micqueh cencah miequintin in nicān tlācah. Cencah miequintin micqueh in nicān tlācah.
6. Momauhtihqueh mochintin in Españoles. Mochintin momauhtihqueh in Españoles.
7. Yehhuāntin īntlaīximach mochi in āxcān nemi. Mochi yehhuāntin īntlaīximach in āxcān nemi.
8. Quincuīlihqueh moch in īnyāōtlatqui. Moch quincuīlihqueh in īnyāōtlatqui.
9. Quitlatia in āmatl tlaōlchipīnīlli. In āmatl quitlatia tlaōlchipīnīlli.
10. Cencah pitzāhuac in tlacōtl in ticpia. In tlacōtl cencah pitzāhuac in ticpia.

37D. *Pronominal Interrogatives as Heads in Structures of Modification.* Translate.

1. Nicmacac in tlein quinec.
2. In āquin quīzaznequi, ōmpa quihuālxihxilih.
3. Ōniquittac in āquin ōichtec.
4. In tlein ōtiquihtoh, ca nelli.
5. Ōquittac in tlein ticchīhuazqueh. [Translate future as future-in-the-past.]
6. Ihciuhcā huel quimati in tlein quimomachtia.

37E. *Further Practice with Constructions Involving Adjectival Modification.* Pronounce and translate.

1. Oncān mihtoa in quēnin ahcico in achto ācalli huāllah.
2. Ixquich oncah in xōchihcualli.
3. Inīn mochi nanacatl ahmō xoxōuhcācualōni.
4. In āquin miec quicua, miec tlamantli quitta tēmāmauhtih.
5. Mochi oncah in nepāpan ichcatl.
6. Ahocāc tlācatl ōquīz in mācēhualli.
7. Mochi quīximati in nepāpan tlazohtetl.
8. Ixquich olīn in huēhuentzin.
9. In chīlli quinamaca in cualli.
10. In pahtli quīximati in micohuani.
11. Cencah miec in quitquiqueh in teōcuitlatl.
12. In quitquiqueh in tētlahpalōliztli cencah miec.
13. Ahzo acah ye huītz cēmeh in tohuānyōlqueh.
14. Cē notiāchcāuh ōtitomictihqueh.

EXERCISE 38. Adverbial Modification (Part One)

38A. *Noun Sentences as Adverbial Modifiers.* Translate.

1. In nochān ōhuālmohuīcac in teōpixqui.
2. Onactihcaca in īnāhual.
3. Nepanōtl mohottah.
4. Huālmauhcāquīzqueh in īmāltepēuh.
5. Zan tequitl ōnātlic.
6. Huetzi in innāhuatīl.
7. Zan nāppōhualilhuitl tlahtohcāt.
8. Cuīcatl tiyōlqueh.
9. Ōcalac in tēlpōchcalli.
10. Ninozohzōhua quechōlli.
11. In īnchān cencah cēhua. [*(cēhua)* is an impersonal verb. Translate *(chān)-tli* as "homeland" here.]
12. Acah īchān ōcalacqueh.
13. In ētlamanixtin huel miz.
14. Īntlāhuīz quimonaquiāyah.

38B. *Apocopated Nouns as Adverbs.* Translate. (Remember that frequently such a noun is equivalent to an English prepositional phrase.)

1. Ca nel ōconittac.
2. Ocōzacatl tlani quihuīcah.
3. Huīptla cēhuaz.
4. Ōntlapal huīcōlloh in tlaptli.
5. In teōtlāc ōtlālolīn.
6. Cencah ye huehcāuh mococoa.
7. In ye huehcāuh yehhuātl in īnteōuh catca.
8. Tlacuāuh tlahtohqueh.

38C. *Multiple-Nucleus Structures in the Adverbial Function.* Translate.

1. Mochintin huih in tōnatiuh īchān.
2. Ixquich cāhuitl mocuāilpihtinemih.
3. Ōcalac in huēi tēlpōchcalli.
4. Zan ōme ilhuitl ōmpa mocēhuihqueh.
5. In ixquich in mētztli monequi.

38D. *The Adverbial Noun as Matrix.* Translate.

1. Cēcemilhuitl in huālnehnenqueh.
2. Cēceyohual in quitzaucqueh.

3. Zan tlamatzin [for *tlamachtzin*] in onquīzqueh.
4. Cencah ihuiān in yahtihuītzeh.
5. Huel cē xihuitl in huālmoquetzaya.
6. Huel iuh cemilhuitl in calacohua.
7. Oc huehca yohuan in quīza.
8. Ca nicān in mihtōtīzqueh.

38E. *Adverbials of Time, Place, and Manner.* Translate.

1. In ihcuāc ittōya, zan momimilohtiuh.
2. Huel ōmpa mochīhua in īnchān in momochitl.
3. Ximocuepacān in ōmpa anhuāllahqueh.
4. In ōquittac ītōnacayōuh, pāqui.
5. In ihcuāc īn, ahhuachquiauhtimani.
6. In oc īchān nemi, ceyohual in tlahtoa in centzontlahtōleh.
7. Cencah pācohua in cuīco.
8. In ōquittaqueh in toyāōhuān, motlalōzquiah.
9. In cānin tlacuah, oncān cochih.
10. In ye iuhqui, niman huehhuetz in tlequiquiztli.

92

EXERCISE 39. Adverbial Modification (Part Two)

39A. *Unkeyed Adverbial Embeds.* Translate.
1. Momati ahzo piltzintli in chōca.
2. Huel ximotlachielti in cātlehhuātl achtopa mocui.
3. Huih in tlahtlācaānazqueh.
4. Momatqueh ca oncān quimictīzqueh.
5. Huih tēnāmiquizqueh.
6. Oc cequintin huāllahqueh in quinpalēhuīzquiah.
7. Ye yauh quinmomacaz in tēteoh.
8. In ixquich mācēhualli cenhuetzi in motamalhuia.

39B. *Keyed Adverbial Embeds.* Translate.
1. Intlā oc piltōntli, oc quihuīcah in pilhuahqueh.
2. Intlā zā nēn quēmman nēcia ahzo octli qui, niman quitzauctihuiah.
3. In mānel huehca nemiah, ihciuhcā onahcitihuetziah.
4. In āxcān, mācihui in aocmō cencah monequi tlāhuīztli, ca zan mo-tocatiuh in tlachīhualli.
5. Intlā canah itlah mochīhuaz, huel oc yohuan in huīlohua.
6. Intlācanelmō tichicāhuac, huel ticmāmāz.
7. Ahīmel, mācihui in ichtiqueh.
8. Intlāca oc tleh quitta quitlāhuāntīz, quinamaca in ītilmah.

39C. *Keyed and Unkeyed Adverbial Embeds.* Translate.
1. Huel ixquich tlācatl ōyah in tēnāmiquito.
2. Momatia ca ōmpa in yāōmiquizqueh.
3. Yauh in māltīz.
4. Ōtlamatqueh, āc yeh in mahuizcuic.
5. Mā tihuiān tātatacazqueh, in oncān tātlizqueh.
6. Huītz tēnāhualittaz.
7. Māca tichtequicān in mā titepachōlohtin.
8. Intlāca tleh mohuen, ahhuel ticalaquiz.
9. Inmānel ōtlālmic, ca oquichtli.
10. Māca xitētlaxīma in mā titetzotzonaloh.
11. In mānel yehhuāntin in tēcōāchīhuah, mihtōtiah.
12. Intlā ye cahmana, in quitlathuīltia, quilhuia, "Xinēchcāhua!"

EXERCISE 40. Complementation

40A. *The Object-Complement Construction.* Translate.
1. Ītlahtohcāhuān mochīhuah in tōnatiuh.
2. Mochintin tlamacazqueh mochīhuah.
3. Āc timomati?
4. Xoxōuhqui niccua.
5. Tētepoztin mochīuhtihuītzeh.
6. Pāpalōmeh mocuepah.

40B. *The Subject-Complement Construction.* Translate.
1. Īcēl ihcatihuītz.
2. Cihuātl ōtlācat in īnconētōn.
3. In tlecuīlli nexxoh catca.
4. At īntlacoch catca.
5. Tomāhuac ihcac in cuahuitl.
6. Tihuēhueh tinēci.

40C. *The Adverbial-Complement Construction.* Translate.
1. Moca xālli. Xālloh.
2. Niman pēhua in tlamīnqui quimīna.
3. Ompēhua motlaloa.
4. Moca zacatl. Zacayoh.
5. Pēhua tepēhui.
6. Titocāhuazqueh ticuīcah.

40D. *The Various Complement Constructions.* Pronounce and translate.
1. Timoca tlālli. Titlālloh.
2. Tixōlopihtin titocuepah.
3. Huel melāhuac quimocaquītīz.
4. Yehhuātl īīxīptla mochīuh.
5. In ye huāllāznequi quiahuitl, ihcuāc pēhua in tlahtoa in īn tōtōtl.
6. Āc ninomati?
7. Ye nihuēhueh ninēci.
8. Ahmō huehcāhuazqueh yāōquīzatīhuih.
9. Pēhua ahhuachquiahui.
10. In ācalchīmalli cuahuitl ahnēci.
11. In īntlaquēn catca ichtli.
12. Yehhuātl pehpenalo in teōpixqui mochīhua.

EXERCISE 41. Relational Nouns (Part One)

41A. *Locative Nouns Formed with the Suffix -n Added to *(cā)-tl.* Analyze and translate.

Example: tēpahpāquiltihqui, tēpahpāquiltihcān
Ø-Ø(tē-pah-pāqui-l-tih-Ø)qui = he is one who has made people happy
Ø-Ø(tē-pah-pāqui-l-tih-Ø-cā-n)Ø = it is a place that makes people happy

1. tōlloh, tōllohcān
2. tlīliuhqui, tlīliuhcān
3. yēctli, yēccān
4. nāhui, nāuhcān
5. cacnamacac, cacnamacacān
6. ιtlaxcalchīuhqui, tlaxcalchīuhcān

7. tēchōctih, tēchōctihcān
8. tēcuiltōnoh, tēcuiltōnoh-cān
9. āhuah, āhuahcān
10. tepēhuah, tepēhuahcān
11. izqui, izquicān

41B. *Locative (or Temporal) Nouns Formed with the Suffix -n Added to the Imperfect-Tense Theme of Active and Impersonal Stems as Well as Those Formed with the Suffix -yān.* Analyze and translate.

Example: tlacuahcuāyah, īntlacuahcuāyān
Ø-tla(cuah-cuā)ya-h = they were grazing
Ø-īn(tla-cuah-cuā-yā-n)Ø = it is their grazing place

1. māltiāya, īneāltiāyān
2. calacohuaya, calacohuayān
3. quīzaya, īquīzayān
4. tlayohuaya, tlayohuayān
5. ātliyah, īmātliyān
6. calaquia, īcalaquiān

7. cēhui, īcēuhyān
8. panohuaya, panohuayān
9. tlaxcalnamacōya, tlaxcalnamacōyān
10. tlapialōya, tlapialōyān
11. yeya, īyeyān

41C. *Locative Nouns Formed with the Relational Suffix -tlah.* Analyze and translate.

Example: tehtetl, tehtetlah
Ø-Ø(teh-te)tl = they are rocks of various shapes and sizes
Ø-Ø(teh-te-tlah)Ø = it is a place of many rocks of various shapes and and sizes, it is a stony area

1. nohpalli, nohpallah
2. tetl, tetlah
3. xohxōchitl, xohxōchitlah
4. calli, callah
5. cahcalli, cahcallah

6. ātl, ānepantlah
7. amehhuāntin, amonepantlah
8. ātl, ātlah
9. tzapotl, tzapotlah
10. yohualli, yohualnepantlah

41D. *Locative Nouns Formed with the Relational Suffix -co ~ -c.* Analyze and translate.

> *Example:* ātlacomōltēntli, ātlacomōltēnco
> Ø-Ø(ā-tla-comō-l-tēn)tli = it is a well rim
> Ø-Ø(ā-tla-comō-l-tēn-co)Ø = on a well rim

1. ātlacomōlli, ātlacomōlco	6. nihti, nihtic
2. quimilli, quimilco	7. īīx, īīxco
3. calmecatl, calmecac	8. tletl, tleco
4. tōptli, tōpco	9. nomā, nomāc
5. īxiquipil, īxiquipilco	10. calpōlli, calpōlco

41E. *Adverbial Nouns Formed with the Relational Suffixes -pa (Directional), -pa (Numeral Adverbial), and -teuh.* Analyze and translate.

> *Examples:* ihhuitl, ihhuiteuh
> Ø-Ø(ihhui)tl = it is a feather
> Ø-Ø(ihhui-teuh)Ø = it is featherlike, it is like a feather

> caxtōlli, caxtōlpa
> Ø-Ø(caxtōl)li = they are fifteen in number
> Ø-Ø(caxtōl-pa)Ø = fifteen times

1. tlacochcalli, tlacochcalco, tlacochcalcopa
2. mācuīlli, mācuīlpa
3. zacatl, zacateuh
4. quiāhuatl, quiāhuac, quiāhuacpa
5. nocealiz, nocealizcopa
6. tlaxcalli, tlaxcalteuh
7. īmāyauhcān, īmāyauhcāmpa
8. nāuhcān, nāuhcāmpa
9. tlaptli, tlapco, tlapcopa
10. īmāopōch, īmāopōchco, īmāopōchcopa

41F. *Adverbial Nouns Formed with Relational Suffixes in Various Sentence Structures.* Pronounce and translate.

1. Ōnicnepantlahtec.
2. In ōmpa calmecac mochintin ōmpa cochih.
3. Nauhcān xeliuhticah.
4. Cuauhtlah īmochīhuayān.
5. Huālquīzah in ithualnepantlah.
6. Texcalco in īchān.
7. Conmana tleco in oncān ithualco.
8. Teohtlālli iihtic ōmic.

9. Ayāc tleh contēnquīxtīz. Zan amihtic.
10. Mā tlapielo in nōhuiān ātēnco.
11. Ōmpa huālpēuh in tōnatiuh īcalaquiāmpa.
12. Ca ye ixquich cāhuitl in cencah īīxco titlachiaznequih.
13. Ēxcān in huih, in ihcuāc miquih.
14. Achi cōntōnco contēca in ātl.
15. Māltiāya yohualnepantlah.
16. Cuix ōticteteuhilpih?

EXERCISE 42. Relational Nouns (Part Two)

42A. *The Inherently Possessed Relational Stems.* Analyze and translate.

Example: amohuān

Ø-amo(huān)Ø = it is your (pl) company; in your company; with you (pl)

1. ītloc	4. mohuān
2. īmpal	5. topampa
3. nicampa	6. mopaltzinco

42B. *Inherently Possessed Relational Stems in Wider Sentence Contexts.* Pronounce and translate.

1. Ahmō īhuān tlatlah in tlahtoāni.
2. Yehhuāntin mochipa totloc cateh.
3. Tlein ticchīhuazqueh, inīc huel tiquīzazqueh?
4. Mā cualli īc ninemini!
5. Zan īpaltzinco titīximaticoh in totēucyo.
6. Ca oc cē; xoconi. Ca cualli in pahtli; īc chicāhuaz in monacayo.
7. Inīc quitqui, īmāyauhcāmpa quiquetza in tecomatl.
8. Achi huel cemmātl inīc huīac.
9. Cualli īc xinemi inīc cualli īc timiquiz.
10. Yeh inīc huēi!
11. Ahhuel niāz mochān, īpampa huel ye tlahcah.
12. Tōtoco itlah īpampa ītlahtlacōl.

42C. *Relational Stems of the Unmarked-Matrix Type.* Analyze and translate.

Example: ānāhuac

Ø-Ø(ā-nāhuac)Ø = it is a water vicinity; near water

1. tlathuināhuac	8. tlāllan
2. īnāhuac	9. ītlan
3. caltzālan	10. īnhuīc
4. ītzālan	11. ilhuicachuīc
5. tepēpan	12. ilhuicapahuīc
6. īpan	13. tlālpan
7. ahtēīxpan	14. īmīxpampa

42D. *Relational Stems of the Unmarked-Matrix Type in Wider Sentence Contexts.* Pronounce and translate.

1. Huel huehcapan cateh in cīcītlaltin.
2. Achtopa quipēhualtia in tzahtzi, niman quinānquiliah in nepāpan tōtōmeh ātlan nemih.

3. Nōhuiān mochīhua tepēpan.
4. Monechicoah in īcalnāhuac tlācah.
5. Oncān tēīxpan quitlāz in īmaxtli.
6. In cānin īmpan yohuatiuh, oncān quitēmoah in ōztōtl.
7. Tlapanco huālhuetziz.
8. Mochintin īmpan cepayauh.
9. Intlā tlahtoāni īpiltzin, īcōzqui ōmpa concāhuayah in teōpan.
10. In ihcuāc mahcia, tētzāhuitl īpan machōya.

42E. *The Deer*

In mazātl cuācuahueh, ca oquichtli. Cuācuauhtihtīcectic; cuācuam-
mātzōltic. In ōtlatziuh īcuācuauh, mocuācuauhtlāza. Cuammāxac ca-
quia in īcuācuauh; niman tzīntlacza; oncān quicuappoztequi in īcua-
cuauh. Īc quipilquīxtihtiuh.

In mazātl in ahmō cuācuahueh, ca cihuātl.[1]

---

[1] Sources for reading passages are given in the key.

EXERCISE 43. Relational Nouns (Part Three). Place Names. Gentile Nouns

43A. *Connective -ti- Relational Nouns.* Analyze and translate.

Example: petlatitlan
Ø-Ø(petla-ti-tlan)Ø = it is a mat side; between mats; beside mats; near mats

1. nāhuilhuitica
2. īca
3. tepēticpac
4. īcpac
5. tletitlan
6. ītlan
7. tetitech
8. ītech

43B. *Connective -ti- Relational Nouns in Wider Sentence Contexts.* Pronounce and translate.

1. Ahtlatica nitlamīna.
2. Tetica ōnicmōtlac. Īca tetl ōnicmōtlac.
3. In tiahcāhuān cencah mopachoah tenāntitlan.
4. Ītech onahcitoh in īmācal.
5. Ōppa ontlachix in īcpac tōtōtl.
6. Mā tlāltitech mahxitīcān in totēucyōhuān.
7. Huēi ātēnco xāltitlan in tlapāni.
8. Cuauhtica ōnichuītec.

43C. *Place Names.* Pronounce and translate.

1. Ahcico cecni Cuāuhtitlan.
2. Ōmpa nemi Teōtlīxco [for *Teōtl Īīxco*] īhuīcpa in ātēnco.
3. Niman ye īc tlehcoh in īcpac Cōātepētl.
4. Yehhuātl in huēi ātl totlan mani nicān Mēxihco.
5. Ācaltica quimonhuīcaqueh in Xīcalānco.
6. Quittītītoh in tlahtoāni Tlīllān calmecac.

43D. *Gentile Nouns.* Pronounce and translate.

1. Intlā nelli amMēxihcah, tleh ītōcā in tlahtoāni Mēxihco?
2. In Tōltēcah nō mihtoah Chīchīmēcah.
3. Inihqueh īn, achi mocuextēcanequih.
4. Quil in Tōltēcah ahcān in huehca quimatiah.
5. Intlā cē Mēxihcatl, huel quinpanahuīz, in mānel mahtlāctin in īyāōhuān.
6. Ca toyāōuh in Tepanēcatl.
7. In Tlaxcaltēcah yēppa mochalānihticatcah in Cholōltēcah.
8. Mochintin micqueh in Tlaxcaltēcah īmOtonhuān.

9. In ixquichtin in Tenōchcah cencah momauhtihqueh.
10. Ōyah in Tlīliuhqui-Tepēcatl.
11. Īc quimatih in ātlahcah, ca cencah quiahuiz in huāllathuiz.
12. In Tlaxcaltēcah tlatzīnpachohtihuih.

43E. *A Blood-Offering Ceremony*
      In ōīpan ommihzoc [in āmatl], niman ye īc huālquīza in ithualne-
pantlah. Achtopa ontlatlāza. In ilhuicac contlāza in īezzo. Niman ye
ōmpa in tōnatiuh īquīzayān, mihtoāya "Tlapcopa," nāppa in contlāza
īezzo. Niman ye ōmpa in tōnatiuh īcalaquiān, mihtoāya "Cihuātlāmpa,"
nō nāppa in contlāza īezzo. Niman ye ōmpa in īmāopōchcopa tlālli,
mihtoāya "Huitznāhuacatlālpan," nō nāppa in contlāza īezzo. Niman
ye ōmpa in īmāyauhcāmpa tlālli, mihtoāya "Mīmixcōah īntlālpan," nō
nāppa in contlāza in īezzo. Zan ōmpa ommocāhuaya, inīc nāuhcāmpa
ommihzo.

43F. *The Tree Squirrel*
      Cuauhtechalōtl, yehhuātl in cuauhtlah nemi techalōtl. Cuauhticpac
in tlacua. Zan mochipa cuauhtitech in nemi, auh inīc motōcāyōtia
"cuauhtechalōtl." Mochi quicua in ocōcintli. Quicua in cuahuitl īyacacelica. Nō quincua in cuauhocuiltin. Quixihxīpēuhtinemi in cuahuitl;
oncān quimāna in cuauhocuiltin. Māpīpītzoa.

EXERCISE 44. Conjunction

44A. *Marked and Unmarked Conjunction.* Pronounce and translate.
1. Mahmāeh, ihicxeh.
2. Motema ēxpa, nāppa.
3. Auh niman quinnōtz in tlaciuhqueh.
4. Ahmō quiz in *vino* in octli.
5. Auh in tlahtoāni quimilhuih, "Ximocēhuīcān."
6. Tzahtzitiquīzah, ihcahuacah, motēnhuītequih.
7. Ca nicān amītzinco amocpactzinco ōnō ceppa nitlachix. [amītzinco = amīxtzinco]
8. In ōpahtic, niman īc calaqui in temazcalco, auh ōmpa coni in iztac pahtli.

44B. *Adverbs That Support Conjunction.* Pronounce and translate.
1. Cecni in oquichtli, īhuān occecni in cihuātl.
2. Cemilhuitl īhuān cenyohual zan connequia in cāmpa yeh ohtli quitocaz.
3. Ahtleh in ītlatqui, ahtleh iāxcā, tēl cualli tlācatl.
4. Nāuhtetl ahnōzo mācuiltetl in īteuh.
5. Zan nō cocōcātlālpan in onoqueh, auh yeceh nō chālchiuhīximatinih.
6. Cuix ōticcōuh, cuix nōzō ōticchīuh?

44C. *The Turkey Vulture*
Tzopilōtl tlīltic, catzāhuac, cuāchīchiltic, xotihtīcectic. Moch ītlacual in tlein micqui, in ihyāc, īhuān in tlahēlli.

44D. *The God Owner at Tecanman*
In Tēcānmān teōhuah, yehhuātl īpan tlahtoāya in ocōtl in tlepilli yez. Īhuān yehhuātl ītequiuh catca, in quinechicoāya in tlāhuitl, in tlīlli, īhuān in pozōlcactli, in xicolli, in tzitzilli, in ītech monequia Xiuhtēuctli, Huēhueh teōtl, in ihcuāc miquia.

44E. *Protection from Hail*
In ihcuāc quiahui, in cencah tecihui, in āquin oncān īmīl, ahnōzo īchīlcuen, ahnōzo īecuen, īchian, tleco nextli quiyāhuac quihuāltepēhua īithualco. Quilmach īc ahmō tecihuīlōz in īmīl; quil īc polihui in tecihuitl.

44F. *The Broken Grinding Stone*
In yehhuātl, metlatl, quimotētzāhuiāyah in nicān tlācah. In ihcuāc

acah oncān teztoc, in[1] huālpoztequi, īc nēcia, quilmach, ye miquiz in ōtecia, ahnōceh yehhuātl, in chāneh, ahnōzo īmpilhuān, ahnōceh cē-meh miquizqueh in īchān tlācah.

[1] *In* = if.

EXERCISE 45. The Notion of Similarity. Comparison

45A. *The Expression of Comparison.* Pronounce and translate.
1. In ītzontecon huēi, ixquich in nicān tohuehxōlouh.
2. In pōchtēcah in ōztōmēcah zan centetl catca in īnmahuizzo.
3. Ahmō cualli ōn, yeh cualli īn.
4. Oc tāchcāuh inīc titlāhuānqui, in ahmō in motah.
5. Oc achi nichicāhuac, in ahmō mach iuhqui tehhuātl.
6. Oc huālcah tāxcāhuah, titlatquihuah, in ahmō nehhuātl.
7. Oc cencah miec in māxcā, in motlatqui in ahmō nehhuātl.
8. Oc yeh huehhuēi in amotlahtlacōl in antlahtohqueh, in ahmō yeh īntlahtlacōl in amotlapachōlhuān.
9. Oc huālcah inīc cuauhtic in ahmō nehhuātl.
10. Cencah huehhuēi in īmācal in quin ōhuāllahqueh, in ahmō mach iuhqui catcah in īmācal in achto ōhuāllahqueh.
11. In cepayahuitl tlacempanahuia inīc iztac; aoctleh iuhqui inīc iztac.
12. Intlā āxcān xōpantlah ticecmiqui, quēn zan yeh ticecmiquiz in cehuetzilizpan?

45B. *The Cuitlamiztli*
    Cuitlamiztli cuauhtlah nemi. Ca zan ye nō yeh in miztli. Inīc motōcāyōtia "cuitlamiztli": in ōcahcic centetl mazātl, quipēhualtia in quicua; quicua; quitequicua; quicuahtoc; huel quitlamia. Ōmilhuitl, ēilhuitl inīc ahmō tlacua;[1] zan quicencua; zan huetztoc; tlatemohuihtoc. Īc mihtoa "cuitlamiztli": īpampa xixicuin īhuān īpampa in ahmō motlātia. In yohualtica quinhuālcua in tōtolmeh; quintlamia, intlānel centēcpantli. In ōixhuic, zā quinmictia īhuān in ichcameh.

[1] "It does not eat anything *else.*"

45C. *The Ringtail*
    Itzcuincuāni, ca zan ye nō yeh in cuitlamiztli. Inīc motōcāyōtia "itzcuincuāni": in yohualtica, huāllauh in cahcallah. Chōca. Auh in ōchōcac, niman mochintin quinānquiliah in chichimeh. Mochintin tzahtzih. In ixquichtin quicaquiliah[1] ītzahtziliz; niman īhuīcpa huih. Auh in ōītlan mocentlālihqueh, in ōcolōlhuihqueh, oncān cāna in quēzquitetl huelitiz. Quincua. Cencah huel ītlacualhuān in chichimeh.

[1] Notice the applicative: "they hear it [i.e., its cry] from it [i.e., the ringtail]."

45D. *Peyote*
    Inīn peyōtl iztac. Auh zan iyoh ōmpa in mochīhua in tlacochcalcopa in teohtlālpan in mihtoa Mictlāmpa. In āquin quicua īn, in ahnōzo

qui, ītech quīza, iuhqui in nanacatl. Nō miec tlamantli quitta in tēmah-
mauhtih, ahnōzo tēhuetzquītih. Ahzo cemilhuitl, ahnōzo ōmilhuitl in
ītech quīza, tēl zan nō concāhua. Yeceh, ca quihtlacoa in īyōllo. Tētlapolōltia; tēīhuintia; tētech quīza.

EXERCISE 46. Denominative Verbs

46A. *The Derivation of Denominative Verbs.* Analyze the following verb words. Identify the substantival source and explain the derivation. Translate.

Example: nātoyapanoa = n(ātoya-pan-oa)∅-∅ = I ford a river. Source: the adverbial noun stem *(ātoya-pan)* formed from *(ātoya)-tl,* "river," and the relational noun stem *(pan).* Derivation: intransitive verbalizing suffix *-oa* (see § 46.9).

1. tōchti
2. nitlamahuizoa
3. tēiztlacahuia
4. mazāti
5. titēmahuiztilia

6. tlaihiyōhuia
7. tēlpōchyahcāti
8. nitlamātlahuia
9. tequihuahcāti
10. tētētzāhuia [/w/ + /w/ > /w/]

46B. *A Rabbit in the House*

Nō īhuān, netētzāhuilōya in tōchin in ihcuāc acah īchān calaquia. Quihtoah in mīllahcah, in mīlpan tlācah, "Ye tlālpolihuiz in īchān. Ahnōzo ye acah cholōz. Ye contocaz in tōchtli, in mazātl īohhui; ye tōchtiz, ye mazātiz; ye motōchtilīz, ye momazātilīz."

46C. *Panning for Gold*

In cānin ātoyapan ōmpa huetzticah īohhui teōcuitlatl, in ātoyatl quitqui, cātoctia teōcuitlatl. Īc, īpampa, in ayamō huālhuih Españoles, in Mēxihcah, in Ānāhuacah, in tlaīximatinih, ahmō quitatacayah in cōztic in iztac teōcuitlatl; zan ātoyaxālli quicuiah, quicuauhxīcalhuiah. Oncān quittayah in cōztic teōcuitlatl, in canah huetztihuītz in iuhqui, ixquich in tlaōlli. Niman ye oncān quicuiah in iuhqui xālli. Zātēpan cātiliāyah; quipītzayah; quihmatiah, quitlāliāyah in cōzcatl, in mācuextli, in nacochtli, in tēntetl.

46D. *A Post-Conquest Poem*

Nonāntzin, ihcuāc nimiquiz
motlecuīlpan xinēchtōca.
Ihcuāc tiāz titlaxcalchīhuaz,
ōmpa nopampa xichōca.
Intlā acah mitzihtlanīz,
"Nonāntzin, tle īca tichōca?"
xiquilhui, "Ca xoxōuhqui in cuahuitl
īhuān nēchchohchōctia
īca cehcencah popōca."

EXERCISE 47. Miscellany (Part One)

47A. *The Owl*
Tecolōtl olōltic, tapayōltic, cuitlaolōltic. Īxtemahmalacachtic; īx-
pechtic. Cuācuahueh ihhuitica. Cuāteolōltic; cuātecontic. Ihhuitilāhuac;
ihhuiōtilāhuac. Īxmihmiquini in tlahcah. Texcalco, cuahuitl iihtic in
tlācati. Yohualtica in tlacuācua, īpampa oc cencah huellachia in yohuan. Tlatomāhua inīc tlahtoa. Quihtoa, "Tecolō, tecolō, ō, ō."

47B. *A Skirmish*
"Mēxihcahé, mā ye cuēl!"
Niman ye īc tlahcahuaca īhuān tlapītzalo. Īhuān chīmallāza in yāō-
tlachixqui.
Niman ye īc quintocah in Españoles, quimmayāuhtihuih, īhuān
quimāntihuih. Caxtōltin in ānōqueh in Españoles, niman īc quinhuāl-
huīcaqueh. Auh in īmācal, niman īc quitzīnquīxtihqueh. Ānepantlah
contēcatoh.
Auh in ōquimahxītīcoh, caxtōltin omēi in oncān miquizqueh, ītōca
Tlacochcalco, niman ye īc quinpehpetlāhuah. Moch quincuīlihqueh in
īnyāōtlatqui, īhuān in īmichcahuīpīl, īhuān in ixquich in īntech catca.
Moch quintepēhualtihqueh. Niman ye īc tlācohtih. Quinmictiah.
Auh in īmicnīhuān quinhuālitztoqueh ānepantlah.

47C. *A Messenger from the Hereafter*
Cē tlācatl cihuātl, īchān Tenōchtitlan, mic īca cocōliztli. Niman motōcac īithualco; īpan quitemanqueh. Ye iuh nāhuilhuitl motōcac in cihuātl micqui, mozcalih yohualtica. Cencah tlamauhtih. In oncān motō-
caca tlatatacco motlapoh, auh in tetl īc motemanca, huehca huehhuetzito.
Auh in yehhuātl cihuātl, in ōiuh mozcalih, niman quinohnōtzato,
quilhuīto in Motēuczōmah in tlein quittac. Quipōhuilih, quilhuih, "Ca
inīc ōninozcalih: nimitzilhuīco, ca ye ixquich. Ca tehhuātl moca tzon-
quīza in tlahtohcāyōtl in Mēxihco. Ca tehhuātl mopan māntiāz in āltepētl Mēxihco. Āquihqueh in ye huītzeh, ca yehhuāntin tlālmācēhua-
quīhuih. Yehhuāntin onozqueh in Mēxihco."
Auh in yehhuātl micca cihuātl, ye nō cempōhualxihuitl oncē īnen,
īhuān oc cē quichīuh īconēuh oquichtli.

EXERCISE 48. Miscellany (Part Two)

48A. *Huitzilopochtli*
Huitzilopōchtli zan mācēhualli, zan tlācatl catca. Nāhualli. Tētzāhuitl. Ahtlācacemēleh. Tēīxcuepani. Quiyōcoyani in yāōyōtl. Yāōtēcani; yāōtlahtoāni.
Ca ītechpa mihtoāya, "Tēpan quitlāza in xiuhcōātl, in mamalhuāztli"—quihtōznequi "yāōyōtl," "teōātl tlachinōlli." Auh in ihcuāc ilhuiquīxtīlōya, malmicohuaya, tlaāltīlmicohuaya. Tēāltiāyah in pōchtēcah.
Auh inīc mochihchīhuaya: xiuhtōtōnacocheh catca; xiuhcōānāhualeh; xiuhtlalpīleh; mātacaxeh; tzitzileh, oyōhualeh.

48B. *The Laughing Falcon*
Huāctli mocōzcacuāuhnehnequi. Inīc tlahtoa: in quēmman, iuhqui in mah acah tlācatl huēhuetzca, [in quēmman] iuhqui in mah tlācatlahtoa. Huel quitēnquīxtia inīn tlahtōlli: "yēccān, yēccān, yēccān." Inīc huetzca, quihtoa "hahahahaha, hahai, hahai, hahai, ai." Oc cencah ihcuāc in quitta ītlacual, huel huēhuetzca.

48C. *Distracted Messengers*
Quilmach Quetzalcōātl, Tōllān tlahtoāni catca. Quil ōmentin cihuah mahāltiāyah in īneāltiāyān. In ōquinhuālittac, īc niman quinhuālihua cequintin quimittazqueh, in āquihqueh mahāltiāyah. Auh in yehhuāntin tītlantin, zan ye quimitzticateh in mahāltiah cihuah. Ahmō mah quinōnōtzatoh. In Quetzalcōātl oc ceppa zātēpan conihua in īxōlouh (quihtōznequi "ītītlan") in quimittaz āquihqueh in mahāltiah. Zan nō iuh quichīuh; ayocmō quicuepato in īnetītlaniz.
Īc oncān tzīntic, nelhuayōhuac in mihtoa "moxohxōlotītlani."

SUPPLEMENTARY READINGS

1. A Nahuatl Version of a Fable by Aesop

In cuācuauhtēntzoneh īhuān coyōtl, in ihcuāc ye āmicqueh, cecni ātlacomōlco oncholohqueh. Auh in ihcuāc ōpachiuhqueh ātlih, in tēntzoneh
niman ye nōhuiāmpa tlahtlachia, quitēmoa in cāmpa huel quīzazqueh.
Auh in coyōtl quilhuih: "Mācamō ximotequipacho, ca ōniquittac in tlein
ticchīhuazqueh inīc huel tiquīzazqueh. Intlā timotlamelāuhcāquetzaz,
īhuān in momā caltech ticmahmanaz,[1] īhuān in motzontecon ticahcocuiz,
inīc huel micampa huehhuetztoz[2] mocuācuauh, in nehhuātl niman mo-
cuitlapan nontlehcoz, inīc huel nonquīzaz ātlacomōlco. Auh in ihcuāc
ōniquīz, niman nimitzhuālānaz."

Auh in tēntzoneh, in ihcuāc ōquihuelcac ītlahtōl coyōtl, niman qui-
tlācamah. Īpan huālquīz in coyōtl, auh in ōquīzaco, niman ye ātlacomōl-
tēnco īca huetzcatinemi. Auh in tēntzoneh cencah ōquitlahuēlchīuh in
ītēcanecayāhualiz coyōtl.

Auh in coyōtl quilhuih in tēntzoneh: "Nocnīhué, intlā izquitetl yeni
moyōllo, in izqui mani motēntzon, oc achto tictēmōzquia in cānin huel
tihuālquīzaz in ayamō toncholoa ātlacomōlco."

Inīn zazanīllahtōlli īc tēmachtīlo in quēnin huel achto monequi tic-
nemilīzqueh in tlein ticchīhuaznequih inīc ahmō zātēpan īpan tihuetziz-
queh in ahnezcalīliztli, xōlopihyōtl.

NOTE: Sources for the supplementary readings are given in the Key.
[1] The reduplicative prefix indicates the plurality of the inanimate verb object.
[2] The reduplicative prefix indicates the plurality of the inanimate subject.

2. Mushroom Visions

In ontlatotōnih in tēcōānōtza, niman ye īc huālquīzah in mihtōtiz-queh–in tlācatēccatl, in ye mochintin cuācuāchictin, in Otomih, in tequi-huahqueh, in tītiāchcāhuān. Auh in yehhuāntin pōchtēcatlahtohqueh, ahmō mihtōtiah; zan onoqueh mopixtoqueh, īpampa ca yehhuāntin in tēcōāchīhuah. Auh in pōchtēcahuēhuētqueh, yehhuāntin tēnāmicqueh, in xōchitica in iyetica, in āmacōzcatl xiuhtezcayoh, auh in ichqueh-quetzalli pepeyocyoh mētzcuitlatica.

Huel yacattihuia in tēcualtīlōya nanacatl in quicuāyah ihcuāc in quih-toāyah tlahtlapītzalizpan. Ayamō tleh tlacualli quicuāyah; zan oc iyoh in cacahuatl coniah yohualtica. Auh in nanacatl neucyoh in quicuāyah. In ihcuāc ye īntech quīza nanacatl, in oncān mihtōtiah, oncān chōcah. Auh in cequintin in oc īnyōllo quimatih, in oncān īnyeyān calaquih, motlāliah caltech. Aocmō mihtōtiah, zā oncān huāltōlohtimotlāliah.

In acah conmottilia ye miquiz; oncān chōcaticah. In acah conmottilia yāōmiquiz. In acah conmottilia tēcuāncualōz. In acah conmottilia tlamāz yāōc. In acah conmottilia yehhuātl in mocuiltōnōz, in motlācamatiz. In acah conmottilia tēcōhuaz, tlācahuah yez. In acah conmottilia tētlaxīmaz, tetzotzonalōz, tehtepachōlōz. In acah conmottilia ihichtequiz, nō tehte-pachōlōz. In acah conmottilia tēcuātepachōz, quitzauctiāz. In acah con-mottilia ātlan miquiz. In acah conmottilia yehhuātl in ihuiān yōcoxcā monemītīz īpan miquiz. In acah conmottilia tlapanco huālhuetziz, micti-huetziz.[1] In zāzo quēxquich tēpan mochīhuaz, mochi oncān conittaya–in ahnōzo ilaquīlōz.

Auh in ōquincāuh nanacatl, monohnōtzah, quimolhuiah in tlein ōcon-mottilihqueh. Auh in yehhuāntin in ahtleh ōquicuahqueh nanacatl, nō quihquimonittiliah[2] in tlein īmpan mochīhuaz īhuān in tlein quichīuh-tinemih. Cequintin in ahzo ihichtequih, in ahzo tētlahtlaxīmah, in zāzo quēzquitlamantli, in ixquich ōmihtoh: in tlamāz, in tequihuahcātiz, in tel-pōchyahcātiz, in yāōmiquiz, in motlācamatiz, in tēcōhuaz, in cuihcuīcaz, in tēāltīz, in tētlaxīmaz, in moquechmecanīz, in ātlan miquiz, in ilaquī-lōz. In zāzo tlein īmpan mochīhuaz, mochi oncān conittaya–in ahzo Ānāhuac miquitīuh.

Auh in ōahcic yohualli xelihui, in ye huel yohualnepantlah, in yehhuātl tēcōānōtza, niman ye īc moxtlāhua. Yehhuātl in āmatl quitlatia tlaōlchi-pīnīlli.

---

[1] Notice the structure-and-meaning conflict: not "die and fall" but "fall and die" (see § 19.4.5).

[2] An infrequent formation. The reduplicative prefix is formed from the specific-object prefix. The individuality of the members of the specific group is highlighted: "each one of them."

3. The Specter Called "Human Bundle of Ashes"

No īhuān, tētzāhuitl catca, tētētzāhuiāya in "Tlācanexquimilli." Iuh mihtoa, "Zan ye mochi yeh īnāhual, īnecuepaliz, īnenēxtīliz in Tezcatlihpōca."

In ihcuāc ittōya, zan momimilohtiuh, quiquinacatiuh, tehtēntiuh. In āquin quittaya, īc quitētzāhuia in ye miquiz, ahzo yāōc, ahnōzo zan tlālmiquiz, ahnōceh itlah ahmō cualli ye quimonāmictīz, īpan huetziz.

In āquin ahmō yōllōchicāhuac, in ahmō yōllōtlahpalihui, in zan mauhcātlācatl, intlā ōquimottītih, zan īīxpampa ēhua, motlaloa. Oncān quitōnalcāhualtia, quihizahuia, inīc ihciuhcā miquiz, ahnōzo itlah ahmō cualli quimonāmictīz.

Auh in āquin huel yōllōtlahpalihui, in motēnēhua "yāōtlahuēlilōc," īc momania, īc mochihchīhua, īc mocencāhua. Niman iuh quimolhuia in yohualtica nāhualtehtēmōz. Nōhuiān nehnemi; quitohtocatinemi in izqui ochpāntli; yohualnehnemi; quitehtēmohtinemi, in ahzo canah itlah quimottītīz, inīc quihtlanilīz ītēnemac, ītēicnēlīliz, huitztli.

Auh intlā ye ōquimottītih in iuhqui in quitehtēmoa, quicuītihuetzi, quiteteuhtzītzquia, ītech mopiloa. Ahocmō quicāhua. Quitlahtōltia. Quilhuia, "Āc tehhuātl, in nocné? Xinēchnōtza. Ahmō mahca titlahtōz. Ca ōnimitzān. Ahmō nimitzcāhuaz." Huehcāuhtica quinemītia in quitlahtōltia.

Ihcuāc quinōtza, quinānquilia, intlā ye cahmana, in ahceh īpan tlathuiznequi, in ahceh quitlathuīltia, quilhuia, "Xinēchcāhua. Ye tinēchihtlacoa. Tlein quinequi moyōllo, nimitzmacaz."

"Tlein tinēchmacaz?"

Quilhuia, "Iz cah. Nimitzmaca cē huitztli."

"Ahmō nicea. Ahmō niccelia."

"Tleh nicchīhuaz?"

Ōme, ēi, nāhui quimaca. Zā nel ahmō īc quicāhua. Quin ihcuāc, in ōquiyōlpachihuītih, in ōquiyōlpachiuhcāyōtih, in ye quilhuia, "Mochi nimitzmaca in necuiltōnōlli. Timahuizzōhuaz[1] in tlālticpac." Ihcuāc quicāhua; ca nel ōconittac in quitēmoa īyōllo—inīc ōēlcihciuhtinenca, ōnēntlamattinenca.

[1] A textual emendation. The source reads (respelled) *Titlamahuizōz*, "You will be amazed at things," which in the context makes no sense.

4. The Matlatzincas (Net Landers)

In Mātlatzincah ītech quīza in īntōcā in īntlatequipanōliz. Inīc cōyah cintli, zan quimātlatēmah, zan quihuītequih. Īhuān inīc tlamāmāyah ahmō xiquipilli quitītlaniah. Zan nō quimātlatēmah in tlaōlli mihtoa "zacatemātl."[1] Ocōzacatl tlani quihuīcah, quīxpechtiah.

Oc cencah nō īc motōcāyōtiah "Mātlatzincah": huel ītech momatiah in temātlatl. In pīpiltotōntin zā cen quitquitinemih in temātlatl. In iuh Chīchīmēcah in mochipa quitquitinemih tlahuītōlli, nō mochipa quitquitinemih in temātlatl. Mochipa īc tlahtlamōtlatinemih. Oc cencah īc yequēneh motōcāyōtiah "Mātlatzincah": in ihcuāc tlācatl, mācēhualli quihuenchīhuayah, im īīxpan quimictiāyah diablo īīxīptla; ahmō itlah inīc quimictiāyah; zan quimātlapātzcayah.

Īhuān īntōcā "Cuācuātah": in zā cē "Cuātatl"; in miequintin "Cuācuātah." Inīc "Cuātatl" motōcāyōtiah, īpampa in mochipa quitquitinemih, in zan mochipa īc mocuāilpihtinemih in temātlatl. In "cuā-" quihtōznequi "tzontecomatl"; in "tatl" quihtōznequi "temātlatl"; iuhquin quihtōznequi "cuātemātleh," ahnōzo quihtōznequi "cuāte," "cuātetl," "iuhquin tetl īntzontecon." Quihtōznequi "tetl ītzontecon."

Inihqueh īn Cuācuātah, in īnchān, in īntlālpan, in ītōcāyōcān Mātlatzinco, cencah cēhua. Īc cencah nō chicāhuaqueh, tlahpaltiqueh, huapāhuaqueh, ichtiqueh in yehhuāntin Cuācuātah. Auh nō in īpampa temātlatl quitītlanih in huehca tēcua, īc cencah nō ahmō tlatlamatcāchīhuah in tlālticpac[2] īhuān in yāōc. Auh in āquin ahtlahtlamati, in tēīxco ehēhua, mihtoa, "motōcāyōtia 'Cuātatl'," īhuān mihtoa "iuhquin Cuāta."

In cualli *vino,* in cualli octli, in cencah ihiyoh, in īpampa ihciuhcā tētech quīz, in ihciuhcā tēīhuintih, in ihciuhcā tēpoloh, nō motōcāyōtia "cuātatl." Mihtoa, "Huel cuātatl īn; huel cuātatl momati."

Nō īhuān motōcāyōtiah "Tōlohqueh"[3] in Mātlatzincah. In zā cē, Tōloh; in miequin Tōlohqueh. Ītech māna in ōmpa cah īntepēuh. Quil ītōcā "Tōlohtzin," "Tōloh Tepētl." Cequin quihtoah, tēl nō yehhuān quihtoah in Tōlohqueh, in āltepētl, ca Tōlohcān, auh Tōlohqueh in tlācah, īpampa in cencah ōmpa mochīhua tōlin.

Inihqueh īn Tōlohqueh, in īhuān īntōcā Mātlatzincah, ca popolocah,

---

[1] An apocopated form for *zacatemātlatl,* although the expected shape would be *zacatemātla.* Apocopation is frequent in naming (see § 48.3).

[2] Compare the use of *(tlāl)-li* in *(tlāl-miqui),* "to die outside of battle, to die during peacetime."

[3] The source has *toluca,* which seems to be an error for *toluque.* The single *l* of the source must be doubled if one accepts the suggestion in the text that the word derives from *(tōl)-in.* Forms such as *Tōlloh* and *Tōllohqueh* would be agentive nouns of possession whose stem means "owner of many rushes" (see § 29.7; /ly/ > /ll/).

tēl oncateh in nāhuatlahtoah. Auh in īntlahtōl, cequin quipolōniah inīc quitēnquīxtiah. In īntlahtōlpan, oncah in *letra* "R".

Iniqueh īn Cuācuātah, ahmō tleh mochīhua in īntlālpan. Zan iyoh in tlaōlli, in etl, in huauhtli. Ahtleh chīlli, ahtleh iztatl. Inihqueh īn, cencah īntlacual in tamalli, in etl. Nō cencah īntlaīl in xocoātōlli. Huel ōmpa mochīhua in īnchān in momochitl. In īntlaquēn, in īntilmah catca ichtli. Īmichtilmah catca; īmichmaxtli catca. Inihqueh īn, nō quimotequitiah, nō quimāhuīltiah in tēxōxaliztli, in tēihpītzaliztli.

In īnteōuh in Tōlohqueh, ītōcā Cōltzin. Miec tlamantli inīc quima-huiztiliāyah. Ayāc quēn īpan.[4] Ahmō tēpan quitēcayah.[5] Nōncuah ilhui-tlayah.[6] Ahmō quimpalēhuiāyah in Mēxihcah, in Tepanēcah.

In ihcuāc tlācamictiāyah, zan quimecapātzcayah in mācēhualtzintli. Mātlac contlāliah. Quipātzcah. In īmātzopāz, in īqueztepōl, in īomicicuil mātlacopa huālquihquīza. Oncān nō huālmotehtepēhua in eztli.

---

[4] Compare the expression *ahquēn nopan*, "it is none of my business."

[5] Compare the expression *tēpan nictēca in tlahtōlli*, "I spread the word to people."

[6] < *(ilhui)-tl*, "day, festival." The denominative verb *(ilhui-tla)* is formed according to § 46.6, *note*, since it is intransitive.

5. An Omen of the Coming of the Spaniards

Ceppa tlahtlamāyah, mānōzo tlamātlahuiāyah in ātlahcah. Centetl cah-ciqueh tōtōtl nextic, iuhquin tocuilcoyōtl. Niman quittītītoh in Motēuc-zōmah Tlīllān calmecac. Ommotzcaloh in tōnatiuh, oc tlahcah. Iuhquin tezcatl īcpac mani, malacachtic, teōilacachtic, iuhquin xapottihcac. Ōmpa onnēcia in ilhuicatl, in cīcītlaltin, in mamalhuāztli. Auh in Motēuczō-mah, cencah quimotētzāhuih in ihcuāc quimittac cīcītlaltin īhuān mamal-huāztli. Auh inīc ōppa ontlachix in īcpac tōtōtl, ye neh quittac iuhqui ōn in mah acahmeh moquequetztihuītzeh, tepēuhtihuītzeh, moyāōchih-chīuhtihuītzeh, quimmāmah māmazah. Auh niman quinnōtz in tlaciuh-queh, in tlamatinimeh. Quimilhuih, "Ahmō anquimatih in tlein ōnoconit-tac, iuhquin acahmeh moquequetztihuītzeh." Auh ye quinānquilīzquiah, in conittaqueh, ōpoliuh. Aoc tleh huel quihtohqueh.

6. First Contact with the Spaniards

Auh in ōittōqueh in āquihqueh ōhuāllahqueh ilhuicaātēnco, in ācaltica ye onotinemih, niman īnohmah yah in Cuetlaxtēcatl Pinōtl, huēi calpixqui. Quinhuīcac oc cequintin calpixqueh: Mictlān Cuauhtlah calpixqui Yāōtzin; inīc ēi Teōcinyohcān calpixqui, ītōcā Teōcinyacatl; inīc nāhui yehhuātl in Cuitlalpihtoc, zan Tetlān nenqui tlayacānqui; inīc mācuīlli Tēntlīl, zan nō tlayacānqui.

Zan oc yehhuāntin īn, in quimittatoh, zan iuhquin mah quintlanamaquīltītoh. Inīc quinnāhualittatoh, inīc quinnemilītoh: quimmacatoh tlazohtilmahtli, tlazohtlanqui; zan huel ītech ītilmah in Motēuczōmah, in aoc āc oc cē quiquēmi—zan huel īneīxcāhuil, huel ītōnal.

Ācaltica in yahqueh, inīc quimittatoh. Inīc iuh quichīuhqueh īn, quihtoh in Pinōtzin, "Mā tiquiztlacahuihtin in tlācatl Motēuczōmahtzin. Ca yāōc in ōannencah.[1] Mā zan tehhuāntin tihuiān; mā tonmiquitih, inīc huel melāhuac quimocaquītīz." (In "Motēuczōmahtzin" īpiltōcā, auh "Tlācatēuctli" in ītlahtohcātōcā.)

Niman ye īc huih in ātl iihtic. Ommācalaquihqueh. Ommātoctihqueh. Quintlanelhuihqueh ātlahcah.

Auh in ōīntech ompachihuitoh Españoles, niman īmīxpan ontlālcuahqueh ācalyacac, in momatqueh, ca yehhuātl in Quetzalcōātl Topiltzin, in ōahcico.

Quinhuālnōtzqueh in Españoles, quimilhuihqueh, "Āc amihqueh? Cāmpa ōanhuāllahqueh? Cān amochān?"

Zan niman quihtohqueh, "Ca ōmpa in Mēxihco tihuāllahqueh."

Quinhuālnānquilihqueh, "Intlā nelli amMēxihcah, tleh ītōcā in tlahtoāni Mēxihco?"

Quimonilhuihqueh, "Totēucyōhuāné, ca Motēuczōmah ītōcā."

Niman ye īc quimmacah in izquitlamantli quitquiqueh: tlazohtilmahtli, iuhqui īn, yehhuātl īn, in nicān motēnēhua: tōnatiuhyoh, xiuhtlalpīlli, tecomayoh, xāhualcuāuhyoh, cōāxāyacayoh, ehcacōzcayoh, tōtolezyoh, ahnōzo āmalacayoh, tezcapōcyoh.

In izquitlamantli īn, in quimonmacaqueh, quinhuālcuepcayōtilihqueh, quinhuālmacaqueh cōzcatl, xoxoctic, cōztic, iuhquin mah māpozōnalnehnequi.[2]

---

[1] The source reads *ca iaocmo annenca*. Anderson and Dibble suggest "possibly *tinenca* (we live) is intended" (XII, 5, fn. 3). This emendation still does not create a meaningful passage. My emendation is merely to see the *m* of *iaocmo* as an error for *in;* this yields *ca iaoc in oannenca*, which fits neatly into the context.

[2] The source reads *in apoçonalnenequj*, where the *in* is an error for the reflexive prefix *m-*.

Auh in ōconcuiqueh, in ōquittaqueh, cencah tlamahuizohqueh.

Īhuān quinhuālnāhuatihqueh, quinhuālilhuihqueh, "Xihuiān. Oc ye lihuih in Caxtillān. Ahmō tihuehcāhuazqueh tahcitihuih in Mēxihco." Niman ye īc huih.

Niman ye nō īc huītzeh, huālmocuepqueh. Auh in ōtlālhuāccāquīzacoh, niman huāllamelāuhqueh in Mēxihco. Cēcemilhuitl, cēceyohual in huālnehnenqueh inīc quinohnōtzacoh in Motēuczōmah, in melāhuac in īhuelyahca³ quilhuīcoh, quicaquītīcoh. Īntlatqui huālmochīuhtiah in ōquicuitoh.

Auh niman ye īc quinohnōtzah, "Totēucyōé, totēlpōtziné, mā xitēchmotlahtlātili. Ca iz catqui ōtiquittaqueh. Iz catqui ōticchīuhqueh. Ca in ōmpa mitzonmotlapieliliah in mocōlhuān in teōātl īīxco. Ca ōtiquimittatoh in totēucyōhuān, in tēteoh, in ātl īihtic. In ixquich motilmahtzin ōtiquimmacatoh. Auh iz catqui tēchmacaqueh īntlatquitzin. Quihtohqueh, 'Intlā nelli ōmpa ōanhuāllahqueh Mēxihco, iz catqui anquimacazqueh in tlahtoāni Motēuczōmah. Īc tēchīximatiz.'"

Moch iuh quilhuihqueh, in iuh quimilhuihqueh ātl īihtic.

Auh in Motēuczōmah quimilhuih, "Ōanquihiyōhuihqueh, ōanquiciauhqueh. Ximocēhuīcān. Ca ōnontlachix in tōpco petlacalco. Ayāc tleh quihtōz, ayāc tleh contēnquīxtīz, ayāc tleh conchitōnīz, ayāc tleh concamacāhuaz, ayāc quitēnēhuaz. Zan amihtic."

³Notice the glottal stop. The source reads *jveliaca,* which Anderson and Dibble translate "to be the first" (XII, 6), apparently presupposing the absolute stem *(huel-yaca)-tl;* but this would entail the possessive theme *-i(huel-yac)-,* not *-i(huel-yaca)-.* Besides, there is no support in the context for the idea of competition. The word is an active action noun, first type (see § 30.5), of the Class D verb *(huel-ya).* In omitting glottal stops (and indications of vowel length), writers of Nahuatl emasculated the language. They set innumerable traps for unwary readers.

7. The Destruction of Cholollan

Auh in Tlaxcaltēcah, yēppa mochalānihticatcah, mocualāncāitzticatcah, motlahuēlitzticatcah, mococōlihticatcah, ahīmel mottayah, ahcān huel monepanoāyah in Cholōltēcah. Īpampa īn, quintēnahnāhuatilihqueh, inīc quinpoyōmictīzqueh [in Españoles]. Quimilhuihqueh, "Ca cencah tlahuēlilōc, ca toyāōuh in Cholōltēcatl. Iuhquin Mēxihcatl īc chicāhuac. Ca īcnīuh in Mēxihcatl."

In ōiuh quicacqueh in Españoles, niman īc ōmpa yahqueh in Cholōllān. Quinhuīcaqueh in Tlaxcaltēcah īhuān in Cempōhualtēcah. Moyāōchihchīuhtiahqueh. In ōahcitoh, niman ye īc tēnōtzalo, tētzahtzilīlo, ixquichtin huāllāzqueh in pīpiltin, in tlahtohqueh, in tēyacānah, in tiahcāhuan, īhuān mācēhualtin. Neteōithualtēmalōc. Auh in ye ōcenquīzqueh ixquichtin, niman quihuāltzahtzaucqueh in calacohuayān, in izquicāmpa calacohua.

Niman ye īc tēxihxilīhua, tēmictīlo, tēhuihhuīteco. Ahtleh īnyōllo īpan catcah in Cholōltēcatl. Ahmō mītica, ahmō chīmaltica quinnāmicqueh in Españoles. Zan iuhquin ichtacāmictīlōqueh; zan tlaīxpopoyōmictīltih, zan tlachtacāmictīltih.[1] Ca nel zan quintēnahnāhuatilihqueh in Tlaxcaltēcah.

Auh in ixquich mochīhuaya, mochi quihuālmacayah, quihuālilhuiāyah, quihuālcaquītiāyah in tlahtōlli in Motēuczōmah. Auh in tītlantin, ixquich huālahcih, ixquich ompēhuah, zan mocuitlacueptinemih; aoc quēmman cactoc in quicaqui, in caquītilo tlahtōlli. Auh in ye ixquich tlācatl mācēhualli, zā mahcomantinemi; zā achca in mocomōnia. Zā iuhquin tlālolīni, zā iuhquin tlālli xoxoquihui, zā iuhquin tlaīxmalacachihui;[2] mahuizcuīhuac.

Auh in ommicohuac Cholōllān, niman huālpēuhqueh in ye īc huītzeh Mēxihco. Olōliuhtihuītzeh, tepēuhtihuītzeh, teuhtli quiquetztihuītzeh.

---

[1] The forms *tlaīxpopoyōmictīltih* and *tlachtacāmictīltih* pose two problems. The first is the *tla-* prefix: both words should show double objects, since they are causative derivations from *tla-(īx-po-poyō-mic-tia)* and *tla-(ichta-∅-cā-mic-tia)*. The second problem is the singular-number suffix: the plurality of the other forms in the context would lead one to expect plurality here. Assuming that we do not here have a serious scribal error (always a possibility), the only solution I can come up with breaks the rules but answers *both* difficulties and furthermore satisfies the semantic pressures of the context. I propose (not with any real confidence) that these are impersonal *tla-* forms. This is a flagrant violation of the rule that the impersonal *tla-* is attached only to intransitive stems (see § 12.6); it means that the impersonal *tla-* is here pre-empting the *tētla-* or *tētē-* required by the double-object stems while at the same time allowing the form to retain the double-object meaning: "people have caused people to wreak havoc on people" and "people have caused people to kill people treacherously" (or, in other words, "havoc was caused to be wreaked on people" and "people were caused to be killed treacherously").

[2] An impersonal *tla-* form.

In īntepoztōpīl, in īntzinācantōpīl iuhquin tlapepetlaca.[3] Auh in īntepoz-
mācuauh, iuhquin ātl monecuiloa; iuhquin tlacacalaca[4] in īntepozhuīpīl,
in īntepozcuācalalah. Auh cequintin huel moch tepoztli motquitihuītzeh,
tētepoztin mochīuhtihuītzeh, pepetlacatihuītzeh. Īc cencah huālmoma-
huizzōtihtiahqueh. Īc cencah huālmotlamauhtilihtiahqueh. Īc cencah
mauhcāittōyah. Īc cencah īmacaxōyah.

Auh in īmitzcuinhuān yacattihuītzeh, quinyacāntihuītzeh, īnyacac
ihcatihuītzeh, īnyacac onotihuītzeh; ihihcīcatihuītzeh; īntēncualac pīpil-
catihuītz.

---

[3] An impersonal *tla-* form.
[4] An impersonal *tla-* form.

8. Sorcerers against the Spaniards

Niman ihcuāc tlaihua in Motēuczōmah; in quimihua mochehhuāntin in ahtlācah—in tlaciuhqueh, in nānāhualtin. Īhuān quimihua in āchcācāuhtin, chicāhuaqueh, in tiahcāhuān in īpan tlahtōzqueh in ixquich īntech monequiz [in Españoles] in cualōni: in tōtolin, in tōtoltetl, in iztac tlaxcalli, īhuān in tlein quihtlanizqueh, īhuān inīc zā oc huel pachihuiz in īnyōllo. Huel quimittazqueh.

Quimihua in māmaltin; īc monemachtih, cuix quizqueh in īmezzo. Auh iuh quichīuhqueh in tītlantin. Auh in ihcuāc ōquittaqueh, cencah motlahēltihqueh; chihchihchah, īxtehtēnmotzoloah, ihihcopih, motzonteconhuihuixoah. Auh in tlacualli eztica cātzelhuihqueh, quehezhuihqueh, ca cencah īnhuīc ēhuac, quintlahēltih, yehīca, ca cencah xoquihyāc in eztli.

Auh inīc iuh quichīuh Motēuczōmah, ca quinteōmah, tēteoh īmpan quimmah, quinteōtocac. Īc nōtzalōqueh, īc tōcāyōtilōqueh "tēteoh ilhuicac huītzeh." Auh in tlīltiqueh, "teōcācatzactin" mihtohqueh. . . .

Auh quil inīc quimihua Motēuczōmah in nānāhualtin, in tlaciuhqueh: inīc quimittazqueh in quēnamihqueh, in ahzo huel quintlācatecolōhuīzqueh, quintlachīhuīzqueh, in ahzo huel quimihpītzazqueh, quinxōxazqueh, in ahzo oc itlah īc quimmōtlazqueh, in ahzo itlah tlācatecolōtlahtōlli īc quintlanōnōchilīzqueh, inīc ahzo cocōlizcuizqueh, mīmiquizqueh, in ahnōceh īc īlōtizqueh.

Auh in yehhuāntin in quichīuhqueh in īntequiuh, in īnnāhuatīl in īntechpa Españoles, zan niman ahhuelitqueh, ahtleh huel quichīuhqueh.

Niman īc huālmocueptihuetzqueh, quinōnōtzacoh in Motēuczōmah. "Inīc iuhqueh, inīc chicāhuaqueh, ahmō titēnāmichuān. Iuhquin ahtitlehmeh."

9. The Spaniards Flee from Tenochtitlan

Auh in ōhuālyohuac, in ōahcic yohualnepantlah, niman ye īc quīzah in Españoles ommotēnqueh, īhuān in ye ixquich Tlaxcaltēcatl. In Españoles yacattihuih, auh in Tlaxcaltēcah tlatoquilihtihuih, tlatzīnpachohtihuih, iuhquin mah īntenānhuān, īntzacuilhuān mochīuhtihuih. Quihuīcatiahqueh cuauhtlapechtli, contēcatiahqueh in ācalohco in īpan ompanotiahqueh.

In ihcuāc īn, ahhuachquiauhtimani, ahhuachtzetzeliuhtimani, ahhuachpixauhtimani. Oc cequi in huel companahuihquch ācalohtli–Tēcpantzinco, Tzapotlah, Ātēnchicalco. Auh in ōahcitoh Mixcōātēchialtitlan, inīc nāuhcān ācalohco, ye oncān ittōqueh in ye quīzah. Cē ātlacuic cihuātl in quimittac. Niman ye īc tzahtzi, quihtoh, "Mēxihcah, xihuālnehnemicān! Ye quīzah, ye nāhualquīzah in amoyāōhuān!" Niman nō cē tlācatl tzahtzic in īcpac Huitzilopōchtli. Huel tēpan motēcac in ītzahtziliz. Ixquich tlācatl quicac. Quihtoh, "Tiahcāhuāné, Mēxihcahé, ye onquīzah in amoyāōhuān! Huāllatotōca[1] in ācalchīmalli īhuān in ohtli īpan!"

Auh in ōcacōc, niman ye īc tlahcahuaca,[2] niman ye īc tlatzomōni.[3] In ācalchīmalehqueh totōcah. Tequitlaneloah. Mācalhuītequih. Mācalhuītectihuih. Tlamattihuih Mictlāntōnco, Mācuīlcuitlapilco. Auh in ācalchīmalli necoc in īmpan huālmonāmic; in īmpan huālmopic in Tenōchcah īmācalchīmal īhuān in Tlatilōlcah īmācalchīmal. Īhuān cequintin icxipan yahqueh, Nonoalco tlamelāuhqueh, Tlacōpampa itztiahqueh, quinyacatzacuilīzquiah.

Niman ye īc contlāzah in ācalchīmalehqueh in tlatzontectli in īmpan in Españoles. Necoccāmpa, necoc in huālhuetzi in tlatzontectli. Auh in yehhuāntin Españoles, nō quinhuālmīnah in Mēxihcah; quihuāllāzah in tepozmītl īhuān in tlequiquiztli. Necoc micohua. Mīnaloh in Españoles īhuān Tlaxcaltēcah. Mīnaloh in Mēxihcah. Auh in Españoles in ōahciqueh in Tlāltēcayōhuahcān, in oncān in Tōltēcaācalohco, oncān iuhquin motepexihuihqueh, motepexitēnqueh. Mochintin oncān onhuetzqueh. Ommotepēuhqueh in Tlaxcaltēcatl, in Tlīliuhqui-Tepēcatl, īhuān in Españoles, īhuān in cahuallohmeh, cequi cihuah. Huel īc tēn in ācalohtli; huel īc tzonēuh. Auh in zā tlatzauctiahqueh, zā tlācapan, zā nacapan in onquīzqueh, in ompanoqueh.

___

[1] An optative form. Since in this instance the optative is identical to the indicative, the expected construction would use the introductory particle mā: Mā huāllatotōca . . . ! Its omission here adds intensity and vehemence to the expression. Notice that the directional prefix here precedes the impersonal tla- form of (to-tō-ca).

[2] An impersonal tla- form.

[3] An impersonal tla- form.

Auh in ōahcitoh Petlacalco, in oc cē oncān ihcaca ācalohtli, zan ihuiān, zan matcā, zan tlamach, zan tlamatzin in onquīzqueh, in īpan cuauhtlapechtli. Oncān pahtitoh; oncān īmihio quicuiqueh; oncān moquichquetzqueh. Auh in ōahcitoh Popōtlān, ōtlathuic, ōtlanēz. Ye oquichēuhtihuih; ye huehca motlamātilihtihuih. Auh niman ye īc quimihcahuatztihuih, quimolōlhuihtihuih, īntech ihcatihuih in Mēxihcah. Quimahāntihuih in Tlaxcaltēcah īhuān in Españoles mictihuih. Auh nō mictīloh in Mēxihcah, in Tlatilōlcah. Necoc micohuatiuh. Tlacōpan quinquīxtihqueh in quintocah. Auh in ōquinquīxtītoh Tlīliuhcān, Xocotl Īihiyōhuihcān, oncān in Xohxocotlah, oncān in yāōmic in Chīmalpopōca, in īpiltzin Motēuczōmah. In īpan quīzatoh, mīntoc tlatzontectica īhuān huihhuītectoc. Zā ye nō oncān in mic Tlāltēcatzin, Tepanēcatl tēuctli, in quinyacānaya, in quintlaīxtlātihtihuia, quimohtlāxilihtihuia, quimohtequilihtihuia, quimohquechilihtihuia in Españoles.

Niman ye īc companahuihqueh in Tepzōlātl, cē ātoyatōntli. Ompanoqueh, onāpanoqueh, in oncān Tepzōlāc. Niman īc ontlehcoqueh in Ācuehco. Ommotlālītoh Otoncalpōlco; cuauhtenānyohtoc, cuauhtenāmehtoc in ithualli. Oncān mocēhuihqueh; mocehcēhuihqueh. Īhuān oncān ihiyōcuiqueh, īmihiyō quicuiqueh. Oncān pahtitoh. Oncān quinnāmiquico in Teōcalhuēyacān in huāltēyacān.

10. A Brief History of the Conquest

In īpan xihuitl 1519, ihcuāc quīzaco in Capitan don Hernando Cortes, cencah miec in ācalli huāllah in oncān huālyetiahqueh in Españoles in yāōquīzqueh. Auh in ōiuh quimah in yehhuātl Motēuczōmah, niman tlaihuah. Yahqueh in ītītlanhuān, auh in quitquiqueh in tētlahpalōliztli cencah miec, īhuān cencah tlazohtli in tlatquitl.
Auh momatqueh, ca yehhuātl in Quetzalcōātl ōhuāllah. Auh in ihcuāc ōahcitoh, niman mochi quimahmacaqueh in quitquiqueh tētlahpalōliztli in yehhuātl, Capitan don Hernando Cortes.
Auh in ihcuāc ye calactihuītzeh in yehhuāntin Españoles, niman quinyāōnāmiquitoh in Tlaxcaltēcah īmOtonhuān. Ahmō zan quēxquichtin, cencah miequintin īc ōquimihcalqueh, ōquinyāōchīuhqueh in Españoles. Auh mochintin micqueh in Tlaxcaltēcah īmOtonhuān. Quimmictihqueh in Españoles. Īc cencah momauhtihqueh in Tlaxcaltēcah, auh in yehhuāntin, in Tlaxcaltēcah, niman īc tlaihuahqueh; quimmacatoh in tlacualli, in ixquich īntech monequi. Īhuān quimpāccātlahpalōtoh, īhuān quinhuīcaqueh in ōmpa īnchān, in Tlaxcallān.
Auh zan quēzquilhuitl, in oncān motlālihqueh, mocēhuihqueh in yehhuāntin, Españoles. Auh in yehhuāntin, Españoles, niman yahqueh in ōmpa Cholōllān. Oncān miequintin quimmictihqueh in Cholōltēcah.
Auh in ihcuāc in ōiuh quicac in yehhuātl Motēuczōmah, cencah momauhtih; īhuān in ixquichtin in Tenōchcah cencah momauhtihqueh. Īc oc ceppa tlaihuah in yehhuātl Motēuczōmah. Yehhuāntin in quimihuah in tētēuctin, in pīpiltin, quināmiquitoh in Capitan don Hernando Cortes; cencah miec in quitquiqueh in teōcuitlatl. Auh oncān in quināmiquitoh in ītzālan Popōca Tepētl īhuān in Iztac Tepētl, in motēnēhua Ithualco. Oncān quinohnōtzqueh; quimacaqueh in ītlahtōl in ītah Motēuczōmah. Īhuān quimacaqueh in ixquich in īntētlahpaloāya, in īntētechahcia, in teōcuitlatl, īhuān occequi.
Auh zan huāllamelāuh in nicān Mēxihco. Inīc ahcico in yehhuātl, don Hernando Cortes, zan huālmoyāōchihchīuhtiah. Auh in Motēuczōmah ōmpa in quināmiquito in caltēnco, in ōmpa Xolohco. Zan quipāccānāmiquito. Īhuān quitlātlauhtih, quitlahpaloh in Capitan don Hernando Cortes. Niman quihuīcac in ōmpa huēi tēcpan. Oncān motlālihqueh in ixquichtin Españoles.
Auh in īquēzquilhuiyōc, in yehhuātl Capitan ōquilpih in Motēuczōmah.
Auh in ihcuāc ōahcico tlahtōlli in ōmpa ātēnco, in īc oc centlamantin ōahcic Españoles, in yehhuātl Capitan ōquinnāmiquito. Cequintin quin-

huīcac Españoles īhuān nicān tlācah. Auh nicān quicāuhtiah in don Pedro Alvarado īhuān oc cequintin Españoles in tēcpan tlapiayah.

Auh in ihcuāc in ōquīz īlhuiuh Huitzilopōchtli, in yehhuātl don Pedro Alvarado īhuān in Españoles in ītlan catcah, miequintin quimmictihqueh in Mēxihcah in quilhuiquīxtiliāyah Huitzilopōchtli. Īc ompēuh in yāōyōtl.

Auh in ihcuāc in ōhuālmocuep in Capitan in ōmpa ātēnco, miequintin quinhuālhuīcac Españoles. Ahmō īc motlacāhualtihqueh in Mēxihcah. Cencah quitotōtzayah in yāōyōtl.

Auh in īpan xihuitl 1520, ihcuāc ōmic in Motēuczōmah. Auh in yehhuāntin Españoles ōquīzqueh; Tlaxcallān yahqueh. Auh huēi cocōliztli mochīuh in nicān Mēxihco; zāzahuatihuac. Īhuān cencah miequintin micqueh in nicān tlācah.

In īpan xihuitl 1521, oc ceppa huāllahqueh in Españoles. Ōmpa ōmotlālihqueh in Tetzcohco. Huehcāuhtica quinyāōchīuhqueh, quimpēuhqueh, quimihcalqueh in Mēxihcah.

In īpan xihuitl 1522, oc ceppa huālmonechicohqueh, huālmocentlālihqueh in Mēxihcah in moyāhuacah, in xitīncah in īpampa yāōyōtl.

KEY TO THE EXERCISES
AND SUPPLEMENTARY READINGS

KEY TO THE EXERCISES

NOTE: This key is selective. It does not always illustrate all the aspects of the task set up for a given exercise, nor does it present the steps underlying the solution of a given task. The proneness of Nahuatl sentences to ambiguity makes it unfeasible for a key of this nature to give all the translational possibilities of an item. The translations given here were chosen in order to exploit the purpose of the exercise. For this reason, the student is advised to be alert to other possible meanings.

EXERCISE 1.

1A.
1. huēi
2. ahco
3. quīza
4. cuēitl
5. ahhuīc
6. tzahtzi
7. Cuāuhtemoctzin

8. tēmāquīxtiāni
9. āxcāitl
10. cuetlāchtli
11. neuctli
12. nocihuāuh
13. quicuāz
14. ōnichōcac

15. quiahuitl
16. mīmicqueh
17. xicmōtla
18. tēuctli
19. quēxquich
20. nehhuātl
21. tōchuah

1C.
1. [u:mpa]
2. [nu:čλi]
3. [tuskaλ]
4. [o:ki¢akʷ]
5. [to:tulin]
6. [kune:λ]
7. [kiyekoa]
8. [kih¢uma]

9. [šu:panλi]
10. [ku:stik]
11. [ki¢upa]
12. [yu:li]
13. [kitoka]
14. [tusan]
15. [šokuλ]
16. [λao:kuya]

17. [a:mušλi]
18. [wi:lu:λ]
19. [ku¢λi]
20. [muči]
21. [tepusλi]
22. [¢upki]
23. [kuyu:λ]
24. [i:tepu¢ko]

1D.
1. azcihuah
2. teuhyoh
3. anhuih, ahuih
4. tlālli

5. ītetztzinco, ītetzinco [also spelled *ītechtzinco*]
6. antzīnquīzah
7. michchōctia, michōctia [also spelled *mitzchōctia*]
8. quixxiccāhua [also spelled *quinxiccāhua*]

9. anyezqueh, ayezqueh
10. tēucyōtl
11. quizzāzaca [also spelled
    quinzāzaca]
12. ohpitzactli
13. xālloh

14. tepochchicōlli, tepochicōlli
15. nimitztzonhuilāna, nimitzon-
    huilāna
16. tepoxxomahtli
17. petlānqui [peλa:ŋki]
18. antlaczah

EXERCISE 2

2A. 1. n-on(temo)∅-∅ = I am going down
       t-on(temo)∅-h = we are going down
    2. am(āhuia)z-queh = you (pl) will be content
       t(āhuia)z-∅ = you (sg) will be content
    3. ∅(huetzca)∅-∅ = he is laughing
       ∅(huetzca)∅-h = they are laughing
    4. n(ixhui)∅-∅ = I am becoming satiated
       t(ixhui)∅-h = we are becoming satiated
    5. ti(miqui)z-queh = we shall die
       ni(miqui)z-∅ = I shall die
    6. n(āhuia)ni-∅ = I am habitually content
       t(āhuia)ni-h = we are habitually content
    7. n(āltiā)ni-∅ = I habitually bathe
       t(āltiā)ni-h = we habitually bathe
    8. am(āltiā)ya-h = you (pl) used to bathe
       t(āltiā)ya-∅ = you (sg) used to bathe
    9. ō-ti(huetzca)ya-∅ = you (sg) used to laugh
       ō-an(huetzca)ya-h = you (pl) used to laugh
    10. an-huāl(choloa)∅-h = you (pl) are fleeing hither
        ti-huāl(choloa)∅-∅ = you (sg) are fleeing hither
    11. t(ixhui)z-∅ = you (sg) will become satiated
        am(ixhui)z-queh = you (pl) will become satiated
    12. ∅(cēhui)ya-∅ = he was calming down
        ∅(cēhui)ya-h = they were calming down
    13. ni(tomāhua)z-∅ = I shall become fat
        ti(tomāhua)z-queh = we shall become fat
    14. ∅(nemi)∅-h = they are living
        ∅(nemi)∅-∅ = he is living
    15. ni-huāl(quīza)ya-∅ = I used to come out
        ti-huāl(quīza)ya-h = we used to come out
    16. an(chōca)ni-h = you (pl) habitually cry
        ti(chōca)ni-∅ = you (sg) habitually cry
    17. ∅-huāl(temo)z-∅ = he will come down
        ∅-huāl(temo)z-queh = they will come down

18. ti(xōtla)∅-∅ = you (sg) have a high fever
    ax(xōtla)∅-h = you (pl) have a high fever

2B. 1. nāhuiaz = I shall be content; nāltīz = I shall bathe; niāz [for *niyāz*] = I shall go; nichicāhuaz = I shall become strong
   2. tāhuiaz = you will be content; tāltīz = you will bathe; tiāz = you will go; tichicāhuaz = you will become strong
   3. tāhuiazqueh = we shall be content; tāltīzqueh = we shall bathe; tiāzqueh = we shall go; tichicāhuazqueh = we shall become strong
   4. amāhuiazqueh = you (pl) will be content; amāltīzqueh = you (pl) will bathe; anyāzqueh = you (pl) will go; anchicāhuazqueh = you (pl) will become strong
   5. āhuiazqueh = they will be content; āltīzqueh = they will bathe; yāzqueh = they will go; anchicāhuazqueh = they will become strong
   6. āhuiaz = he will be content; āltīz = he will bathe; yāz = he will go; chicāhuaz = he will become strong

2C. 1. temo = he is descending; quīza = he is going out; choloa = he is fleeing; temoni = he customarily descends; quīzani = he customarily goes out; āltiāni = he customarily bathes; yāni = he customarily goes
   2. temoh = they are descending; quīzah = they are going out; choloah = they are fleeing; temonih = they customarily descend; quīzanih = they customarily go out; āltiānih = they customarily bathe; yānih = they customarily go
   3. titemoh = we are descending; tiquīzah = we are going out; ticholoah = we are fleeing; titemonih = we customarily descend; tiquīzanih = we customarily go out; tāltiānih = we customarily bathe; tiānih [for *ti-yānih*] = we customarily go
   4. titemo = you (sg) are descending; tiquīza = you are going out; ticholoa = you are fleeing; titemoni = you customarily descend; tiquīzani = you customarily go out; tāltiāni = you customarily bathe; tiāni [for *tiyāni*] = you customarily go
   5. nitemo = I am descending; niquīza = I am going out; nicholoa = I am fleeing; nitemoni = I customarily descend; niquīzani = I customarily go out; nāltiāni = I customarily bathe; niāni [for *niyāni*] = I customarily go
   6. antemoh = you (pl) are descending; anquīzah = you are going out; ancholoah = you are fleeing; antemonih = you customarily descend; anquīzanih = you customarily go out; amāltiānih = you customarily bathe; anyānih = you customarily go

2D. 1. cēhuiz = he will calm down
    azcēhuizqueh = you (pl) will calm down

    2. tihuetzcaz = you will laugh
       tihuetzcazqueh = we will laugh
    3. niāz = I shall go
       yāzqueh = they will go
    4. temoz = he will descend
       titemozqueh = we will descend
    5. cholōzqueh = they will flee
       nicholōz = I shall flee
    6. amixhuizqueh = you (pl) will become satiated
       tixhuiz = you (sg) will become satiated

2E. 1. nāhuiaya = I used to be content
       āhuiayah = they used to be content
    2. amāltiāyah = you (pl) used to bathe
       āltiāya = she used to bathe
    3. miquia = he was dying
       miquiah = they were dying
    4. nitemoya = I was descending
       antemoyah = you (pl) were descending
    5. choloāyah = they were fleeing
       nicholoāya = I was fleeing
    6. tixōtlayah = we had a high fever
       tixōtlaya = you had a high fever

2F. 1. you used to be content, you customarily are content, you will be content
    2. you used to bathe, you customarily bathe, you will bathe
    3. he was dying, he customarily dies [e.g., the impersonator of a god in a yearly ceremony], he will die
    4. you (pl) were fleeing, you customarily flee, you will flee
    5. they had a high fever, they customarily have a high fever, they will have a high fever
    6. we used to cry, we customarily cry, we will cry
    7. you were laughing, you customarily laugh, you will laugh
    8. I was descending, I customarily descend, I shall descend
    9. you (pl) used to go out, you customarily go out, you will go out
   10. I was living, I customarily live, I shall live

2G. 1. they were dying, you (pl) customarily die, we shall die
    2. we were bathing, you (pl) customarily bathe, they will bathe
    3. they were content, you (pl) customarily are content, we shall be content
    4. you used to flee, I customarily flee, he will flee

5. we were descending, you (pl) customarily descend, they will descend
6. I had a high fever, he customarily has a high fever, you will have a high fever

2H. 1. you (pl) are crying; tichōca = you (sg) are crying
2. we shall laugh; nihuetzcaz = I shall laugh
3. you (pl) were going down; tontemoya = you (sg) were going down
4. they will become satiated; ixhuiz = he will become satiated
5. we were dying; nimiquia = I was dying
6. you (pl) will come down; tihuāltemoz = you (sg) will come down
7. they used to go out; ōonquīzaya = he used to go out
8. we are content; nāhuia = I am content

2I. 1. you used to jump; ōtihuālcholoāya = you used to jump hither; ōton-choloāya = you used to jump thither
2. he customarily descends; huāltemoni = he customarily comes down; ontemoni = he customarily goes down
3. you (pl) will exit; anhuālquīzazqueh = you will come out; amonquī-zazqueh = you will go out
4. we used to exit; ōtihuālquīzayah = we used to come out; ōtonquīza-yah = we used to go out
5. he will flee; huālcholōz = he will flee hither; oncholōz = he will flee thither
6. I shall descend; nihuāltemoz = I shall come down; nontemoz = I shall go down

EXERCISE 3

3A. 1. ō-n-on(temo)∅-c = I have gone down
ō-t-on(temo)∅-queh = we have gone down
2. ō-am(āhuix)ca-h = you (pl) had become content
ō-t(āhuix)ca-∅ = you (sg) had become content
3. ō-∅(chōca)∅-queh = they have cried
ō-∅(chōca)∅-c = he has cried
4. t-on(choloh)∅-∅ = you (sg) jumped thither
am-on(choloh)∅-queh = you (pl) jumped thither
5. ō-ti(huetzca)∅-queh = we have laughed
ō-ni(huetzca)∅-c = I have laughed
6. ō-∅(ixhui)ca-∅ = he had become satiated
ō-∅(ixhui)ca-h = they had become satiated
7. ō-ti-huāl(quīz)∅-queh = we have come out
ō-ni-huāl(quīz)∅-∅ = I have come out
8. ō-∅(mic)ca-h = they had died
ō-∅(mic)ca-∅ = he had died

9. ō-n(āhuix)∅-∅ = I have become content
   ō-t(āhuix)∅-queh = we have become content
10. ō-am(ixhui)∅-queh ‒ you (pl) have become satiated
    ō-t(ixhui)∅-c = you (sg) have become satiated
11. ∅(nēz)∅-∅ = it appeared
    ∅(nēz)∅-queh = they appeared
12. ō-∅(nen)ca-h = they had lived
    ō-∅(nen)ca-∅ = he had lived
13. n(āltih)∅-∅ = I bathed
    t(āltih)∅-queh = we bathed
14. ō-az(cēuh)∅-queh = you (pl) have become calm
    ō-ti(cēuh)∅-∅ = you (sg) have become calm
15. ō-∅(huetz)ca-h = they had fallen
    ō-∅(huetz)ca-∅ = he had fallen
16. ∅(yōl)∅-∅ = he lived
    ∅(yōl)∅-queh = they lived

3B. 1. azcezqueh = you (pl) became willing; anchōcaqueh = you cried; amāl-
       tihqueh = you bathed; anyahqueh = you went
    2. nicez = I became willing; nichōcac = I cried; nāltih = I bathed; niah
       [for *niyah*] = I went
    3. ticezqueh = we became willing; tichōcaqueh = we cried; tāltihqueh =
       we bathed; tiahqueh [for *tiyahqueh*] = we went
    4. ticez = you (sg) became willing; tichōcac = you cried; tāltih = you
       bathed; tiah [for *tiyah*] = you went
    5. cez = he became willing; chōcac = he cried; āltih = he bathed; yah =
       he went
    6. cezqueh = they became willing; chōcaqueh = they cried; āltihqueh =
       they bathed; yahqueh = they went

3C. 1. ōtihuetzcacah = we had laughed; ōtihuetzcah = we had fallen; ōtāl-
       tihcah = we had bathed; ōtiahcah [for *ōtiyahcah*] = we had gone
    2. ōhuetzcacah = they had laughed; ōhuetzcah = they had fallen; ōāltih-
       cah = they had bathed; ōyahcah = they had gone
    3. ōnihuetzcaca = I had laughed; ōnihuetzca = I had fallen; ōnāltihca =
       I had bathed; ōniahca [for *ōniyahca*] = I had gone
    4. ōhuetzcaca = he had laughed; ōhuetzca = he had fallen; ōāltihca = he
       had bathed; ōyahca = he had gone
    5. ōanhuetzcacah = you (pl) had laughed; ōanhuetzcah = you had fallen;
       ōamāltihcah = you had bathed; ōanyahcah = you had gone
    6. ōtihuetzcaca = you (sg) had laughed; ōtihuetzca = you had fallen;
       ōtāltihca = you had bathed; ōtiahca [for *ōtiyahca*] = you had gone

3D. 1. nitemoc = I descended; temoqueh = they descended
2. cholohqueh = they fled; ticholoh = you fled
3. nixhuic = I became satiated; tixhuiqueh = we became satiated
4. tāhuixqueh = we became contented; tāhuix = you became contented
5. tāltihqueh = we bathed; tāltih = you bathed
6. nitlācat = I was born; antlācatqueh = you (pl) were born
7. titlatziuhqueh = we became lazy; tlatziuh = he became lazy
8. azcezqueh = you (pl) became willing; nicez = I became willing

3E. 1. ōanhuetzcah = you (pl) had fallen; ōhuetzca = she had fallen
2. ōnitōlohca = I had nodded; ōtōlohcah = they had nodded
3. ōchōcacah = they had cried; ōchōcaca = he had cried
4. ōtimiccah = we had died; ōmicca = she had died
5. ōnicēuhca = I had calmed down; ōazcēuhcah = you (pl) had calmed down
6. ōtihuetzcacah = we had laughed; ōtihuetzcaca = you had laughed
7. ōpācca = she had become happy; ōnipācca = I had become happy
8. ōaxxōtlacah = you (pl) had had a high fever; ōxōtlaca = he had had a high fever

3F. 1. you had become willing, you have become willing, you are willing, you will be willing
2. it had appeared, it appeared, it is appearing, it will appear
3. I had become happy, I have become happy, I am happy, I shall be happy
4. he had been born, he has been born, he is being born, he will be born
5. they had lived, they have lived, they are living, they will live
6. you (pl) had become sated, you have become sated, you are sated, you will be sated
7. they had become strong, they have become strong, they are strong, they will be strong
8. he had lived, he has lived, he is living, he will live
9. you (pl) had become satiated, you have become satiated, you are satiated, you will be satiated
10. they had slept, they have slept, they are sleeping, they will sleep
11. I had bathed, I have bathed, I am bathing, I shall bathe
12. I had become content, I have become content, I am content, I shall be content
13. we had jumped, we have jumped, we are jumping, we shall jump
14. we had descended, we have descended, we are descending, we shall descend
15. it had spilled, it has spilled, it is spilling, it will spill [*also,* they (*inan*) had spilled, etc.]

3G. 1. I have bathed; ōtāltihqueh = we have bathed
    2. you had become willing; ōazcezcah = you (pl) had become willing
    3. he has slept; ōcochqueh = they have slept
    4. I had returned; ōtīlōtcah = we had returned
    5. I have cried; ōtichōcaqueh = we have cried
    6. you have become sad; ōantlaōcoxqueh = you (pl) have become sad

3H. 1. they have become willing, we are willing, you (pl) will be willing
    2. we have returned, you (pl) are returning, they will return
    3. I have descended, you are descending, he will descend
    4. you have lived, he is living, I shall live
    5. you have jumped, I am jumping, he will jump
    6. we have become satiated, you (pl) are satiated, they will become satiated
    7. you bathed, I am bathing, he will bathe
    8. they have become sad, you (pl) are sad, we shall become sad

EXERCISE 4

4A. 1. I used to enter, I customarily enter, I shall enter
    2. he became sick, he is sick, he will be sick
    3. you sang, you are singing, you will sing
    4. it was straight, it is customarily straight, it will be straight
    5. they ascended, they are ascending, they will ascend
    6. you (pl) were afraid, you are customarily afraid, you will be afraid
    7. we became angry, we are angry, we shall be angry
    8. I had been hurrying, I customarily hurry, I shall hurry
    9. we crossed the river, we are crossing the river, we shall cross the river
    10. you shouted, you are shouting, you will shout

4B. 1. am- . . . -queh; -(āltī)z-; You (pl) will bathe.
    2. $\emptyset$- . . . -$\emptyset$; -(cochi)ya-; He was sleeping.
    3. $\emptyset$- . . . -h; -(pāqui)$\emptyset$-; They are happy.
    4. ti- . . . -$\emptyset$; -huāl(cholō)z-; You will flee hither.
    5. $\emptyset$- . . . -$\emptyset$; ō- . . . -(mic)ca-; He had died.
    6. ax- . . . -h; -(xōtla)ni-; You (pl) customarily have a high fever.
    7. ni- . . . -$\emptyset$; ō- . . . -(huetz)ca-; I had fallen.
    8. t- . . . -queh; -(īlōt)$\emptyset$-; We returned.
    9. an- . . . -h; -(yōl)ca-; You (pl) had lived.
    10. $\emptyset$- . . . -$\emptyset$; -(melāhua)$\emptyset$-; It is straight.
    11. ni- . . . -$\emptyset$; -(cea)$\emptyset$-; I am willing.
    12. $\emptyset$- . . . -queh; ō- . . . -huāl(ac)$\emptyset$-; They have come in.

4C. 1. I became angry. Ahōnicualān. Ahmō ōnicualān. = I did not become angry.
2. He will sing. Ahcuīcaz. Ahmō cuīcaz. = He will not sing.
3. Shall we cross the river? Cuix ahtonpanozqueh? Cuix ahmō tonpanozqueh? = Shall we not cross the river?
4. Were you afraid? Ahtimahuia? Ahmō timahuia? = Weren't you afraid?
5. It perished. Ahōpoliuh. Ahmō ōpoliuh. = It did not perish.
6. Did you become sick? Cuix ahōticocōx? Cuix ahmō ōticocōx? = Didn't you become sick?

4D. 1. It started off. Ca ōompēuh. = It indeed started off.
2. We shall not go up. Ca ahtontlehcozqueh. = We shall indeed not go up.
3. They did not come in. Ca ahmō huālacqueh. = They indeed did not come in.
4. I shall hurry. Ca nihcihuiz. = I shall indeed hurry.
5. He isn't going in. Ca ahonaqui. = He indeed isn't going in.
6. You shouted. Ca titzahtzic. = You indeed shouted.

4E. 1. You (pl) entered. Ōamacqueh? Cuix ōamacqueh? = Did you (pl) enter?
2. They are not hurrying. Ahihcihuih? Cuix ahihcihuih? = Aren't they hurrying?
3. I shouted. Ōnitzahtzic? Cuix ōnitzahtzic? = Did I shout?
4. You were not sick. Ahmō ticocōyaya? Cuix ahmō ticocōyaya? = Weren't you sick?
5. You are customarily afraid. Timahuini? Cuix timahuini? = Are you customarily afraid?
6. He has not gone up. Ahōontlehcoc? Cuix ahōontlehcoc? = Hasn't he gone up?

4F. 1. Have you become sick? —No, I haven't.
2. Will she become angry? —Yes, sir, she will.
3. Are you afraid? —Yes, I am.
4. Will you (pl) begin? —No, we won't.
5. Did he cross the river? —No, he did not.
6. Are you willing? —Yes indeed, sir, I indeed am.

4G. 1. Will you (pl) go in?
2. Didn't you (pl) become sick?
3. I am indeed angry.
4. Yes, he indeed became afraid.
5. He indeed has not crossed the river.
6. You (pl) used to sing, didn't you?
7. No, we had not gone up.

   8. Did he shout?
   9. Will they exit?
  10. We did not cross the river.
  11. Is he singing?
  12. You indeed were angry.
  13. Yes, sir, I shouted.
  14. Will they ascend?
  15. I do not have a high fever.
  16. Will he go in?

EXERCISE 5

5A. 1. We were leaving frightenedly.
    2. Will you sleep well? [Second version can also mean "Will you be able to sleep?"]
    3. He shouted angrily.
    4. I shall hurry upstairs.
    5. Does he live by himself?

5B. 1. He always laughs. You occasionally laugh.
    2. He has already crossed the river. I have not yet crossed over.
    3. Do you still customarily sing? —I no longer customarily sing.
    4. They sleep in one place. They sleep everywhere.
    5. Will you (pl) live there? —No, we shall live here.
    6. Did he hurry much? —No, he hardly hurried at all.
    7. He is able to ascend. He will not be able to descend.

5C. 1. He descends. He does not descend. He does not descend there.
    2. He descends. He descends with difficulty. He descends without difficulty.
    3. We are willing. We are not willing. We are still not willing.
    4. We are willing. We are still willing. We are no longer willing.
    5. You are singing. You are not singing. You are not singing now.
    6. You are singing. You are already singing. You are not yet singing.

5D. 1. You are customarily very happy. Cuix cencah tipāquini? = Are you customarily very happy?
    2. We could not start off. Cuix ahhuel ompēuh? = Couldn't he start off?
    3. We shall not be completely afraid. Ahmō ticemmahuizqueh? = Shall we not be completely afraid?
    4. You (pl) live chastely there. Cuix ōmpa anchipāhuacānemih? = Do you (pl) live chastely there?
    5. He is also willing. Nō cea? = Is he also willing?
    6. It has already perished. Cuix ye ōpoliuh? = Has it already perished?

5E. 1. They fall on both sides.
   2. Then they fell down.
   3. Day after tomorrow she will sing happily.
   4. They had always lived chastely.
   5. We were able to go up.
   6. I indeed went out angrily.
   7. Will you go back tomorrow?
   8. They will no longer come in.
   9. Are they coming down slowly?
   10. I just now calmed down.
   11. He died quickly.
   12. Did you every become afraid?
   13. I left first.
   14. He will cross the river there.
   15. It customarily appears during the day.
   16. They were crying strongly.
   17. Are you (pl) still sick?
   18. I am still content.
   19. Perhaps it will be born tomorrow.
   20. We hardly got our fill.
   21. We were living together.
   22. He just now got a high fever.
   23. I shall bathe tomorrow.
   24. He cannot sleep at night.

EXERCISE 6

6A. 1. He is descending. He is descending here. He is descending right here.
   2. They are going out. They are going out now. They are going out right now.
   3. I hurried. I hurried without reason. I hurried quite without reason.
   4. He will ascend. He will ascend many times. He will ascend very many times.
   5. He died. He died in the night. He died yesterday night.
   6. We shall be sad. We shall always be sad. We shall be sad at all times.
   7. It is falling. It is falling now. It is falling right now. It fell just a minute ago.
   8. You will cross the river. You will be able to cross the river. You will not be able to cross the river. You will absolutely not be able to cross the river.

6B. 1. He will die day after tomorrow evening.
   2. We hurried very frightenedly.

3. Are you (pl) sick once in a while?
4. It is not yet ascending very strongly.
5. Perhaps he lives far away.
6. You used to laugh quite seldom.
7. It is crossing the river very slowly indeed.
8. I absolutely am not willing.
9. He is sleeping better now.
10. He is bathing right now.
11. They left immediately.
12. Afterward he fled.
13. They absolutely cannot sing.
14. He has already returned.
15. Has it already become satiated? —Perhaps.
16. I have a high fever again.

6C. 1. Did he laugh many times? Quēzquipa cuix ōhuetzcac? = How many times did he laugh?
2. Shall we become lazy there? Cān titlatzihuizqueh? = Where shall we become lazy?
3. Will he cross the river day after tomorrow? Īc cuix panoz? = When will he cross the river?
4. Will you sleep here? Cān ticochiz? = Where will you sleep?

6D. 1. Where do they live? Ōmpa nemih. = They live there.
2. When will it appear? Mōztla nēciz. = It will appear tomorrow.
3. How does he sing? Tlacuāuh cuīca. = He sings loudly.
4. How strong are you? Cencah nichicāhua. = I am very strong.
5. How many times did he fall? Ōppa ōhuetz. = He fell twice.
6. When were you born? Ach īquin. = I don't know when.

6E. 1. Where did you cross the river?
2. In how many places did it appear?
3. How shall we go down?
4. When did he go out?
5. Where will you (pl) go up?
6. How many times did he bathe?
7. When will you jump?
8. Where did he fall?
9. When will you go out?
10. Where did they sleep?
11. How did he ascend?
12. At what time will you bathe?
13. I don't go out anywhere.
14. Where ever do you live?

EXERCISE 7

7A. 1. I seek something, I seek it ~ I seek them
2. you hunt something, you hunt it, you hunt them
3. he gives things to people, he gives it to people ~ he gives them to people

4. he gives things to people, he gives it to s.o., he gives them to people
5. he gives things to people, he gives things to me, he gives things to you, he gives things to himself, he gives things to him, he gives things to us, he gives things to you (pl), he gives things to them
6. I see s.th., I see it, I see them
7. I see s.th., I see it ~ I see them
8. I see s.o., I see myself, I see you, I see him, I see us, I see you (pl), I see them
9. you say s.th., you say it ~ you say them [e.g., words]
10. he eats s.th., he eats it ~ he eats them
11. he eats s.th., he eats it, he eats them
12. you make s.th., you make it ~ you make them
13. he creates (~ engenders) s.o., he creates you

7B. 1. I see him, I see them
2. you call me, you call us
3. I frown in anger, we frown in anger
4. he hears you, he hears you (pl)
5. he waited for him, he waited for them
6. you saw yourself, you saw yourselves [*also,* you saw one another]
7. you heard me, you heard us
8. I called you, I called you (pl)
9. he will frown in anger, they will frown in anger
10. we shall wait for him, we shall wait for them
11. they will send me, they will send us
12. you (pl) will say s.th. to him, you (pl) will say s.th. to them
13. we used to see you, we used to see you (pl)
14. you (pl) used to eat it, you (pl) used to eat them
15. they were saying s.th. to me, they were saying s.th. to us
16. he used to see himself [*also,* it used to be seen, they used to be seen], they used to see themselves [*also,* they used to see one another]

7C. 1. you waited for him, I am waiting for you, he will wait for me
2. I saw myself, you see yourself, he will see himself [*also,* it will be seen].
3. you saw us, I see you (pl), he will see them
4. I heard them, he hears you (pl), you will hear us
5. they frowned in anger, we are frowning in anger, you (pl) will frown in anger
6. we sent you (pl), they are sending us, you (pl) will send them
7. we saw him, you (pl) see me, they will see you
8. you (pl) heard him, we hear you (sg), they will hear us

7D. 1. he calls you, he gives it to you ~ he gives them to you
2. he says it to me, he waits for me

   3. I say it, I say it to him ~ I say them to him
   4. you take it, you give it to him ~ you give them to him
   5. they say it to you (pl), they see you (pl)
   6. they send it, they say it to him
   7. they give it to him ~ they give them to him, they hunt him
   8. he will say it to them, he will send them

7E. 1. they will call us; tēnōtzazqueh = they will call s.o.
   2. he gave it to me ~ he gave them to me; ōtētlamacac = he gave s.th. to
      s.o.
   3. I used to say it; ōnitlahtoāya = I used to say things, I used to speak
   4. he will say it to you; tētlalhuīz = he will say things to s.o., he will
      speak to s.o.
   5. he saw them; ōtēittac ~ ōtlattac [*tla-* here represents an animate re-
      ferent] = he saw s.o. ~ he saw s.th.
   6. we shall give it to him ~ we shall give them to him; titētlamacazqueh =
      we shall give s.th. to s.o.
   7. I made it; ōnitlachīuh = I made s.th.
   8. I said it to him; ōnitētlalhuih = I said s.th. to s.o., I spoke to s.o.

7F. (Only the functions of subject and predicate are illustrated here. The subfunctions of the predicate are easily recognizable.)
   1. ∅- . . . -∅; ah- . . . qui(tēmō)z-; He will not seek it.
      ∅- . . . -∅; ah- . . . -(temo)z-; He will not descend.
   2. t- . . . -h; -amēch-∅(maca)∅-; We give it to you (pl). We give them to
      you (pl).
   3. ni- . . . -∅; ō- . . . -c-huāl(nōtz)ca-; I had called him hither.
   4. ti- . . . -∅; -quin-tla(lhuī)z-; You will say something to them.
   5. no- . . . -∅ (*for* ni- . . . -∅); -c-on(ihuā)z-; I shall send it thither.
   6. ti- . . . -∅; -tē(chia)∅-; You are waiting for someone.
      ti- . . . -∅; -tēch(chia)∅-; You are waiting for us.
   7. ti- . . . -queh; -tē-tla(lhuī)z-; We shall say something to someone.
   8. ∅- . . . -∅; -tēch(ihua)∅-; He sends us.
      ∅- . . . -∅; -tla(chīhua)∅-; He makes it.
   9. ∅- . . . -c; ō- . . . -qui(cui)∅-; He took it.
      ∅- . . . -c; ō- . . . -c-on(cui)∅-; He reached over and took it.
   10. ti- . . . -∅; ō- . . . -quim-on(nōtz)∅-; You went and called them.
   11. ∅- . . . -queh; -qui-huāl-∅(maca)z-; They will give it to him. ~ They will
       give them to him. [The *-huāl-* indicates that the speaker somehow as-
       sociates himself with the referent behind the *-qui-*, the receiver of the
       giving.]
   12. ti- . . . -h; -c(māma)∅-; We are carrying it on our backs.

7G. 1. When did you (pl) send him?
2. He said it to me angrily.
3. Will you go to see him tomorrow?
4. Where did you hear it?
5. Aren't you seeking it? —Yes, sir, I am.
6. He spoke loudly.
7. I cannot carry it on my back.
8. How many times did you wait for me?
9. Whither did you carry it (on your back)?
10. He cannot speak. He is very sick.
11. We are eating now. Have you already eaten?
12. Do you enjoy hearing it?
13. He was doing it uselessly.
14. I just now said it to you.
15. We never make it any more.
16. I do not enjoy seeing it.
17. I looked upwards.
18. Didn't I give them to you yesterday?
19. He blasphemed. He will surely die.
20. Afterwards we became angry.
21. He placed it here.
22. Didn't he become upset?

EXERCISE 8

8A. 1. if only he had bathed, if only he would bathe
2. would that he had guarded it, would that he guard it
3. I wish I had counted it, I wish I were counting it
4. if only we had sat down, if only we would sit down
5. would that you had buried it, would that you bury it
6. I wish they had run, I wish they would run
7. if only you (pl) had bought it, if only you (pl) would buy it
8. I wish you (pl) had carried it on your backs, I wish you (pl) would carry it on your backs.
9. if only he had requested it, if only he would request it
10. I wish it had amazed him, I wish it would amaze him

8B. 1. I wish I had stepped on it, I wish we had stepped on it; I wish I were stepping on it, I wish we were stepping on it
2. would that you had sat down, would that you (pl) had sat down; would that you would sit down, would that you (pl) would sit down
3. if only he had carried it, if only they had carried it; if only he would carry it, if only they would carry it

4. if only we had smelted it, if only I had smelted it; if only we would smelt it, if only I would smelt it

5. would that you (pl) had eaten, would that you (sg) had eaten; would that you (pl) would eat, would that you (sg) would eat

6. I wish they had followed it, I wish he had followed it; I wish they would follow it, I wish he would follow it

7. if only you had pasted it, if only you (pl) had pasted it; if only you would paste it, if only you (pl) would paste it

8. would that he had thrashed them, would that they had thrashed them; would that he thrash them, would that they thrash them

8C. 1. I was selling things. Mā nitlanamacani. = I wish I had sold things.
2. You buried it. Mā xictōcani. = If only you had buried it.
3. He will seat them. Mā quintlālīz. = If only he will seat them.
4. I remain aloof. Mā ninopia. = If only I would remain aloof.
5. We shall not count things. Māca titlapōhuazqueh. = If only we shall not count things.
6. You (pl) carry it. Mā xiquitquicān. = If only you (pl) would carry it.
7. I followed them. Mā niquintocani. = If only I had followed them.
8. He did not run. Mācamo motlaloāni. = If only he had not run.
9. He will buy them. Mā quicōhuaz. = If only he will buy them.
10. We did not sit down. Māca titotlāliānih. = If only we had not sat down.

8D. 1. You are buying it. Mā xiccōhua! = Buy it!
2. We shall not smelt things. Mācamō titlapītzazqueh! = Let's not smelt things in the future!
3. He requests it. Mā quihtlani! = Let him request it!
4. You (pl) do not tread upon it. Māca xiquiczacān! = Do not tread upon it!
5. You are running. Mā ximotlalo! = Run!
6. I am not returning. Māca ninocuepa! = Let me not return!
7. We are putting it down. Mā tictlālīcān! = Let's put it down!
8. They will not sell it. Mācamō quinamacazqueh! = Let them not sell it in the future!
9. You remain aloof. Mā ximopia! = Remain aloof!
10. You (pl) will not go out. Mācamō anquīzazqueh! = Do not go out (pl) in the future!
11. They are following them. Mā quintocacān! = Let them follow them!
12. You are returning it. Mā xiccuepa! = Return it!

8E. 1. If only you would say it to them. Say it to them.
2. If only we shall request it. Let's request it in the future.
3. May I never perish. May I never die.

4. Let him not spill them.
5. If only you would sell it now. Sell it now.
6. Would that I had done it.
7. Oh, if only you would see it!
8. If only we had guarded it!
9. If only you will not smelt something. Do not smelt something in the future.
10. Please hear him!
11. If only you will not go out. Do not go out in the future.
12. Let's nevertheless say it!
13. Count them later.
14. Don't eat (pl) it!
15. Don't go out.
16. If only they would follow it. If only they would bury it.
17. Don't buy (pl) it. —We have already bought it.
18. Wait a moment.
19. Have (pl) a good time.
20. Let me not be surprised.

EXERCISE 9

9A. 1. let me beware of leaving it, let's beware of leaving it
2. beware of stretching out on the ground, beware (pl) of stretching out on the ground
3. let him beware of frowning in anger, let them beware of frowning in anger
4. let's beware of disturbing him, let me beware of disturbing him
5. let them beware of paddling, let him beware of paddling
6. beware (pl) of breaking it, beware (sg) of breaking it
7. let me beware of squeezing juice from it, let's beware of squeezing juice from it
8. beware of wearing it, beware (pl) of wearing it
9. let him beware of closing it, let them beware of closing it
10. let's beware of burning fields over, let me beware of burning fields over
11. beware (pl) of baking it, beware (sg) of baking it
12. let them beware of standing up, let him beware of standing up

9B. 1. *Admon:* Beware of making it. *Pret opt:* If only you had made it.
2. *Pret opt:* If only you had not stood up. *Admon:* Beware of not standing up; i.e., Be sure to stand up.
3. *Admon:* Let's beware of stopping off. *Pres opt:* Let's stop off.
4. *Admon:* Beware of spitting. *Pres opt:* Spit.

5. *Admon:* Let him beware of burning fields over. *Pret opt:* If only he had burned fields over.
6. *Admon:* Let him beware of baking it. *Pres opt:* Let him bakc it.
7. *Admon:* Let me beware of being surprised. *Pres opt:* Let me be surprised. *Pret opt:* If only I had not been surprised.
8. *Admon:* Beware (pl) of standing it upright. *Pret opt:* If only you (pl) had stood it upright.
9. *Admon:* Let's beware of lying down. *Pres opt:* Let's lie down.
10. *Pres opt:* Stay. *Admon:* Beware of staying.
11. *Admon:* Let them beware of not tumbling it to the ground. *Pret opt:* If only they had not tumbled it to the ground.
12. *Pres opt:* Stretch it out on the ground. *Admon:* Beware of stretching it out on the ground.

9C. 1. You are standing it upright. Mā ticquetz. = Beware of standing it upright.
2. You (pl) are not paddling. Mānēn ahantlanelohtin. = Beware (pl) of not paddling; i.e., Be sure to paddle.
3. I am beginning. Mā nipēuh. = Let me beware of beginning.
4. We are not disturbing him. Mānen ahticahmantin. = Let's beware of not disturbing him; i.e., Let's be sure to disturb him.
5. They are baking something. Mā tlaxcahtin. = Let them beware of baking things.
6. He burns it over. Mā quichinoh. = Let him beware of burning it over.
7. He is hunting. Mā tlamah. = Let him beware of hunting.
8. I am stretching out on the ground. Mā ninotēcah. = Let me beware of stretching out.
9. We are throwing it to the ground. Mā ticmāyauhtin. = Let's beware of throwing it to the ground.
10. You (pl) are breaking it. Mā anquipoztectin. = Beware (pl) of breaking it.
11. I am wearing it. Mā nicquēn. = Let me beware of wearing it.
12. You are closing it. Mā tictzauc. = Beware of closing it.

9D. 1. Beware of falling somewhere.
2. Beware (pl) of confining me.
3. Let them beware of baking it here.
4. Beware of going out tomorrow.
5. Let him beware of not stirring it; i.e., Let him be sure to stir it.
6. Beware (pl) of becoming upset.
7. Let them beware of not crossing the river slowly; i.e., Let them be sure to cross the river slowly.
8. Do not break it. Beware of breaking it.

9. Let's beware of upsetting them.
10. Beware of standing up quickly.

EXERCISE 10

10A. 1. ni(cah)∅-∅ = I am; ti(cat)∅-eh = we are
2. ō-ti(huītz)a-h = we came; ō-ni(huītz)a-∅ = I came
3. ∅(on-o)∅-c = he is lying there; ∅(on-o)∅-queh = they are lying there
4. ni(yauh)∅-∅ = I am going; ti(hui)∅-h = we are going
5. ō-an-qui(mat)∅-queh = you (pl) knew it; ō-ti-c(mah)∅-∅ = you knew it
6. n(on-o)ca-∅ = I lay there; t(on-o)ca-h = we lay there
7. ti(huītz)∅-∅ = you come; an(huītz)∅-eh = you (pl) come
8. ni(hui)a-∅ = I used to go; ti(hui)a-h = we used to go
9. ∅(ā)∅-c = he is present; ∅(ā)∅-queh = they are present
10. ni-n(ahco-c)∅-∅ = I got up from the ground; ti-t(ahco-c)∅-queh = we got up from the ground

10B. 1. ō-ni(cat)ca-∅ = I was; ti(cah)∅-∅ = you are; ∅(ye)z-∅ = he will be
2. ō-∅(cat)ca-∅ = he used to be; ni(ye)ni-∅ = I customarily am; ti(ye)z-∅ = you will be
3. ō-ni(yah)ca-∅ = I had gone; ō-∅(hui)a-∅ = he went; ō-∅(yah)∅-∅ = he went; ti(yauh)∅-∅ = you are going; ni(yā)z-∅ = I shall go
4. ō-ni(yā)ya-∅ = I used to go; ti(yā)ni-∅ = you customarily go; ∅(yā)z-∅ = he will go
5. ō-∅(ihca)ca-∅ = it stood; n(ihca)∅-c = I am standing; t(ihca)z-∅ = you will stand
6. ō-n(ihca)ya-∅ = I used to stand; t(ihca)ni-∅ = you customarily stand; ∅(ihca)z-∅ = it will stand
7. ō-t(on-o)ca-∅ = you lay there; ∅(on-o)∅-c = it lies there; n(on-o)z-∅ = I shall lie there
8. ō-n(on-o)ya-∅ = I used to lie there; t(on-o)ni-∅ = you customarily lie there; ∅(on-o)z-∅ = he will lie there
9. ō-∅(huāl-lah)ca-∅ = he had come; ti(huāl-hui)a-∅ = you came; ō-ti-(huāl-lah)∅-∅ = you came; ni(huāl-lauh)∅-∅ = I am coming; ∅(huāl-lā)z-∅ = he will come
10. ō-∅(huāl-lā)ya-∅ = he used to come; ni(huāl-lā)ni-∅ = I customarily come; ti(huāl-lā)z-∅ = you will come
11. ō-ni-c(ahco-c)ca-∅ = I had lifted it; ō-ti-c(ahco-c)∅-∅ = you lifted it; ∅-c(ahco-cui)∅-∅ = he is lifting it; ni-c(ahco-cui)z-∅ = I shall lift it
12. ō-ni-c(ahco-cui)ya-∅ = I used to lift it; ∅-c(ahco-cui)ni-∅ = he customarily lifts it; ti-c(ahco-cui)z-∅ = you will lift it
13. ō-∅(man)ca-∅ = it extended; ∅(mani)∅-∅ = it extends; ∅(mani)z-∅ = it will extend

14. ō-∅(mani)ya-∅ = it used to extend; ∅(mani)ni-∅ = it customarily ex-
    tends; ∅(mani)z-∅ = it will extend

10C. 1. ō-ti(cat)ca-h = we used to be; an(cat)∅-eh = you (pl) are; ∅(ye)z-queh
       = they will be
   2. ō-ti(yah)ca-h = we had gone; ō-∅(hui)a-h = they went; ō-∅(yah)∅-
      queh = they went; an(hui)∅-h = you (pl) are going; ti(yā)z-queh = we
      shall go
   3. ō-ti(yā)ya-h = we used to go; an(yā)ni-h = you (pl) customarily go;
      ∅(yā)z-queh = they will go
   4. ō-∅(ihca)ca-h = they stood; t(ihca)∅-queh = they are standing; am-
      (ihca)z-queh = you (pl) will stand
   5. ō-am(on-o)ca-h = you (pl) used to lie there; ∅(on-o)∅-queh = they
      are lying there; t(on-o)z-queh = we shall lie there
   6. ō-∅(huāl-lah)ca-h = they had come; an(huāl-hui)a-h = you (pl) came;
      ō-an(huāl-lah)∅-queh = you (pl) came; ti(huāl-hui)∅-h = we are com-
      ing; ∅(huāl-lā)z-queh = they will come
   7. ō-∅(huāl-lā)ya-h = they used to come; ti(huāl-lā)ni-h = we customar-
      ily come; an(huāl-lā)z-queh = you (pl) will come
   8. ō-ti-c(ahco-c)ca-h = we had lifted it; ō-an-c(ahco-c)∅-queh = you (pl)
      lifted it; ∅-c(ahco-cui)∅-h = they are lifting it; ti-c(ahco-cui)z-queh =
      we shall lift it

10D. 1. If only I were lying down. (~ Let me lie there.) If only we were ly-
        ing down. (~ Let's lie there.)
    2. If only he had hanged. If only they had hanged.
    3. Let's be. Let me be.
    4. Come. xi(huāl-hui)∅-ān = Come (pl).
    5. If only they had been. If only it had been.
    6. Lie (pl) there. Lie (sg) there.
    7. If only he had gone. If only they had gone.
    8. t-on(hui)∅-ān = Let's go away. n-on(yauh)∅-∅ = Let me go away.
    9. Stand. Stand (pl).
   10. ∅-c(ahco-cui)∅-cān = Let them lift it. ∅-c(ahco-cui)∅-∅ = Let him lift
       it.
   11. If only we had gone. If only I had gone.
   12. Go. xi(hui)∅-ān = Go (pl).

10E. 1. Let's beware of going. Let me beware of going.
    2. Let him beware of hanging. Let them beware of hanging.
    3. Let them beware of not knowing it. Let him beware of not know-
       ing it.
    4. Let me beware of lifting it. Let's beware of lifting it.

5. Let them beware of lying there. Let him beware of lying there.
6. Beware of not going! Beware (pl) of not going.
7. Let him beware of being. Let them beware of being.
8. Let me beware of standing. Let's beware of standing.

10F. 1. Where is it? —It is there. Where is it? —It is here.
2. They no longer came.
3. Where did he go? —I don't know where.
4. I came yesterday.
5. Let him come here.
6. Please go away in the afternoon.
7. Was he able to get up from the ground?
8. Stand there.
9. Will it be hanging here tomorrow?
10. He came from nearby [*lit*, from not far away].
11. I shall go first.
12. He is absent today.
13. Where else can you possibly go?
14. He will come later.
15. You will just be idle.
16. By no means did he know it; i.e., He was not worried about it.
17. He went just this moment.
18. I do not go well anywhere; i.e., I am unhappy.
19. There isn't any, any more. There aren't any, any more.
20. They came once again.
21. He lifted it little by little.
22. It is lying crosswise.

EXERCISE 11

11A. 1. ni-c(āna)∅-∅ = I am taking hold of it ~ them; ∅(ān-o)∅-∅ = it is being taken hold of ~ they are being taken hold of; ∅(āna-lo)∅-∅ = it is being taken hold of ~ they are being taken hold of
2. ti-c(huīca)∅-∅ = you are carrying it ~ them; ∅(huīc-o)∅-∅ = it is being carried ~ they are being carried
3. ∅-qu(i)∅-∅ = he is drinking it; ∅(ī-hua)∅-∅ = it is being drunk
4. ni-quim(ihcali)∅-∅ = I am fighting them; ∅(ihcalī-hua)∅-h = they are being fought; ∅(ihcalī-lo)∅-h = they are being fought
5. ti-tēch(īmacaci)∅-∅ = you fear us; t(īmacax-o)∅-h = we are feared
6. ∅-amēch(tītlani)∅-∅ = he is sending you (pl); an(tītlan-o)∅-h = you (pl) are being sent; an(tītlanī-lo)∅-h = you (pl) are being sent
7. ti-c(nequi)∅-h = we want it ~ we want them; ∅(nec-o)∅-∅ = it is wanted ~ they are wanted

8. an-qui(poloa)∅-h = you (pl) are losing it ~ them; ∅(polō-lo)∅-∅ = it is being lost ~ they are being lost

9. ∅-qui(tlatia)∅-h = they are burning it ~ them; ∅(tlatī-lo)∅-∅ = it is being burnt ~ they are being burnt

10. ti-quin(tlātia)∅-h = we are hiding them; ∅(tlāti-lo)∅-h = they are being hid

11. an-tēch(tlāza)∅-h = you (pl) are deposing us; ti(tlāx-o)∅-h = we are being deposed; ti(tlāza-lo)∅-h = we are being deposed

12. ∅-amēch(toca)∅-h = they are following you (pl); an(toc-o)∅-h = you (pl) are being followed

13. ti-c(nāmiqui)∅-∅ = you are meeting him; ∅(nāmic-o)∅-∅ = he is being met

14. ∅-qui(namaca)∅-∅ = he is selling it ~ them; ∅(namac-o)∅-∅ = it is being sold ~ they are being sold

11B. 1. it is wanted; ∅- . . . -∅ = it < -qui- = it
2. you are being seized; t- . . . -∅ = you < -mitz- = you
3. they are being carried; ∅- . . . -h = they < -quin- = them
4. I am being self-hidden; ni- . . . -∅ = I < -no- = myself
5. you (pl) are being fought; am- . . . -h = you (pl) < -amēch- = you (pl)
6. I am feared; n- . . . -∅ = I < -nēch- = me
7. we are being destroyed; ti- . . . -h = we < -tēch- = us
8. you (pl) are being self-deposed; an- . . . -h = you (pl) < -mo- = yourselves [The *mo-* would automatically be second person plural because the subject in the active form would be *am-.*]

11C. 1. I shall accompany you (pl); -amēch- = you (pl) > an- . . . -queh = you (pl)
2. you drank it; -qu- = it > ∅- . . . -c = it
3. he fought me; -nēch- = me > ni- . . . -c = I
4. we shall destroy them; -quim- = them > ∅- . . . -queh = they
5. we hid ourselves; -to- = ourselves > ti- . . . -queh = we [The reflexivity of the active object *-to-* will show up in the passive form in the object prefix *-ne-.*]
6. he will take hold of it ~ them; -c- = it ~ them > ∅- . . . -∅ = it ~ they
7. he sent you; -mitz- = you > ti- . . . -c = you
8. he customarily throws himself to the floor; -mo- = himself > ∅- . . . -∅ = he [The reflexivity of the active object *-mo-* will show up in the passive form in the object prefix *-ne-.*]

11D. 1. they are accompanying us; tihuīcoh = we are being accompanied
2. I am meeting them; nāmicoh = they are being met
3. you are making it ~ them; chīhualo = it is being made ~ they are being made

4. we are drinking it; īhua = it is being drunk
5. I am carrying it ~ them; huīco = it is being carried ~ they are being carried
6. they are fighting you (pl); amihcalīhuah ~ amihcalīloh = you (pl) are being fought
7. he wants it; neco = it is wanted
8. he is destroying us; tipolōloh = we are being destroyed
9. they are saying it to me; nilhuīlo = I am being told it [English prefers "it is being said to me."]
10. we are taking charge of it; netequitīlo = it is being taken charge of
11. you (pl) want it; neco = it is wanted
12. we are giving it ~ them to you; timaco = you are given it ~ them
13. I am losing it ~ them; polōlo = it is being lost ~ they are being lost
14. he is throwing it ~ them; tlāxo ~ tlāzalo = it is being thrown ~ they are being thrown
15. they are deposing themselves; netlāxoh ~ netlāzaloh = they are being self-deposed
16. you are burning it ~ them; tlatīlo = it is being burnt ~ they are being burnt

11E. 1. it had been burnt, it has been burnt, it was being burnt, it is being burnt, it is customarily burnt, it will be burnt
2. I had been accompanied, I have been accompanied, I was being accompanied, I am being accompanied, I am customarily accompanied, I shall be accompanied
3. it had been wanted, it has been wanted, it was wanted, it is wanted, it is customarily wanted, it will be wanted
4. we had been sent, we have been sent, we used to be sent, we are being sent, we are customarily sent, we shall be sent
5. if only they had been destroyed, if only they were being destroyed, if only they will be destroyed
6. let's beware of being accompanied
7. it had been drunk, it has been drunk, it was being drunk, it is being drunk, it is customarily drunk, it will be drunk
8. if only I had been given it ~ them, if only I were given it ~ them, if only I shall be given it ~ them
9. it had been thrown, it has been thrown, it was being thrown, it is being thrown, it is customarily thrown, it will be thrown
10. beware of being self-hidden

11F. 1. How was he captured?
2. Have you (pl) already been given something?
3. It will no longer be wanted. It will no longer be wanted.

   4. When was it seized?
   5. Perhaps it will be done slowly.
   6. They used to be much feared.
   7. It was heard at that time.
   8. Does it grow there? [*Lit*, Does it make itself there?]
   9. They were already seen there.
  10. It is scattered down everywhere. ~ They are scattered down every-
       where.
  11. Have they already been pierced with arrows?
  12. It is much said. ~ It is often said. [*Also*, He is very obliging.]

EXERCISE 12

12A. 1. it is cold [speaking of weather]
      2. it was drizzling [an imperfect-tense form: Ø(pixahui)ya-Ø]
      3. it is raining heavily
      4. it is close-woven ~ they are close-woven
      5. it ~ they became full
      6. it blotted ~ they blotted
      7. it was becoming night
      8. it is dripping ~ they are dripping
      9. it is ~ they are
     10. it is raining
     11. it ~ they will come to an end
     12. it was hailing [an imperfect-tense form: Ø(tecihui)ya-Ø]
     13. it was hot [speaking of weather]
     14. it ~ they will grow [*lit*, it will make itself ~ they will make them-
          selves]
     15. it will dawn
     16. it ~ they made a grating sound

12B. 1. We are arriving. All are arriving.
      2. You (pl) are becoming tired. Everyone is becoming tired.
      3. They are departing. All are departing.
      4. You will grind grain. Someone will grind grain.
      5. They are beginning. All are beginning. All are beginning.
      6. We are hearing something. All are hearing something.
      7. You (pl) are waiting for someone. All are waiting for someone.
      8. They are making something. Everyone is making something.
      9. They are frowning in anger. Someone is frowning in anger.
     10. You (pl) are taking things. People are taking things. People are tak-
          ing things.

12C. 1. you (pl) are seeking s.th.; tlatēmolo = all are seeking things
2. they are speaking; tlahtōlo = all are speaking
3. we are frowning in anger; nezōmalo = people are frowning in anger
4. you (pl) are stepping on things; tlacxo ~ tlaczalo = people are stepping on things
5. we are requesting s.th.; tlahtlano ~ tlahtlanīlo = people are requesting s.th.
6. they are selling things; tlanamaco = everyone is selling things
7. you (pl) are astonished; neizahuīlo = all are astonished
8. we are carrying things; tlatco ~ tlatquīhua = all are carrying things
9. they are guarding things; tlapialo = people are guarding things
10. we are following s.o.; tētoco = s.o. is following s.o.

12D. 1. it is being bought ~ they are being bought; people are buying things
2. it is being composed ~ they are being composed; s.o. is composing
s.th.
3. they are being buried; s.o. is burying s.o.
4. it is being blown on ~ they are being blown on; people are blowing
on things
5. they are being astonished; s.o. is astonishing s.o.
6. we are being confined; s.o. is confining s.o.
7. I am being self-upset; people are becoming upset
8. he is being self-upset; people are becoming upset
9. people are becoming tired
10. people are ~ everyone is

12E. 1. things had begun, things began, things were beginning, things are beginning, things customarily begin, things will begin
2. if only things had begun, if only things would begin, if only things
will begin
3. let things beware of beginning
4. people had left things, people left things, people were leaving things,
people are leaving things, people customarily leave things, people
will leave things
5. if only people had left things, if only people would leave things, if
only people will leave things
6. let people beware of leaving things
7. people had baked things, people baked things, people were baking
things, people are baking things, people customarily bake things,
people will bake things
8. if only people had baked things, if only people would bake things,
if only people will bake things
9. let people beware of baking things

12F. 1. it is appearing ~ they are appearing; things are appearing
      2. it is perishing ~ they are perishing; things are perishing
      3. it is becoming night; it is becoming night
      4. it is lying there ~ they are lying there; things are lying there
      5. it is blazing ~ they are blazing; things are blazing

12G. 1. People live happily there.
      2. Do people cross the river there?
      3. All fell down quickly.
      4. It had not yet dawned.
      5. All ran frightenedly.
      6. I wish all were able to return.
      7. All are becoming satisfied here.
      8. It was hot yesterday.
      9. Let people beware of going out.
     10. It will not be cold tomorrow.

EXERCISE 13

13A. 1. I am arriving; I am overtaking it
      2. it entered; he caused it to enter
      3. it will become restored; you will pay it
      4. it is extending (over a surface); he is causing it to extend (over a sur-
          face), i.e., he is setting it down
      5. it is turning around; he is causing himself to turn around, i.e., he is
          returning
      6. I became feverish; I heated it
      7. he is becoming tired; he is wearing himself out for it
      8. it is entering; it is being put in [*lit,* it is causing itself to enter]
      9. he is spitting; he is spitting on it
     10. it was consumed; he consumed it
     11. it is becoming full; he is putting s.th. into a container
     12. it became pierced with an arrow; he shot it with an arrow
     13. it will break; I shall break it
     14. we are bathing; we are bathing
     15. they are calming down; they are resting
     16. it was becoming beaten; he was threshing it
     17. I became drunk; you got me drunk
     18. he is bathing; he is bathing him

13B. 1. it is dripping; he is sprinkling it
      2. it popped off; I popped it off
      3. they are becoming fat; he is fattening them

4. it was flaring up; they were rioting
5. it made a grating sound; we clashed with one another
6. it is becoming stuck on; I am pasting it on
7. it became straight; we straightened it
8. it is drizzling; you (pl) are broadcasting them, i.e., the seeds

13C. 1. Beware (pl) of inserting them. Beware (pl) of entering.
2. They were broadcasting seeds yesterday. It was drizzling yesterday.
3. Is it still full? Is he still putting it into the container?
4. Let's beware of not overtaking them. Let's beware of not arriving.
5. It was always dripping. He was always sprinkling it.
6. Were you able to pay it? Has it already become restored?
7. Let it quickly be consumed. Consume it quickly.
8. Where did he set it down? Where was it sitting?
9. Give me a rest. If only I could calm down.
10. I used to always take a rest there. I used to always calm down there.
11. I was not able to warm it. I was not able to get warmed up.
12. Then everything became stuck on. Then it was pasted on. ~ Then they were pasted on.
13. I reached right there. I overtook him right there.
14. It no longer enters. They no longer put it in.
15. I shall bathe tomorrow. I shall bathe tomorrow. I shall bathe them tomorrow.

EXERCISE 14

14A. 1. it is descending; I am causing it to descend, i.e., I am lowering it [*also*, I am digesting it]
2. you are crossing the river; he is carrying you across the river [*also*, he is surpassing you ~ he is overtaking and passing you]
3. it is beginning; I am causing it to begin ~ I am starting it
4. you are afraid; I am frightening you
5. I am appearing; I am revealing myself
6. we are doing out; he is causing us to go out, i.e., he is dismissing us
7. things are going out ~ things are getting out; I am letting things out ~ I am putting things out
8. you (pl) are dying; he is killing you (pl)
9. they are crying; I am making them cry
10. people are crossing the river; I am carrying people across the river [*also*, I am surpassing people ~ I am overtaking and passing people]
11. you (pl) are arriving; we are causing you (pl) to arrive ~ we are taking you (pl) to a place
12. I am laughing; you are making me laugh

14B. 1. I see it; you cause me to see it, i.e., you show it to me
2. you hear it; I cause you to hear it, i.e., I inform you of it
3. I remain aloof [*lit,* I guard myself]; I cause him to guard me, i.e., I entrust myself to his keeping
4. we see s.th.; he shows us s.th.
5. I am pondering; I am getting ready
6. they know it; I inform them of it
7. I am meeting it; I am causing myself to meet it, i.e., I am bringing it upon myself
8. we are leaving it; we are causing ourselves to leave it, i.e., we are abstaining from it
9. I am scattering it; they are causing me to scatter it, i.e., they are ripping it from me
10. you (pl) are losing it; I am causing you to lose it, i.e., I am ridding you of it

14C. 1. I am afraid; nēchmauhtia = he is frightening me
2. it is beginning; ticpēhualtia = you are starting it
3. you are arriving; timitzahxītiah = we are taking you to a place
4. everything is descending; tlatemohuia = he is lowering things
5. you are appearing; timonēxtia = you are revealing yourself
6. it is descending; anquitemohuiah = you (pl) are lowering it

14D. 1. we are losing it; titēchpolōltia = you are causing us to lose it
2. I hear them; annēchincaquītiah = you (pl) are making me hear them
3. people are scattering things; nitētlatepēhualtia = I am causing people to scatter things
4. we are pondering; titonemachtiah = we are getting ready
5. you (pl) know it; anquimomachtiah = you (pl) are studying it
6. they are eating; quintlacualtiah = they are feeding them

14E. 1. If only you had made him make it (~ them).
2. He was made to make something yesterday.
3. I can't digest it.
4. Did he get ready?
5. Perhaps it will show itself to him somewhere.
6. It is not being taught to people any more.
7. Then they showed it (~ them) to him.
8. It will not befall him there.
9. It is just causing people to lose things.
10. Let him beware of making people laugh.
11. First he will feed it (~ them) to him.
12. Then they took them there.
13. They revealed themselves here.

14. It does not eat them. It only kills them.
15. It frightened him greatly.

EXERCISE 15

15A. 1. he is going in order to see him; Ø-quim-on-Ø(itti-lia)Ø-Ø = he is going in order to see him for them [The *-on-* prefix here suggests outgoing movement.]
2. I speak aloud; ni-mitz(nāhuat-ia)Ø-Ø = I am giving you a command; ni-c-Ø(nāhuat-i-lia)Ø-Ø = I am giving you a command with regard to it [e.g., I tell you to say I'm not home]
3. you are shaking s.th. down; ti-nēch-tla(tzel-huia)Ø-Ø = you are shaking s.th. down for me
4. we are taking it; ti-mitz-Ø(cuī-lia)Ø-h = we are taking it from you
5. I am making it; ni-mitz-Ø(chīhui-lia)Ø-Ø = I am making it for you
6. I am doing s.th.; ni-mitz(tla-chīhu-ia)Ø-Ø = I am doing s.th. to you, i.e., I am putting a spell on you
7. you are asking s.th.; ti-nēch-tla(htlan-ia)Ø-Ø = you are asking me s.th.
8. you are requesting s.th.; ti-nēch-tla(htlani-lia)Ø-Ø = you are requesting s.th. from me
9. I am saying it; ni-mitz-Ø(il-huia)Ø-Ø = I am saying it to you
10. I am selling it; ni-mitz-Ø(namaquī-l-tia)Ø-Ø = I am selling it to you [exception: causative form, applicative meaning]
11. they are sick; Ø-mo(cocō-lia)Ø-h = they are sick toward one another, i.e., they hate one another
12. he is telling stories; Ø-quin-tla(quechi-lia)Ø-Ø = he is telling them stories
13. he is throwing it; Ø-qui-Ø(tlāxi-lia)Ø-Ø = he is throwing it from her, i.e., he is causing her to have an abortion
14. I am cutting it; ni-c-Ø(tequi-lia)Ø-Ø = I am cutting it for him, i.e., I am setting up an ambush for him
15. you are living; ti-c(nemi-lia)Ø-Ø = you are dwelling on it ~ you are considering it

15B. 1. you are closing it; tinēchtzacuilia = you are closing it for me
2. I am saying it; nicnolhuia = I am saying it to myself
3. they are shouting; quintzahtziliah = they are shouting to them
4. you (pl) are guarding s.th.; antēchtlapialiah = you (pl) are guarding s.th. for us
5. we hear it; tictēcaquiliah = we hear it from people
6. he is going (in order) to see it; commottilia = he is going (in order) to see it for himself
7. he is calling it; amēchnōchilia = he is calling it for you (pl)
8. it is hailing; quitecihuia = it is hailing on it

15C. 1. Won't it be hailed on?
    2. Then they answer him.
    3. Think about it.
    4. They heard it from me yesterday afternoon.
    5. Formerly they used to hate one another.
    6. When did you do it for them?
    7. Do not shake it down for him.
    8. He went there to see it for himself. ~ At that time he went to see it for himself.
    9. Beware of taking it from them.
   10. He was giving it to him. [The -*huāl*- indicates that the speaker allies himself with the receiver.]
   11. Let's beware of paying it to him.
   12. Then people were shouted to.

15D. 1. $\emptyset$(quīz)$\emptyset$-queh = they went out; $\emptyset$-qu(i)z-queh = they will drink it
    2. $\emptyset$-quim(āna)$\emptyset$-$\emptyset$ = he is taking hold of them; $\emptyset$-qui(mana)$\emptyset$-$\emptyset$ = he is setting it down
    3. ō-$\emptyset$(man)ca-$\emptyset$ = it had been sitting; ō-$\emptyset$-m(ān)ca-$\emptyset$ = it had been taken hold of [*lit,* it had taken hold of itself]
    4. $\emptyset$-tēch-$\emptyset$(ilhuih)$\emptyset$-$\emptyset$ = he said it to us; $\emptyset$-tē(chix)$\emptyset$-$\emptyset$ = he waited for s.o.
    5. $\emptyset$-tēch(ihua)$\emptyset$-$\emptyset$ = he is sending us; $\emptyset$-tē(chīhua)$\emptyset$-$\emptyset$ = he is engendering people
    6. ti-c(cua)$\emptyset$-h = we are eating it [*also,* ti-c(cuah)$\emptyset$-$\emptyset$ = you ate it] ; ō-ti-c(cuah)$\emptyset$-$\emptyset$ = you have eaten it

EXERCISE 16

16A. 1. he is hiding it; he is hiding it for himself, i.e., he (H) is hiding it ~ he is hiding it (H)
    2. you are guarding s.th. for me; ti-nēch-mo-tla(pia-li-lia)$\emptyset$-$\emptyset$ = you are guarding s.th. for me for you, i.e., you (H) are guarding s.th. for me
    3. he is frightening things; he is frightening things for himself, i.e., he (H) is frightening things
    4. they are getting the cramps; they are causing themselves to get the cramps, i.e., they (H) are getting the cramps
    5. I am receiving it; I am receiving it for myself, i.e., I am receiving it (H)
    6. he is helping me; he is helping me for himself, i.e., he (H) is helping me
    7. they are spearing you (pl); they are spearing you (pl) for themselves, i.e., they (H) are spearing you (pl) ~ they are spearing you (H, pl)
    8. you are tying me up; you are tying me up for yourself, i.e., you (H) are tying me up

9. we are doing him a favor; we are doing him a favor for ourselves, i.e., we are doing him (H) a favor

10. he is throwing rocks at s.th.; he is throwing rocks at s.th. for himself, i.e., he (H) is throwing rocks at s.th.

11. he is undressing him; he is undressing him for himself, i.e., he (H) is undressing him ~ he is undressing him (H)

12. she is bewitching me; she is bewitching me for herself, i.e., she (H) is bewitching me

16B. 1. he is girding himself; he (H) is girding himself
      2. he is remaining aloof; he (H) is remaining aloof
      3. you (pl) are poor; you (H, pl) are poor
      4. he is frowning in anger; he (H) is frowning in anger
      5. you are reviving; you (H) are reviving
      6. you are stretching out; you (H) are stretching out

16C. 1. I am stuttering; I (P) am stuttering
      2. he causes him to stutter; he (P) is causing him to stutter ~ he is causing him (P) to stutter
      3. we are hitting you with rocks; we (P) are hitting you with rocks ~ we are hitting you (P) with rocks
      4. you are eating; you (P) are eating
      5. he is spearing them; he (P) is spearing them ~ he is spearing them (P)
      6. I am tearing it; I (P) am tearing it ~ I am tearing it (P)

16D. 1. Hide (H) me! [*Also, metaphorically speaking,* Kill (H) me!]
      2. Here I (P) am guarding something.
      3. Will you (H) say it to her? ~ Will you say it to her (H)?
      4. Rest (H, pl)!
      5. He (R) was able to help me; i.e., He (R) helped me.
      6. Whither shall I take you (H, pl)?
      7. They (H) speared him yesterday afternoon. ~ They speared him (H) yesterday afternoon.
      8. Wait (pl) a little longer for him (H). [The absence of *mā* or *tlā* makes it unlikely that the subject refers to an honored entity.]
      9. Please have (H) mercy on me.
    10. He (H) never did us a favor.

EXERCISE 17

17A. 1. it is sifting down; it is drizzling
      2. he is eating; he is chewing
      3. he is stuttering; he is speaking a foreign language
      4. he is spearing him; he is spearing them again and again

5. he is spitting; he is sputtering
6. it is becoming polished; it is glittering
7. he is taking a rest; each one is taking a rest
8. they are undressing him; they are undressing them ~ they are undressing each of them
9. he is doing him a favor; he is imploring him
10. I am calling you; I am conversing with you
11. I am calling him for you; I am advising him for you
12. it is happening; he is adorning himself
13. he is hunting; he is fishing with a seine
14. I am living; I am walking
15. it is jingling; it is rattling

17B. 1. Kill (H) us.
2. There he became repeatedly thrashed.
3. They come chasing things.
4. Walk (pl) hither.
5. There people are repeatedly thrashed.
6. Then they closed them [e.g., doors or windows].
7. He was rocking it a lot.
8. Perhaps somewhere it will be struck repeatedly.
9. Yesterday he hastened him away.
10. Afterwards they gave them severally commands regarding people.
11. Then there was repeated spearing of people.
12. During the night it was still smoking.
13. Immediately there is an outcry.
14. Immediately he stirred them up to an outcry.
15. It is always whining.
16. They used to make it run a great deal.
17. Once they were seining.
18. Did they walk in this direction?
19. We have already each rested.
20. Afterwards they gave it (~ them) to each of them.

EXERCISE 18

18A. 1. he will show it to him; Ø-qu-Ø(ittī-tī-t-o)Ø-Ø = he went in order to show it to him
2. he will see it; Ø-qu(itta-t-o)Ø-Ø = he went in order to see it
3. I shall hollow it out; ni-c(comōlō-t-īuh)Ø-Ø = I am going in order to hollow it out
4. we shall be rich; ti-to(cuiltōnō-c-o)Ø-h = we came in order to be rich

5. you will shell it (~ them); ti-c(ōya-qu-īuh)∅-∅ = you will come in order to shell it (~ them)

6. you (pl) will curve it (~ them); an-qui(huītōlō-t-o)∅-h = you (pl) went in order to curve it (~ them)

7. I shall dig it; ni-c(tataca-c-o)∅-∅ = I have come in order to dig it

8. we shall govern you (pl); t-amēch(pachō-qu-īhui)∅-h = we shall come in order to govern you (pl)

9. he will conquer them; ∅-quim(pēhua-t-īuh)∅-∅ = he will go in order to conquer them

10. you will seine fish; ti(tlah-tla-mā-t-īuh)∅-∅ = you will go in order to seine fish

11. I shall open it; ni-c(tlapō-t-o)∅-∅ = I went in order to open it

12. I shall open it for you; ni-mitz-∅(tlapō-l-huī-t-o)∅-∅ = I went in order to open it for you

18B. 1. I went to commit adultery with you; I am going in order to commit adultery with you

2. you came in order to stoop over (~ bow down); you will come in order to stoop over (~ bow down)

3. he went in order to prepare s.th.; he is going in order to prepare s.th.

4. he went in order to dance; he is going in order to dance

5. we have come in order to gather things together; we shall come in order to gather things together

6. they have come in order to join together; they will come in order to join together

7. you (pl) went in order to grip it (~ them); you (pl) will go in order to grip it (~ them)

8. they came in order to interpret the influence of the heavenly bodies; they will come in order to interpret the influence of the heavenly bodies

18C. 1. if only he would go in order to cast spells on people (~ let him go . . .); if only they would go in order to cast spells on people (~ let them go . . .)

2. if only he would come to greet me (~ let him come . . .); if only they would come to greet me (~ let them come . . .)

3. if only you would go to hang him (~ go hang him); if only you (pl) would go to hang him (~ go (pl) hang him)

4. if only I would go to excavate (~ let me go . . .); if only we would go to excavate (~ let's go . . .)

5. if only I would come to control things (~ let me come . . .); if only we would come to control things (~ let's come . . .)

18D. 1. Go (pl) say it to him.
    2. Perhaps he (H) has come to show himself to you (i.e., to appear to you) everywhere.
    3. Perhaps I shall go to get it for you.
    4. Please come (H, pl) help me.
    5. They will come to shell things during the day.
    6. We shall first come at that time in order to conquer them. [Notice *ōmpa* in temporal meaning.]
    7. I absolutely did not come to hurt you.
    8. Let's go at night in order to dig it.
    9. They have come indeed from far away in order to dance.
   10. Let them not go in order to hang him.
   11. Perhaps he is going there in order to die.
   12. They went severally in order to fall at a distance.
   13. Immediately he went in order to converse with him.
   14. He came to that place in order to meet them.
   15. I have come in order to say it to you secretly.

EXERCISE 19

19A. 1. you will stand up straight
    2. he is speaking pleasantly
    3. they greeted me happily
    4. they were killed stealthily
    5. they were looking at you (pl) frightenedly
    6. he will die quickly

19B. 1. it rolled over; it goes rolling over and over
    2. it whined; it goes whining along
    3. it bellied; it goes bellying along
    4. he captured something; he goes along capturing things [from *tla-(ma)*]
    5. he found s.th. out; he goes along finding things out [from *tla-(mati)*]
    6. he became arrow-pierced; he lies arrow-pierced
    7. he is standing; he goes along standing
    8. they are here; they go along being here [Notice locative rather than directional meaning of *huāl-*; see § 2.6.3.]
    9. it began to rain; it is raining
   10. they remained aloof; they are sitting (~ lying) aloof
   11. he cried; he is crying
   12. he took it; he takes it abruptly
   13. it became perforated; it stands perforated
   14. they set them upright; they come along setting them upright

19C. 1. Ø-m(ān-Ø-ti-yah)ca-Ø = he had gone growing; he has gone growing; he goes growing; he will go growing
   2. I stood standing; I stand standing; I shall stand standing
   3. they came continually panting; they come continually panting
   4. they lay dispersed; they lie dispersed; they will lie dispersed
   5. it was bright, clear weather; it is bright, clear weather; it will be bright, clear weather
   6. he had lived calmly; he has lived calmly; he is living calmly; he will live calmly

19D. 1. it is becoming perforated
   2. it will gradually become black
   3. it remains split
   4. it was beginning to stink
   5. it is becoming light ~ dawn is coming on
   6. it gradually became calm [e.g., the wind]
   7. it is gradually becoming fat
   8. it is slowly becoming night

19E. 1. we shall make it; we want to make it
   2. I shall be able; I would be able
   3. they will dance; they would dance
   4. you will blink; you wanted to blink
   5. he will twist it; he will want to twist it
   6. he will lie fallen; he wanted to lie fallen
   7. I shall devise it; I would devise it
   8. they will be looking at one another; they want to be looking at one another

19F. 1. He simply went in order to meet her happily.
   2. People are going along dying on both sides.
   3. Then they abruptly came back.
   4. Never more does it lie quiet.
   5. They (H) came frightening things greatly.
   6. He would already answer him.
   7. They are beginning to nod right there.
   8. They are making things most imprudently.
   9. Formerly they were clashing with one another.
   10. Yesterday they went to greet them happily.
   11. He just goes around becoming upset.
   12. They were looked upon with great fear.
   13. You would seek it first.
   14. He goes around putting it to flight everywhere.

15. He lies there thoroughly beaten.
16. They were always looking at one another with hatred.
17. They went quite in the lead. ~ They could go leading the way.
18. Dawn is about to break. [*Lit,* It already wants to become dawn.]
19. They sit there looking at them. [The *huāl-* indicates that the speaker allies himself with the people referred to by *quin-.*]
20. They just went looking.

EXERCISE 20

20A. 1. n-∅(oquich)tli = I am a man; t-∅(oquich)tli = you are a man; ∅-∅-(oquich)tli = he is a man
   2. ni-∅(pil)li = I am a noble; ti-∅(pil)li = you are a noble; ∅-∅(pil)li = he is a noble
   3. ti-∅(pōchtēca)h = we are merchants; am-∅(pōchtēca)h = you are merchants; ∅-∅(pōchtēca)h = they are merchants
   4. ti-∅(tlāca)h = we are persons; an-∅(tlāca)h = you are persons; ∅-∅-(tlāca)h = they are persons
   5. ni-∅(cihuā)tl = I am a woman; ti-∅(cihuā)tl = you are a woman; ∅-∅-(cihuā)tl = she is a woman
   6. ti-∅(tah)tin = we are fathers; an-∅(tah)tin = you are fathers; ∅-∅(tah)-tin = they are fathers
   7. ti-∅(tē-tēuc)tin = we are lords; an-∅(tē-tēuc)tin = you are lords; ∅-∅-(tē-tēuc)tin = they are lords
   8. ni-∅(tlācoh)tli = I am a slave; ti-∅(tlācoh)tli = you are a slave; ∅-∅-(tlācoh)tli = he is a slave

20B. 1. ∅-∅(tepē)tl = it is a mountain; ∅-∅(tē-tepe)h = they are mountains
   2. ti-∅(pil)li = you are a noble; am-∅(pī-pil)tin = you are nobles
   3. ni-∅(pōchtēca)tl = I am a merchant; ti-∅(pōchtēca)h = we are merchants
   4. ∅-∅(mī)tl = it is an arrow ~ they are arrows
   5. ti-∅(cihuā)tl = you are a woman; az-∅(cihua)h = you are women
   6. ∅-∅(cōā)tl = it is a snake; ∅-∅(cō-cōa)h = they are snakes
   7. ∅-∅(chichi)∅ = it is a dog; ∅-∅(chichi)meh = they are dogs
   8. ∅-∅(cītlal)in = it is a star; ∅-∅(cī-cītlal)tin = they are stars
   9. ∅-∅(tepoz)tli = it is copper; it is of copper, they are of copper
   10. ∅-∅(tlāca)tl = he is a person; ∅-∅(tlāca)h = they are persons

20C. 1. *Subj:* ∅- . . . -tli; *pred:* -∅(mētz)-; It is the moon.
   2. *Subj:* ∅- . . . -tin; *pred:* -∅(cī-cītlal)-; They are stars.
   3. *Subj:* ni- . . . -tl; *pred:* -∅(pōchtēca)-; I am a merchant.
   4. *Subj:* an- . . . -h; *pred:* -∅(tē-teo)-; You are gods.
   5. *Subj:* ti- . . . -tl; *pred:* -∅(tlāca)-; You are a person.

6. *Subj:* ∅- . . . -meh; *pred:* -∅(tōtol)-; They are turkeys.
7. *Subj:* ∅- . . . -tl; *pred:* -∅(tla)-; It is a sling. ~ They are slings.
8. *Subj:* t- . . . -tin; *pred:* -∅(oquich)-; We are men.

20D. 1. We are turkeys. Ahtitōtoltin. Ahmō titōtoltin. = We are not turkeys.
    2. It is a snake. Ahcōātl. Ahmō cōātl. = It is not a snake.
    3. You are a dog. Ahtichichi. Ahmō tichichi. = You are not a dog.
    4. You are coyotes. Ahancōcoyoh. Ahmō ancōcoyoh. = You are not coyotes.
    5. It is a nonsling; i.e., It is a spear thrower. Ahahtlatl. Ahmō ahtlatl. = It is not a nonsling; i.e., It is not a spear thrower.
    6. You are a man. Ahtoquichtli. Ahmō toquichtli. = You are not a man.

20E. 1. They are turkeys. Tōtolmeh? Cuix tōtolmeh? = Are they turkeys?
    2. You are a god. Titeōtl? Cuix titeōtl? = Are you a god?
    3. You are women. Azcihuah? Cuix azcihuah? = Are you women?
    4. It is a spear thrower. ~ They are spear throwers. Ahtlatl? Cuix ahtlatl? = Is it a spear thrower? ~ Are they spear throwers?
    5. It is a base. Tzīntli? Cuix tzīntli? = Is it a base?
    6. You are merchants. Ampōchtēcah? Cuix ampōchtēcah? = Are you merchants?

20F. 1. It is an arrow. ~ They are arrows. Ca mītl. = It is indeed an arrow. ~ They are indeed arrows.
    2. We are nobles. Ca tipīpiltin. = We are indeed nobles.
    3. It is a spear thrower. ~ They are spear throwers. Ca ahtlatl. = It is indeed a spear thrower. ~ They are indeed spear throwers.
    4. They are snakes. Ca cōcōah. = They are indeed snakes.
    5. You are lords. Ca antētēuctin. = You are indeed lords.
    6. They are not slaves. Ca ahmō tlātlācohtin. = They are indeed not slaves.

20G. 1. Are you a lord? −Yes, I am.
    2. Are you slaves? −No, we aren't.
    3. Is it an arrow? −No, it is not.
    4. Are they gods? −Yes, sir, they are indeed gods.
    5. Are you Peter? −No, sir, I am not.

20H. 1. We are no longer slaves.
    2. They are not dogs. They are coyotes.
    3. They perhaps are lords.
    4. I am just a woman.
    5. They are absolutely not stars.
    6. Are you only just a merchant?
    7. He is indeed inhuman. [∅-∅(ah-tlāca)tl]
    8. Perhaps they are not nobles.

EXERCISE 21

21A. 1. ni-mo(cnīuh)∅ = I am your friend; ti-mo(cnī)huān [for *ti-mo(cnīuh)-huān*] = we are your friends
   2. ∅-no(mā)∅ = it is my hand ~ they are my hands
   3. ∅-īn(nān)∅ = she is their mother; ∅-īn(nā)huān [for *∅-īn(nān)huān*] = they are their mothers
   4. ∅-mo(tōch)∅ = it is your rabbit; ∅-mo(tōch)huān = they are your rabbits
   5. ∅-ī(oh)hui = it is his road ~ they are his roads
   6. ∅-ī(teō)uh = he is his god; ∅-ī(teō)huān = they are his gods
   7. ∅-no(cuāuh)∅ = it is my eagle; ∅-no(cuā)huān [for *∅-no(cuāuh)huān*] = they are my eagles
   8. ∅-no(cuauh)∅ = it is my tree ~ they are my trees
   9. ∅-amo(tēuc-yo)∅ = he is your (pl) master; ∅-amo(tēuc-yō)huān = they are your (pl) courtiers
   10. ∅-to(tlāca)uh = he is our slave; ∅-to(tlāca)huān = they are our slaves

21B. 1. ∅-no(cal)∅ = it is my house ~ they are my houses; ∅-to(cal)∅ = it is our house ~ they are our houses
   2. ∅-ī(chīmal)∅ = it is his shield ~ they are their shields; ∅-īn(chīmal)∅ = it is their shield ~ they are their shields
   3. ∅-n(ā)uh = it is my water; ∅-t(ā)uh = it is our water
   4. ∅-ī(mā)∅ = it is his hand ~ they are his hands; ∅-īm(mā)∅ = they are their hands
   5. ∅-m(oh)hui = it is your road ~ they are your roads; ∅-am(oh)hui = it is your (pl) road ~ they are your (pl) roads
   6. ∅-no(petl)∅ = it is my mat ~ they are my mats; ∅-to(petl)∅ = it is our mat ~ they are our mats
   7. ∅-mo(tecon)∅ = it is your jar ~ they are your jars; ∅-amo(tecon)∅ = it is your (pl) jar ~ they are your (pl) jars
   8. ∅-ī(te)uh = it is his rock ~ they are his rocks; ∅-īn(te)uh = it is their rock ~ they are their rocks; ∅-ī(teuh)∅ = it is his dust; ∅-īn(teuh)∅ = it is their dust
   9. ∅-no(yac)∅ = it is my nose; ∅-to(yac)∅ = they are our noses; it is a nose of one of us; i.e., it is a nose
   10. ∅-ī(tōcā)∅ = it is his name ~ they are his names; ∅-īn(tōcā)∅ = it is their name ~ they are their names
   11. ∅-no(yāō)uh = he is my enemy; ∅-to(yāō)uh = he is our enemy
   12. ∅-mo(tenān)∅ = it is your wall ~ they are your walls; ∅-amo(tenān)∅ = it is your (pl) wall ~ they are your (pl) walls
   13. ∅-ī(māx)∅ = it is its crotch ~ they are its crotches ~ it is their crotch

~ they are their crotches [The possessor could also be animate ("it is his crotch") with the corresponding plural possessor form *∅-īm-(māx)∅*, "they are their crotches."]

14. *∅-no(chān)∅* = it is my home ~ they are my homes; *∅-to(chān)∅* = it is our home ~ they are our homes

21C. 1. you are my friends; I am your (pl) friend
   2. he is their grandfather; they are his grandfathers
   3. he is my father; he is our father; they are our fathers
   4. they are your (sg) turkeys; it is your (pl) turkey
   5. I am his wife; we are his wives; we are their wives
   6. you are my mother; you are our mother; you are our mothers
   7. we are his enemies; he is our enemy

21D. 1. *Subj:* ∅- . . . -∅; *pred:* -īx(xo)-; They are their feet.
   2. *Subj:* n- . . . -∅; *pred:* -ī(cnīuh)-; I am his friend.
   3. *Subj:* ∅- . . . -huān; *pred:* -to(tlāca)-; They are our slaves.
   4. *Subj:* ∅- . . . -∅; *pred:* -amo(cxi)-; They are your (pl) feet.
   5. *Subj:* ∅- . . . -∅; *pred:* -ī(neuc)-; It is his honey.
   6. *Subj:* t- . . . -huān; *pred:* -īm(oquich)-; We are their husbands.
   7. *Subj:* ti- . . . -∅; *pred:* -no(cōl)-; You are my grandfather.
   8. *Subj:* ∅- . . . -uh; *pred:* -īn(te)-; It is their rock. ~ They are their rocks. *Subj:* ∅- . . . -∅; *pred:* -īn(teuh)-; It is their dust.

21E. 1. She is not my mother. Nonān. = She is my mother.
   2. They are indeed our enemies. Toyāōhuān. = They are our enemies.
   3. Are you his wife? Tīcihuāuh. = You are his wife.
   4. Is it his dog? Īchichi. = It is his dog.
   5. I am indeed not your friend. Ahnimocnīuh. = I am not your friend.
   6. Isn't it my arrow? ~ Aren't they my arrows? Ahnomīuh. = It is not my arrow. ~ They are not my arrows.
   7. It is not our mat. ~ They are not our mats. Topetl. = It is our mat. ~ They are our mats.
   8. It is not your turkey. Motōtol. = It is your turkey.
   9. Is it your house? ~ Are they your houses? Mocal. = It is your house. ~ They are your houses.
   10. Isn't it your (pl) home? ~ Aren't they your (pl) homes? Amochān. = It is your (pl) home. ~ They are your (pl) homes.

21F. 1. Perhaps it is his water.
   2. It is indeed his rock. ~ They are indeed his rocks.
   3. Aren't you my friend?
   4. They are indeed their dogs.
   5. Is he your lord? —No, he isn't.

6. They are not our hands. They are our feet. (~ It is not a hand. It is a foot. ~ They are not hands. They are feet.)
7. It is just our jar. ~ They are just our jars.
8. He is not his father. He is his grandfather.
9. It is absolutely not his road. ~ They are absolutely not his roads.
10. Are they still his friends?

EXERCISE 22

22A. 1. it is a sling: it is a hand, it is a net; $\emptyset$-$\emptyset$(māxa)tl = it is a crotch; $\emptyset$-$\emptyset$-(māx-tla)tl = it is a breechcloth [*lit,* a crotch sling]
2. it is a house: he is a god, it is a temple; it is a mat, it is a hamper (~ a wickerwork chest [*lit,* a structure made of mats]); it is water, it is a boat [*lit,* a structure made for water]
3. it is a lip: it is water, it is a water-edge (~ it is a shore); it is a house, it is the edge of a house; it is an eye, it is the lip of an eyelid
4. it is a rock: it is an eye, it is an eyeball; it is a turkey, it is a turkey egg; it is a lip, it is a labret (a lip ornament)
5. it is a tree: it is a hand, it is a club (~ a sword); it is a head, it is a horn [*lit,* a head tree]
6. it is water: it is the sky, it is an ocean; he is a god, it is divine water (ocean, blood, flood)
7. it is excrement: he is a god, it is gold [*lit,* god excrement]; it is the moon, it is mica [*lit,* moon excrement]
8. it is a child: it is a bird, it is a baby bird; it is a deer, it is a fawn
9. it is a child: it is a fire, it is a torch [*lit,* a child of the fire]; it is a back, it is a tail [*lit,* the child of a back]
10. it is a stick: it is a rock, it is a stiff switch; it is rubber, it is a flexible switch

22B. 1. it is a name; (pil)-li = a prince; it is the name of a prince, i.e., it is a princely title
2. it is hair; (tēn)-tli = a lip; it is hair at the lips, i.e., it is a beard
3. it is a wall; (cuahui)-tl = tree; it is a wooden wall, i.e., it is a palisade
4. it is a hill; (ā)-tl = water; it is water and a hill (it is a town)
5. it is an arrow; (tepoz)-tli = copper, iron; it is a metal arrow (it is a bolt for a crossbow)
6. it is a bone; (huitz)-tli = a thorn; it is a needle
7. it is a cultivated field; (xōchi)-tl = flower; it is a flower garden
8. it is water; (nex)-tli = ash, ashes; it is lye

22C. 1. (ā)-tl = water; (cal)-li = house; (oh)-tli = road
$(a+b)+c;$ (ā-cal)-li + (oh)-tli
it is a road for boats; i.e., it is a canal

2. (te)-tl = rock; (māi)-tl = hand; (tla)-tl = sling
   a+(b+c); (te)-tl + (mā-tla)-tl
   it is a sling (for hurling stones)
3. (ā)-tl = water; (cal)-li = house; (yaca)-tl = nose
   (a+b)+c; (ā-cal)-li + (yaca)-tl
   it is the prow of a boat
4. (ilhuica)-tl = sky; (ā)-tl = water; (tēn)-tli = edge
   (a+b)+c; (ilhuica-ā)-tl + (tēn)-tli
   it is the edge of the ocean; i.e., it is the seashore
5. (ā)-tl = water; (tepē)-tl = mountain, hill; (tenāmi)-tl = wall
   (a+b)+c; (ā-l-tepē)-tl + (tenāmi)-tl
   it is the wall of a town (~ city)

22D. 1. it is a town; Ø-Ø(ā-l-tepē-tōn)tli = it is a small town
2. she is my mother; Ø-no(nān-tzin)Ø = she is my mother (H) ~ she is my dear mother
3. they are our puppies; Ø-to(chichi-conē-pi-pīl)huān = they are our dear little puppies
4. it is a boat; Ø-Ø(ā-cal-zol)li = it is a dilapidated boat
5. he is my father; Ø-no(tah)tzin = he is my father (H) ~ he is my beloved father
6. it is a horn; Ø-Ø(cuā-cuahui-tōn)tli = it is a small horn
7. he is my child; Ø-no(conē-tzin)Ø = he is my dear child
8. it is a turkey; Ø-Ø(tōtol-pōl)Ø = it is a big old turkey
9. it is a tail; Ø-Ø(cuitla-pil-tōn)tli = it is a little tail
10. he is a youth; Ø-Ø(tēl-pō-tzin)tli [for *Ø-Ø(tēl-pōch-tzin)tli*] = he is a fine young man

22E. 1. They are not our baby birds.
2. Is he your father (H)? —Yes indeed, sir, he is indeed my father (H).
3. Perhaps it is their war canoe. ~ Perhaps they are their war canoes.
4. It is just absolutely not his princely title.
5. Is it your (pl) gold?
6. Perhaps it is lye.
7. Today it is a temple.
8. Perhaps it is mica.
9. Is it a metal arrow? —No, it is only a wooden arrow.
10. It is my very city. ~ It is my city itself.

EXERCISE 23

23A. 1. it is a holiday, they are causing it to come out; Ø(ilhui-quīx-tia)Ø-h = they are celebrating a holiday, Ø-qu(ilhui-quīx-ti-lia)Ø-h = they are celebrating a holiday in his honor

    2. it is a road, you (pl) are hurling it; am(oh-tlāza)∅-h = you (pl) are blocking a road, an-quim(oh-tlāxi-lia)∅-h = you (pl) are blocking a road to them, you (pl) are misdirecting them

    3. he is a person, you are killing him; ti(tlāca-mic-tia)∅-∅ = you are sacrificing a human being ~ you are performing a human sacrifice

    4. it is a job, I am leaving it; ni(tequi-cāhua)∅-∅ = I am leaving a job, I am retiring

    5. it is water, ni-qu(i)∅-∅ = I am drinking it; n(ā-tl-i)∅-∅ = I am drinking water

    6. it is anger, he is taking it; ∅(tlahuēl-cui)∅-∅ = he is becoming angry

    7. it is a road, they are setting it up; ∅(oh-quetza)∅-h = they are establishing a road, ∅-tēch(oh-quechi-lia)∅-h = they are establishing a road for us

    8. it is water, he is fetching it; ∅(ā-tla-cui)∅-∅ = he is fetching water

23B. 1. it is a cord, I am squeezing it; ni-c(meca-pātzca)∅-∅ = I am squeezing it with cords

    2. it is water, they are crossing a river; ∅(ā-pano)∅-h = they are crossing a river

    3. it is rubber, you are sprinkling it; ti-c(ōl-chipīnia)∅-∅ = you are sprinkling it with (liquid) rubber

    4. it is a boat, they are striking one another; ∅-m(ā-cal-huītequi)∅-h = they are bumping into one another in boats

    5. it is dew, it is drizzling; ∅(ahhuach-pixahui)∅-∅ = it is misting rain

    6. it is work, you are bending over; ti-mo(tequi-pachoa)∅-∅ = you are worrying

    7. it is something clear-sounding, we are speaking; ti(nāhua-tla-htoa)-∅-h = we are speaking by means of something clear-sounding, i.e., we are speaking Nahuatl

    8. they are their noses, I am taking them; ni-quin(yac-āna)∅-∅ = I am taking them by their noses, i.e., I am leading them

    9. it is a house, you are entering; ti(cal-aqui)∅-∅ = you are entering (a house)

    10. it is its rump, it is trampling; ∅(tzīn-tla-cza)∅-∅ = it is trampling to the rear

    11. they are lips, you (pl) raise it; an-qui(tēn-ēhua)∅-h = you (pl) are raising it to the lips, i.e., you are pronouncing it ~ you are mentioning it

    12. they are his eyes, he is dead; ∅(īx-mih-miqui)∅-∅ = he is dead at the eyes, i.e., he is blind

    13. it is a mouth, I am leaving it; ni-c(cama-cāhua)∅-∅ = I am letting it slip out (of my mouth)

23C. 1. you are a guest, I am creating you; ni-mitz(cōā-chīhua)∅-∅ = I am making you a guest, i.e., I am inviting you
   2. he is a god, we know him; ti-c(teō-mati)∅-h = we know him to be a god
   3. it is an eagle with a necklace, i.e., it is a king vulture, it is mimicking; ∅-mo(cōzca-cuāuh-neh-nequi)∅-∅ = it resembles a king vulture
   4. it is a child, it is going out; ∅(pil-quīza)∅-∅ = it is (~ they are) being rejuvenated, ∅-qui(pil-quīx-tia)∅-∅ = it causes it (~ them) to be rejuvenated
   5. you are a fool, you are returning; ti-mo(xōlopih-cuepa)∅-∅ = you are becoming a fool
   6. they are slaves, we know them; ti-quin(tlācoh-mati)∅-h = we think they are slaves
   7. you are my friends, I am following you (pl); n-amēch(icnīuh-toca)-∅-∅ = I consider you my friends
   8. it is an evil omen, you (pl) know it; an-qui(tētzām-mati)∅-h = you (pl) consider it an evil omen

23D. 1. ni-quim(īxi-mati)∅-∅; embed = adverb; I know them by the face
   2. ∅-m(ā-cal-aqui-a)∅-∅; embed = adverb; it causes itself to enter into a boat
   3. ti(tequi-tla-neloa)∅-∅; embed = adverb; you row with effort
   4. ∅(īx-teh-tēn-motzoloa)∅-h; embed = direct object; they grapple the borders of the eyes
   5. ∅(tlāl-polihui)∅-∅; embed = adverb; it perishes in the earth
   6. ni-n(oquich-quetza)∅-∅; embed = adverb of compared manner; I stand up like a man
   7. ∅-mo(cuā-cuauh-tlāza)∅-∅; embed = adverb; it throws itself from the horns
   8. ti-c(cōā-nōtza)∅-h; embed = adverb; we are calling him as a guest
   9. ∅-tēch(yaca-tzacui-lia)∅-h; embed = direct object; they are closing the point to us
   10. t(ā-miqui)∅-∅; embed = adverb; you are dying from (lack of) water ~ you are dying for water
   11. am-mo(cuitla-cuepa)∅-h; embed = adverb; you (pl) are turning toward the back
   12. ∅-qui(tēn-quīx-tia)∅-h; embed = adverb; they cause it to leave at the lips
   13. ti-c(teō-toca)∅-h; embed = complement; we follow him as if he were a god
   14. ∅-mo(quech-mecania)∅-∅; embed = adverb; he uses a rope upon himself at the neck

15. ni-mitz(tlahuēl-chīhua)∅-∅; embed = adverb; I create you with anger
16. ∅-tē(īx-cuepa)∅-∅; embed = adverb; he turns people at the eyes (~ by means of the eyes?); he fools people's eyes
17. ∅(yāō-tēca)∅-∅; embed = direct object; he lays down an enemy ~ a war
18. ∅(yāō-tla-htoa)∅-h; embed = adverb; they speak about enemies ~ war

23E. 1. Did it sink? —No, they sank it.
2. Perhaps he will be drowned.
3. He had always gone around just sighing.
4. Formerly they looked at each other with hatred.
5. Then it retreats. They caused it to retreat.
6. It just eats it diligently.
7. At that time is was drizzling rain. [Notice the present-tense form translated as past tense. See § 47.1.]
8. They warred against them greatly.
9. Then they went to meet him in battle.
10. He just goes along retreating.
11. They are shaking their heads strongly.
12. He just came preparing himself for battle.

EXERCISE 24

24A. 1. t-∅(ac-ah)∅ = you are s.o.
2. an-∅(tleh)meh = you (pl) are s.th.
3. ∅-∅(quē-x-qui-ch-tōn)∅ = it is a small amount
4. am-∅(mie-qui-n)tin = you (pl) are many
5. n-∅(itl-ah)∅ = I am s.th.
6. ∅-∅(iz-qui-n)∅ = they are as many
7. ∅-∅(yeh-yeh-huā)tl = they are those various ones
8. ∅-∅(a-chi-tōn)∅ = it is a little
9. am-∅(eh-huā-n)tin = you are those
10. ∅-∅(cā-tle-in)∅ = which one is it?
11. ∅-∅ (ix-a-chi-n)∅ = they are many
12. ∅-∅(yeh-huā-m-po-pōl)∅ = they are those worthless ones
13. am-∅(mo-chi-n)∅ = you (pl) are all
14. an-∅(quē-x-qui-ch)tin = how many are you?
15. az-∅(ce-qui-n)tin = you (pl) are some (of a group)
16. ni-∅(tl-e-im-pōl)∅ = what a miserable thing I am!

24B. 1. They are nothing.
2. He is the very one. ~ He himself is the one.
3. They are as many again. ~ They are an equal number.
4. Perhaps you are some people.

    5. Are they the ones?
    6. It is quite as much. ~ They are quite as many.
    7. We are a multitude. ~ We are a crowd.
    8. They are nothing.
    9. You (pl) are a sufficient number.
  10. How fortunate we are!
  11. Are you (pl) something?
  12. It is just a little.

EXERCISE 25

25A. 1. they are 15 + 2 (seventeen) in number
      2. they are (2 × 20) + 5 + 4 (forty-nine) in number
      3. they are 10 + 1 (eleven) in number
      4. they are 5 + 4 (nine) in number
      5. they are (3 × 20) + 3 (sixty-three) in number
      6. they are 5 + 1 (six) things
      7. they are 20 + 10 + 2 (thirty-two) in number
      8. they are (10 × 20) + 15 + 3 (two hundred eighteen) in number
      9. they are (1 × 20) + 10 + 4 (thirty-four) in number
   10. they are (4 × 20) + 5 (eighty-five) in number

25B. 1. They are only twelve in number.
      2. Are they still three in number? ~ Are they three more?
      3. From time to time they are four in number.
      4. They are already fifteen in number.
      5. How many are you? —We are four.
      6. Today they are only fifteen. Yesterday they were eighteen.
      7. They are no longer six in number.
      8. Are we five in number? —No, we are only three.
      9. They are only thirty-three in number.
   10. Are they sixty in number?
   11. Then they sat down as one; i.e., Then they sat down together.
   12. They are truly twenty in number.
   13. Are they three in number? —No, they are only two.
   14. It just eats it completely up.

EXERCISE 26

26A. 1. It is crying. It-is-crying it-is-one-in-number; i.e., One is crying.
      2. They are shouting. They-are-shouting they-are-all; i.e., All are shout-ing.
      3. They have been seen. They-have-been-seen they-are-the-ones, i.e., *They* have been seen.

   4. It is indeed nothing. It-is-indeed-nothing it-is-its-price; i.e., Its price
      is indeed nothing; i.e., It does not cost anything. ~ It is worthless.
   5. We have been here. Here we-have-been we-are-many; i.e., Many of
      us have been here.
   6. They are two in number. They-are-two-in-number they-are-its-lips,
      i.e., Its lips are two in number. ~ It has two lips.
   7. It grows there. There it-makes-itself it-is-red-pepper; i.e., Red pepper
      grows there.
   8. It hurts people. It-hurts-people it-is-peyote; i.e., Peyote hurts people.
   9. It is sold. It-sells-itself it-is-pine-wood; i.e., Pine wood is sold.
  10. He sat down. ~ It was set down. It-set-itself-down it-is-fire; i.e., A
      fire was lit.

26B. 1. They shell them. They-shell-them they-are-dried-ears-of-maize; i.e.,
        They shell dried ears of maize.
     2. He saw them. He-saw-them they-are-stars; i.e., He saw stars.
     3. They captured it. They-captured-it it-is-one-in-number; i.e., They
        captured one.
     4. He is sending them. He-is-sending-them they-are-all-of-them; i.e., He
        is sending all of them.
     5. They made it. They-made-it this; i.e., They made this.
     6. He carried them. He-carried-them still they-are-a-few; i.e., He carried
        a few others.
     7. They went in order to give it (~ them) to them. They-went-in-order-
        to-give-it-to-them it-is-a-blanket; i.e., They went in order to give a
        blanket to them. ~ They-went-in-order-to-give-them-to-them they-
        are-blankets; i.e., They went in order to give blankets to them.
     8. They are throwing it (~ them) hither. They-are-throwing-it-hither
        it-is-a-metal-arrow; i.e., They are shooting a bolt in this direction. ~
        They-are-throwing-them-hither they-are-metal-arrows; i.e., They are
        shooting bolts in this direction.
     9. It lies looking at them. It-lies-looking-at-them they-are-deer; i.e., It
        lies looking at the deer.
    10. I am making it (~ them). I-am-making-it it-is-a-sandal; i.e., I am mak-
        ing a sandal. ~ I-am-making-them they-are-sandals; i.e., I am making
        sandals.
    11. They gave it (~ them) to them. They-gave-it-to-them it-is-a-neck-
        lace; i.e., They gave them a necklace. ~ They-gave-them-to-them
        they-are-necklaces; i.e., They gave them necklaces.
    12. He split it. He-split-it it-is-pine-wood; i.e., He split pine wood.

26C. 1. It is my staff. It-is-my-staff I-am-the-one; i.e., It is *my* staff.
     2. It is your paper. It-is-your-paper you-are-the-one; i.e., It is *your* paper.

3. It is their blanket. ~ They are their blankets. It-is-their-blanket they-are-three-in-number; i.e., It is the blanket of the three. ~ They-are-their-blankets they-are-three-in-number; i.e., They are the blankets of the three.

4. They are its (~ their) worms. They-are-its-worms it-is-a-tree; i.e., They are the tree's worms. ~ They-are-their-worms they-are-trees; i.e., They are the trees' worms.

5. It is their boat. ~ They are their boats. It-is-their-boat they-are-the-ones; i.e., It is *their* boat. ~ They-are-their-boats they-are-the-ones; i.e., They are *their* boats.

6. It is its sand. It-is-its sand it-is-a-river; i.e., It is a river's sand.

7. It is our road. It-is-our-road we-are-the-ones; i.e., It is *our* road.

8. They are its eggs. They-are-its-eggs it-is-a-fish; i.e., They are a fish's eggs.

9. They are their blouses. They-are-their-blouses they-are-women; i.e., They are the women's blouses.

10. They are your (pl) friends. They-are-your-friends you-are-men; i.e., They are the friends of you men.

26D. 1. Her husband hates *me*. [*nehhuātl* = suppl obj; *īoquichhui* = suppl subj]

2. Your dog killed my turkeys. [*notōtolhuān* = suppl obj; *mochichi* = suppl subj]

3. Will your friend sell me pine wood? [*ocōtl* = suppl obj (in cross reference with silent direct object); *mocnīuh* = suppl subj]

4. His father is always drinking pulque. [*ītah* = suppl subj; *octli* = suppl obj]

5. My mother is looking for my sandals. [*nocac* = suppl obj; *nonān* = suppl subj]

6. *Your* maguey hemp has already been put on board the boat. [*mochhui* = suppl subj; *tehhuātl* = suppl poss]

7. My friends' child's name is nothing; i.e., My friends' child has no name. [*ītōcā* = suppl subj of *ahtleh; īmpiltōn* = suppl poss of *ītōcā; nocnīhuān* = suppl poss of *īmpiltōn*]

8. I shall not help my town's enemies. [*īyāōhuān* = suppl obj; *nāltepēuh* = suppl poss]

26E. 1. Peyote is being eaten. [*peyōtl* = suppl subj]

2. You have three. [*ētetl* = suppl obj]

3. All go out. [*mochintin* = suppl subj]

4. A lot is spilling out. [*miec* = suppl subj]

5. My shield goes being; i.e., I have my shield with me. [*nochīmal* = suppl subj]

6. Let *him* beware of standing up. [*yehhuātl* = suppl subj]
7. My father is indeed their friend. [*notah* = suppl subj]
8. Burn the paper. [*āmatl* = suppl obj]

26F. 1. Five are needed. How many are needed? [*mācuīlli* and *quēxquich* = suppl subjects]
2. You will buy sandals. What will you buy? [*cactli* and *tleh* = suppl objects]
3. My son upset you. Who upset you? [*nopiltzin* and *āc* = suppl subjects]
4. He will gather pine wood. What will he gather? [*ocōtl* and *tleh* = suppl objects]
5. Is it your grandfather's blanket? Whose blanket is it? [*mocōl* and *āquin* = suppl possessors]
6. He is taking four. How many is he taking? [*nāuhtetl* and *quēzquitetl* = suppl objects]

26G. 1. Let your dog beware of entering.
2. His sons are indeed three in number. ~ He has three sons.
3. What will you give me?
4. Beware of ruining my necklace.
5. The gold's road is falling there; i.e., The vein of gold comes to the surface there.
6. Let's sink their boat(s).
7. There all fell down.
8. What shall I do?
9. Its head is of stone.
10. I shall not accept anything from you.
11. Let's just go.
12. Nothing is growing there.
13. Who are you?
14. They weren't able to say anything else.
15. No one will utter anything. ~ No one will say anything.
16. Again all came (being).
17. Someone will shortly flee.
18. They took everything from them.
19. Your mother is not your mother. Your father is not your father.
20. They always have their slings with them.

EXERCISE 27

27A. 1. It continually strips the bark off of them. It continually strips the bark off of the trees. [*in cuahuitl* = suppl obj]

2. It captures them there. It captures the wood-worms there. [*in cuauh-ocuiltin* = suppl obj]
3. It breaks. The metate breaks. [*in metlatl* = suppl subj]
4. They will die. His slaves will die. [*in ītlācahuān* = suppl subj]
5. They used to not dig for it. They used to not dig for the gold. [*in teōcuitlatl* = suppl obj]
6. They are already leaving! Your (pl) enemies are already leaving! [*in amoyāōhuān* = suppl subj]
7. It will not be hailed on. His field will not be hailed on. [*in īmīl* = suppl subj]
8. We indeed went in order to see them. We indeed went in order to see our courtiers ~ our lords. [*in totēucyōhuān* = suppl obj]
9. They crossed it. They crossed the stream. [*in ātoyatōntli* = suppl obj]
10. They come in the lead. Their dogs come in the lead. [*in īmitzcuin-huān* = suppl subj]
11. He is indeed only one in number. Their god is indeed only one in number. ~ They have only one god. [*in īnteōuh* = suppl subj]
12. It grows well there. Popcorn grows well there. [*in momochitl* = suppl subj]
13. You will be unable to buy it. You will be unable to buy this. [*inīn* = suppl obj]
14. It will go being taken. The city will go being taken. [*in āltepētl* = suppl subj]
15. It is indeed mine. That is indeed mine. [*inōn* = suppl subj]

27B. 1. He is indeed my grandfather (H). *He* is indeed my grandfather. [*in yehhuātl* = suppl subj]
2. Let's beware of upsetting him. Let's beware of upsetting this one. [*inīn* = suppl obj]
3. It carries it. It carries gold. The river carries gold. [*in ātoyatl* = suppl subj]
4. They went separately to fall at a distance. The rocks went separately to fall at a distance. [*in tetl* = suppl subj]
5. I shall climb up. *I* shall climb up. [*in nehhuātl* = suppl subj]
6. It is indeed Coltzin. His name is indeed Coltzin. Their god's name is indeed Coltzin. [*ītōcā* = suppl subj; *in īnteōuh* = suppl poss of *ītōcā*]
7. They are not dancing. *They* are not dancing. [*in yehhuāntin* = suppl subj]
8. I want to eat it. I want to eat the meat. [*in nacatl* = suppl obj]
9. They are throwing them hither. They are shooting the bolts hither. *They* are shooting the bolts hither. [*in yehhuāntin* = suppl subj]

10. He heard it with much pleasure. The boy heard it with much pleasure. The boy heard the anecdote with much pleasure. [*in zazanīlli* = suppl obj]
11. They rested there. *They* rested there. [*in yehhuāntin* = suppl subj]
12. It is being dribbled down. The blood is being dribbled down. [*in eztli* = suppl subj]
13. They go around being. Their lip ornaments go around being; i.e., They have their lip ornaments with them. The men's lip ornaments go around being; i.e., The men have their lip ornaments continually with them. [*īntēnteuh* = suppl subj; *in oquichtin* = suppl poss of *īntēnteuh*]
14. They became very afraid. All became very afraid. [*in ixquichtin* = suppl subj]

27C. 1. The crane sees the frog. The frog sees the crane.
   2. The man killed the woman. The woman killed the man.
   3. My friend gave it (~ them) to the child. The child gave it (~ them) to my friend.
   4. The vampire bat frightened the owl. The owl frightened the vampire bat.
   5. The page hated the man. The man hated the page.
   6. This one is sending that one. That one is sending this one.

27D. 1. What did you (pl) do? [absence of specific nuclear obj prefix]
   2. Where is his home? [*cān* as proxy matrix]
   3. The men were setting the blankets down for him. [suppl subj and nuclear subj disagree with regard to person]
   4. Did you steal (something)? Did you steal the necklace? [no prefix for indefinite obj; prefix for definite object]
   5. Did you and the merchant say it to one another? ["named-partner" construction]
   6. All crossed the water there. [lack of agreement in number between suppl subj and nuclear subj]
   7. It was an evil omen. [dummy matrix for purpose of expressing time other than present]
   8. My friend and I conversed. ["named-partner" construction]

27E. 1. Who are you, my fellow?
   2. Do not worry, my friend.
   3. Here you are lying down (H), my sons; i.e., You are present here, my sons.
   4. Remain well aloof, my son. ~ Guard yourself well, my son.
   5. My son, hear it. ~ My son, listen.
   6. Master, please take it (H).

7. Here you are, my son; i.e., Welcome, my son.
8. My children, please fall (H) down here; i.e., My children please sit (H) down.
9. Oh you who are Mother of the Gods, please deign to give it to him!
10. You mothers, whom verily do you still see (H)?

27F. 1. They were acquainted with the stars.
2. Our enemies withdrew their boat(s).
3. His home (~ homeland) will soon be destroyed.
4. Their friends sit looking at them. ~ They sit looking at their friends.
5. The shamans were absolutely helpless (~ useless).
6. The wood is smoking a lot.
7. He will shortly follow the rabbit's road.
8. My father's friend did nothing else but go meet them happily.
9. Your grandfathers indeed are guarding things for you (H) there.
10. The nobles' children will come.
11. Perhaps the wizards will be able to bewitch them.
12. Does the coyote's fire go along being? i.e., Does the coyote carry his fire with him? [*In coyōtl* is the suppl poss of *ītleuh,* which is the suppl subj of *yetinemi.*]
13. The reeds grow abundantly there.
14. The women are just already looking at them. ~ They are just already looking at the women; i.e., They don't do anything but look at the women.
15. The women's blouses were nothing; i.e., The women wore no blouses.

EXERCISE 28

28A. 1. They are coming out. The ones who will dance are coming out; i.e., The dancers are coming out. [*mihtōtīzqueh* = suppl subj]
2. They are there. The ones who speak Nahuatl are there; i.e., There are Nahuatl speakers. [*nāhuatlahtoah* = suppl subj]
3. I sent them. I sent the ones who went. [*ōyahqueh* = suppl obj]
4. They were seen. The ones who came were seen. [*āquihqueh ōhuāl-lahqueh* = suppl subj]
5. They will see them. They will see what kind of people they are. [*quēnamihqueh* = suppl obj]
6. They will come. The ones who are leading people will come; i.e., The leaders will come. [*tēyacānah* = suppl subj]
7. Once again they reassembled. Once again the ones who had become dispersed came back together. [*moyāhuacah* = suppl subj]
8. Soon it will enter. Soon that which goes warming will enter; i.e., Soon the sun will set. [*tōnatiuh* = suppl subj]

9. She will soon die. The one who was grinding will soon die. [*ōtecia* = suppl subj]

10. They are fifteen in number. The ones who were captured are (~ were) fifteen in number. [*ōānōqueh* = suppl subj]

11. He deceived them. Their lord deceived them. As for these, their lord deceived them. [*ihqueh īn* = suppl poss of *īntēucyo*]

12. Here it is. Here is what you (pl) gave him. [*anquimacazqueh* = suppl subj. The referent of the silent direct object and that of the $\emptyset$- . . . -*qui* are identical.]

13. They indeed speak a foreign language. *Those* indeed speak a foreign language. [*ihqueh ōn* = suppl subj]

14. I saw it. I saw what you did (~ made). [*ōticchīuh* = suppl obj. The referent of the -*c*- and that of the -*qu*- are identical.]

28B. 1. He said to him, "Don't worry." [The quote is suppl direct obj and serves as the referent of the silently present nuclear direct obj of the matrix.]

2. "Cuatatl" means "his head is of stone." [*tetl ītzontecon* = suppl obj]

3. One says, "This is *cuatatl* itself." [The quote is suppl subj. The adverb *huel* is translated here as "itself"; cf. § 24.5.1.]

4. She says to him, "Leave me." [*Xinēchcāhua* is the suppl direct obj and serves as the referent of the silently present nuclear direct obj.]

5. They say, "Let it beware of coming to an end quickly." [The quote is suppl obj.]

6. Everywhere they were asked, "Who are you? Where do you come from?" [The quote is suppl obj functioning as referent of the silently present nuclear obj of *ilhuīlōqueh*.]

28C. 1. Think about how you have lived. [Embed is suppl obj and functions as referent of the -*c*- of *xicnemili*.]

2. It was said that he hid everything from him. [*Mochi quitlātilih* is suppl obj and serves as the referent of the -*qu*- of *quil*.]

3. It is necessary that we give them directions. [Embed is suppl subj and serves as the referent of the $\emptyset$- . . . -$\emptyset$ subject affixes of *monequi*.]

4. It is said that his field will not be hailed on. [*Ahmō tecihuīlōz in īmīl* is suppl obj and serves as the referent of the -*qu*- of *quil*.]

5. He was observing closely where he would go (going). [Embed is suppl obj and serves as referent of the -*qu*- of *quittaya*.]

6. There is told how they fashioned their boat(s). [Embed is suppl subj and serves as referent of the $\emptyset$- . . . -$\emptyset$ subj affixes of *mihtoa*.]

7. We do not know whether it will be done tomorrow. [Embed is suppl obj and serves as the referent of the -*c*- of *ticmatih*.]

8. How it ended is not well known. [Embed is suppl subj and serves as referent of the $\emptyset$- . . . -$\emptyset$ subj affixes of *macho*.]

9. I want to pave it with stones. [*Nictemanaz* is suppl obj and serves as the referent of *-c-* of *nicnequi.*]

10. Someone envisions that he will crush someone's head with a rock. [*Tēcuātepachōz* is suppl obj and serves as the referent of the *-c-* of *conmottilia.*]

11. They tell one another what they have envisioned. [Embed is suppl obj and serves as the referent of the *-qui-* of *quimolhuiah.*]

12. It is said that their god goes summoning them. [*Quinnōtztiuh in īnteōuh* is suppl obj and serves as the referent of the *qu-* of *quil.*]

28D. 1. Here is what you are seeking.
2. It is necessary that you (pl) know his name.
3. Those are becoming rich.
4. He has come in order to say to them, "Help (H) the city."
5. Here is what we did (~ made).
6. He said to them, "Please come!"
7. It seemed, it was said, that the one who was grinding would soon die.
8. They answered, (saying,) "What is his name?"
9. These are reviving.
10. I want to eat beans.
11. Do you know in what manner you are carried?
12. Here is mentioned who are the Otomis.

EXERCISE 29

29A. 1. ō-ni(cal-pix)∅-∅ = I have guarded a house; ni-∅(cal-pix-∅)qui = I am one who has guarded a house, I am a steward

2. ō-ti(temo)∅-c = you have descended; ti-∅(temo-∅)c = you are one who has descended, you are a descender

3. ō-ti-tla(namaca)∅-queh = we have sold things; ti-∅(tla-namaca-∅)queh = we are ones who have sold things, we are sellers

4. ō-∅(tlan)∅-∅ = it has come to an end; ∅-∅(tlan-∅)qui = it is a thing that has come to an end, it is a finished thing

5. ō-ni-tla(tqui)∅-c = I have carried things; ni-∅(tla-tqui-∅)c = I am one who has carried things, I am a carrier

6. ō-∅(mic)∅-queh = they have died; ∅-∅(mī-mic-∅)queh = they are ones who have died, they are dead people

7. ō-ti(tlahuēli-lō)∅-c = you have been detested; ti-∅(tlahuēlilō-∅)c = you are one who has been detested, you are a scoundrel

8. ō-an(cualān)∅-queh = you (pl) have become angry; an-∅(cualān-∅)queh = you (pl) are ones who have become angry, you are angry people

9. ō-ni(tla-chix)∅-∅ = I have looked; ni-∅(tla-chix-∅)qui = I am one who has looked, I am a sentinel

10. ō-ti(pāc)∅-queh = we have become happy; ti-∅(pāc-∅)queh = we are ones who have become happy, we are happy people
11. ō-ni(mauh)∅-∅ = I have become frightened; ni-∅(mauh-∅)qui = I am one who has become frightened, I am a coward
12. ō-ti(tla-xca)∅-c = you have baked (things); ti-∅(tla-xca-∅)c = you are a baker
13. ō-∅(yah)∅-∅ = he has gone; ∅-∅(yah-∅)qui = he is one who has gone, he is a traveler
14. ō-ti(tla-neloh)∅-∅ = you have rowed; ti-∅(tla-neloh-∅)∅ = you are one who has rowed, you are a rower

29B. 1. ti-∅(cal-pix-∅)queh = we are stewards; t-ī(cal-pix-∅-cā)huān = we are his stewards
2. ni-∅(yah-∅)qui = I am a goer; ni-ti(yah-∅-cā)uh [for *ni-tē(yah-∅-cā)-uh*] = I am a warrior
3. ti-∅(tla-htoh-∅)qui = you are a speaker, you are a king; ti-no(tla-htoh-∅-cā)uh = you are my king
4. ni-∅(no-mach-tih-∅)qui = I am a student; n-ī(ne-mach-tih-∅-cā)uh = I am his student
5. ∅-∅(mo-zcalih-∅)queh = they are reformed persons; ∅-ī(ne-izcalih-∅-cā)huān = they are his reformed persons
6. ∅-∅(ihciuh-∅)qui = he is one who hurries; ∅-īm(ihciuh-∅-cā)uh = he is their one who hurries
7. ti-∅(tē-yac-ān-∅)qui = you are a leader of people; ti-to(tē-yac-ān-∅-cā)uh = you are our leader of people
8. ni-∅(tla-melāuh-∅)qui = I am a straightener; ni-mo(tla-melāuh-∅-cā)uh = I am your straightener
9. ∅-∅(tla-ciuh-∅)queh = they are astrologers; ∅-ī(tla-ciuh-∅-cā)huān = they are his astrologers
10. am-∅(m-ihtōtih-∅)queh = you are dancers; am-īn(ne-ihtōtih-∅-cā)huān = you are their dancers

29C. 1. ∅-∅(nacoch)tli = it is an ear pendant, they are ear pendants; ti-∅-(nacoch-eh-∅)∅ = you are an ear-pendant owner
2. ∅-∅(oyōhual)li = it is a bell, they are bells; ∅-∅(oyōhual-eh-∅)queh = they are bell owners
3. ∅-∅(neuc)tli = it is honey; ∅-∅(neuc-yoh-∅)∅ = it is covered with honey
4. ∅-∅(cuā-cuahui)tl = it is a horn, they are horns; ∅-∅(cuā-cuahu-eh-∅)-∅ = it is a horn owner, i.e., it is a cow, it is a bull, it is a goat
5. ∅-∅(ez)tli = it is blood; ∅-∅(ez-zoh-∅)∅ = it is covered with blood
6. ∅-∅(cicuil)li = it is a vest, they are vests; ni-∅(cicuil-eh-∅)∅ = I am a vest owner

7. Ø-Ø(popō)tl = it is a broom, they are brooms; Ø-Ø(popō-huah-Ø)Ø = he is a broom owner

8. Ø-Ø(malaca)tl = it is a spindle, they are spindles; Ø-Ø(malaqu-eh-Ø)-queh = they are spindle owners

9. Ø-Ø(xoco)tl = it is a fruit, it is fruit; Ø-Ø(xoco-huah-Ø)Ø = he is a fruit owner

10. Ø-Ø(xā-yaca)tl = it is a mask, they are masks; Ø-Ø(xā-yaqu-eh-Ø)Ø = he is a mask owner

11. Ø-Ø(mix)tli = it is a cloud, they are clouds; Ø-Ø(mix-xoh-Ø)Ø = it is covered with clouds

12. Ø-Ø(teō)tl = he is a god; ti-Ø(teō-huah-Ø)queh = we are god owners, we have a god

13. Ø-Ø(tequi)tl = it is tribute; Ø-Ø(tequi-huah-Ø)queh = they are tribute owners, i.e., they are valiant warriors

14. Ø-Ø(te-mā-tla)tl = it is a sling for stones; Ø-Ø(te-mā-tl-eh-Ø)Ø = he is a sling owner

15. Ø-Ø(ā-malaca)tl = it is a vortex; Ø-Ø(ā-malaca-yoh-Ø)Ø = it is covered with vortexes, i.e., it is decorated with a vortex design

29D. 1. ti-Ø(tlahuēli-lō-Ø)c = you are a scoundrel; ti-Ø(tlahuēli-lō-Ø-cā-pōl)Ø = you are a lousy scoundrel

2. Ø-Ø(mic-Ø)qui = he is a dead person; Ø-Ø(mic-Ø-cā-tōn)tli = he is a small dead person

3. an-Ø(teō-pix-Ø)queh = you are priests; an-Ø(teō-pix-Ø-cā-tzi-tzin)Ø = you are honorable priests

4. ni-Ø(mīl-eh-Ø)Ø = I am a cultivated-field owner; ni-Ø(mīl-eh-Ø-cā-tōn)tli = I am an unimportant field owner

5. Ø-ī(ne-mach-tih-Ø-cā)huān = they are his students; Ø-ī(ne-mach-tih-Ø-cā-pi-pīl)huān = they are his beloved students

29E. 1. Ø-Ø(tla-melāuh-Ø)qui = he is an erect person; ti-mo(tla-melāuh-Ø-cā-quetza)z-Ø = you will stand up erect

2. Ø-Ø(tla-htoh-Ø)qui = he is a king; an(tla-htoh-Ø-cā-tla-htoa)Ø-h = you (pl) are speaking in a kingly fashion

3. Ø-Ø(pāc-Ø)qui = he is one who is happy; Ø-quim(pāc-Ø-cā-tlahpalō-t-o)Ø-h = they went to greet him happily

4. Ø-Ø(mauh-Ø)qui = he is a coward; Ø-quim(mauh-Ø-cā-itta)Ø-h = they are looking at them frightenedly

5. Ø-Ø(tlahuēli-lō-Ø)c = he is a scoundrel; ti-nēch(tlahuēli-lō-Ø-cā-mati)-Ø-Ø = you consider me a scoundrel

29F. 1. What is his kingly name? ~ What is his name as a king?

2. The old men are not dancing.

3. The god (-image) carriers went (~ traveled).
4. The war-canoe owners ran.
5. The blanket is covered (~ decorated) with the snake-mask (design).
6. A turkey vender is a turkey owner.
7. He carried the stewards (with him).
8. The merchant elders met people.
9. The rulers' labrets are gold labrets.
10. They were observed with much fear.
11. These are cultivated-field owners.
12. The goat [*lit,* lip-hair owner ~ beard owner] looks and looks every-where.
13. The child has a mother.
14. Someone envisions that he will be a slave owner.
15. Ø(cuauh-tenām-eh-Ø-t-o)Ø-c = It lies owning a wooden wall; i.e., It is surrounded by a palisade. Ø(cuauh-tenān-yoh-Ø-t-o)Ø-c = It lies own-ing a wooden wall in every part; i.e., It is ringed by a palisade. [In both instances these are connective -*ti*- compounds; consequently, the embeds are verb words reduced to their preterit themes, not preterit agentive nouns.]

EXERCISE 30

30A. 1. ni(tla-htoā)ni-Ø = I customarily speak; ni-Ø(tla-htoā-ni)Ø = I am one who customarily speaks, I am a speaker, I am a ruler
2. Ø(itzcuin-cuā)ni-Ø = it customarily eats dogs; Ø-Ø(itzcuin-cuā-ni)Ø = it is one who customarily eats dogs, it is a dog-eater, i.e., it is a ring-tail
3. an-tla(mati)ni-h = you (pl) customarily know things; an-Ø(tla-mati-ni)h = you are ones who customarily know things, you are savants
4. Ø-tē(cuā)ni-h = they customarily eat people; Ø-Ø(tē-cuā-ni)meh = they are ones who customarily eat people, they are people-eaters, i.e., they are wild beasts ~ they are cannibals
5. ni-no(tlātiā)ni-Ø = I customarily hide myself; ni-Ø(no-tlātiā-ni)Ø = I am one who customarily hides himself, I am one who is hidden
6. ti(chōca)ni-Ø = you customarily cry; ti-Ø(chōca-ni)Ø = you are one who customarily cries, you are a weeper
7. Ø-tla(i)ni-Ø = he customarily drinks something; Ø-Ø(tla-i-ni)Ø = he is one who customarily drinks something, he is a drinker
8. ti-to(zcaliā)ni-h = we customarily revive; ti-Ø(to-zcaliā-ni)h = we are ones who customarily revive, i.e., we are able persons
9. ni(pano)ni-Ø = I customarily cross rivers; ni-Ø(pano-ni)Ø = I am one who customarily crosses rivers, i.e., I am a boat passenger

10. Ø(nemi)ni-h = they customarily dwell; Ø-Ø(nemi-ni)meh = they are ones who customarily dwell, they are inhabitants, they are dwellers
11. ti-tla(mati)ni-Ø = you customarily know things; ti-Ø(tla-mati-ni-tōn)-Ø = you are a small one who customarily knows things, you are a minor savant, you a low-quality savant
12. Ø(tlāhuāna)ni-Ø = he customarily becomes tipsy; Ø-Ø(tlāhuāna-ni-pōl)Ø = he is a drunkard

30B. 1. Ø(tlāl-pōhua-lō)ni-Ø = all customarily measure land; Ø-Ø(tlāl-pōhua-lō-ni)Ø = it is an instrument for surveying
2. Ø(tex-ō)ni-Ø = all customarily grind; Ø-Ø(tex-ō-ni)Ø = it is an instrument for grinding, it is a pestle, it is a pounder
3. Ø-tla(cōhua-lō)ni-Ø = all customarily buy things; Ø-Ø(tla-cōhua-lō-ni)-Ø = it is a means for buying things, it is a coin
4. Ø-ne(mach-ti-lō)ni-Ø = all customarily learn; Ø-Ø(ne-mach-ti-lō-ni)Ø = it is a means for learning, it is a textbook
5. Ø-ne(lpi-lō)ni-Ø = all customarily gird themselves; Ø-Ø(ne-lpi-lō-ni)Ø = it is a belt
6. Ø-tla(tlapō-lō)ni-Ø = all customarily open things; Ø-Ø(tla-tlapō-lō-ni-tōn)Ø = it is a small key
7. Ø-ne(tlāli-lō)ni-Ø = all customarily sit down; Ø-Ø(ne-tlāli-lō-ni)Ø = it is a seat
8. Ø-tla(pātzc-ō)ni-Ø = all customarily squeeze out s.th.; Ø-Ø(tla-pātzc-ō-ni)Ø = it is a juice press, it is a milk pail
9. Ø-tla(pātzca-lō)ni-Ø = all customarily squeeze out s.th.; Ø-Ø(tla-pātzca-lō-ni)Ø = it is a juice press
10. Ø-tla(tlāx-ō)ni-Ø = all customarily hurl s.th.; Ø-Ø(tla-tlāx-ō-ni)Ø = it is a catapult

30C. 1. ni-tla(nequi)ya-Ø = I used to want s.th.; Ø-no(tla-nequi-ya)Ø = it is my will
2. ti-tla(cuā)ya-Ø = you used to eat s.th.; Ø-mo(tla-cuā-ya)Ø = it is your eating utensil, they are your eating utensils
3. Ø(cea)ya-Ø = he used to be willing; Ø-ī(cea-ya)Ø = it is his will
4. ti-tla(mā-toca)ya-h = we used to examine s.th. by touch; Ø-to(tla-mā-toca-ya)Ø = it is our sense of touch
5. Ø-tē(mīna)ya-Ø = it used to sting people; Ø-ī(tē-mīna-ya)Ø = it is its stinger
6. am-mo(mānā-huiā)ya-h = you used to defend yourselves; Ø-amo(ne-mānā-huiā-ya)Ø = it is your defense, they are your weapons

30D. 1. ō-Ø(palēhui-lō)ca-Ø = it had been helped; Ø-ī(palēhui-lō-ca)Ø = it is its alleviation

   2. ō-ni(tlapō-lō)ca-∅ = I had been opened; ∅-no(tlapō-lō-ca)∅ = it is my openness
   3. ō-t(īxi-mach-ō)ca-h = we had been recognized; ∅-t(īxi-mach-ō-ca)∅ = it is our recognition (by others)
   4. ō-∅(mic-tī-lō)ca-∅ = he had been murdered; ∅-ī(mic-tī-lō-ca)∅ = it is his murder
   5. ō-∅-ne(mic-tī-lō)ca-∅ = he had killed himself; ∅-ī(ne-mic-tī-lō-ca)∅ = it is his suicide

30E. 1. ō-∅(ihtlacauh)ca-h = they had become spoiled; ∅-īm(ihtlacauh-ca)∅ = it is their defect, they are their defects
   2. ō-∅-mo(cuep)ca-∅ = he had returned; ∅-ī(ne-cuep-ca)∅ = it is his return
   3. ō-ni(yōl)ca-∅ = I had lived; ∅-no(yōl)ca-∅ = it is my means of living, i.e., it is my sustenance
   4. ō-ti(nēz)ca-h = we had appeared; ∅-to(nēz-ca)∅ = it is the means by which we (continue) to appear, i.e., it is our trace, they are our traces
   5. ō-ti(huel-nēz)ca-∅ = you had appeared pleasing; ∅-mo(huel-nēz-ca)∅ = it is your good appearance

30F. 1. Their traces are also many. Their traces are everywhere.
   2. The woman received the curative.
   3. The metal ax is never left out.
   4. Do you wish to be the king's warriors?
   5. It is useless. ∼ They are useless. ∼ There is no need for it (∼ them).
   6. He is eating them like a man-eater. He is eating them like a wild beast.
   7. Here are the defects of the Otomis.
   8. It is eating the new growth (∼ fresh sprouts) of the tree(s).
   9. The god is a war commander.
   10. It is customarily blind during the day. ∼ It is blind during the day.

EXERCISE 31

31A. 1. he is shouting, it is his act of shouting, it is an act of shouting
   2. you are greeting people, it is your act of greeting people, it is an act of greeting people
   3. we are causing ourselves to appear, it is our self-revelation, it is self-revelation
   4. you (pl) are bewitching people, it is your (pl) act of bewitching people, it is an act of bewitching people
   5. he is returning, it is his act of returning, it is an act of returning
   6. I am afraid, it is my fear, it is fear

31B. 1. you (pl) are sending me as a messenger, I am being sent as a messenger, I am a messenger
2. they are eating it, it is being eaten, it is a good thing [*originally,* it is a thing that can be eaten]
3. we are commanding it, it is being commanded, it is our command
4. he is closing it, it is being closed, it is s.th. that can close, i.e., it is a door
5. he sees it, it is seen, it is a courtyard
6. we are boiling it, it is being boiled, it is foam
7. I dye it, it is being dyed, it is a thing that can be used for dyeing, i.e., it is black clay
8. they are meeting him, he is being met, he is an equal
9. they are standing it upright, it is being stood upright, it is a long, green feather [*originally,* it is a thing that can be stood upright]
10. I am giving it to s.o., it is being given to s.o., it is my gift

31C. 1. The courtyard lies owning a wooden wall; i.e., The courtyard is encircled by a palisade.
2. The messengers did this.
3. He is sending the shamans.
4. The merchants survive their captives. All survive their captives.
5. They busy themselves with casting spells on people.
6. He will request from him his favor.
7. Perhaps they will take sick.
8. Already your enemies are leaving in disguise (i.e., stealthily).
9. They also amuse themselves with bewitching people.
10. We are not equals.

EXERCISE 32

32A. 1. I am spitting, people are spitting, it is spittle
2. you (pl) are digging s.th., people are digging s.th., it is a pit
3. we are setting s.th. down, people are setting s.th. down, it is a thing
4. they are tying s.th., people are tying s.th., it is a knot
5. we are eating s.th., people are eating s.th., it is food
6. you (pl) are content, people are content, it is a toy
7. we are shelling s.th., people are shelling s.th., it is shelled corn
8. it is sun shining, it is the heat of the sun ~ it is the dry season (i.e., fall and winter) ~ it is a day
9. we are speaking, people are speaking, it is a word ~ it is an utterance
10. you (pl) are drinking s.th., people are drinking s.th., it is a drink
11. they are dripping s.th., people are dripping s.th., it is a besplattered thing

12. they are bathing him, he is being bathed, he is a bathed one [The missing step is *tlaāltīlo.* The source is *tē-(āltia).*]
13. we are baking s.th., people are baking s.th., it is a tortilla ~ it is bread
14. it is becoming dark, it is night
15. we are wealthy, people are wealthy, it is wealth

32B. 1. they are shaving their heads, their heads are being shaved, they are ones whose heads have been shaved, i.e., they are high-ranking warriors

   2. they are boiling water, people are boiling water, it is water foam ~ it is amber

   3. I am minding my own business, people are minding their own business, it is a private thing

   4. we are sweeping the road, all are sweeping the road, it is a wide road [The embed is *(oh)-tli,* "road." The matrix is *tla-(ichpāna),* "to sweep something." The /h/ of the embed is deleted, entailing the loss of the initial supportive /i/ of the matrix.]

   5. he is a god, it is a command, it is a divine command

   6. you (pl) are resting your hands, i.e., you are dancing; people are dancing; you are plebeians [The source verb is an incorporated-noun-as-object compound with the embed *(māi)-tl,* "hand," and the matrix *tla-(cēhua),* "to rest s.th., to cool something off."]

32C. 1. People filled the temple courtyard.
   2. It resembles amber. ~ It resembles foam.
   3. Who is a baker?
   4. Will you make tortillas?
   5. People used to survive their ceremonially bathed ones. The merchants used to bathe people ceremonially.
   6. He is sending an ambassador [*lit,* a word-carrier].
   7. They used to inform him of his words. [The *-huāl-* indicates that the speaker of this sentence allies himself with the individual referred to by the indirect object prefix *-qui-.*]
   8. Then the shaved-heads (i.e., the high-ranking warriors) come out.
   9. They are giving them an equal number of things.
   10. It is his very own private matter.
   11. Beans are the special food of *these.*
   12. They are simply putting the shelled corn into nets.

EXERCISE 33

33A. 1. he wore s.th., it is clothing
   2. it puffed with fire, it is a gun

    3. he summoned people, he is one who has been summoned
    4. he set s.th. upright, it is a neatly stacked pile of firewood
    5. I made s.th., it is my artifact
    6. it lived, it is a living being
    7. *it has owned life in every part; it is a thing filled with vitality, i.e., it is a heart; it is his heart
    8. *he prized s.th., it is a thing that is cherished ~ it is a precious thing

33B. 1. he is a vender, it is merchandise
    2. he is an explicator, it is an explicated thing
    3. he is a maker, it is an artifact
    4. he is a dweller, it is a life
    5. he is a stacker, it is a neatly stacked pile of firewood
    6. he is one who is angered, it is anger

33C. 1. I am carrying s.th., it is my property, it is property
    2. a breeze is blowing, it is a breeze
    3. it is hailing, it is hail
    4. it is hanging s.th. over filth, it is a turkey vulture
    5. it is scolding s.th. from a rock, it is a chipmunk
    6. he is taking s.th., it is s.th. taken
    7. he is putting s.th. on, it is clothing
    8. he is eating s.th., it is an opossum [*originally,* it is a thing that is eaten]

33D. 1. it is an utterance, it is history
    2. he is human, it is humanity
    3. he is a man, it is a heroic deed
    4. she is a mother, it is motherhood
    5. he is a person worthy of honor, it is honor (~ dignity)
    6. it is a lip, it is fame
    7. he is a king, it is a kingdom
    8. he is a fool, it is foolishness
    9. it is a sheep, it is a thing pertaining to sheep (i.e., an ovine thing)
   10. he is a father, it is fatherhood

33E. 1. it is their blood; it is their lifeblood (part of their bodies)
    2. it is his feather; it is its feather(s) ~ it is its plumage (part of the bird)
    3. it is your bone; it is your bone (part of your body)
    4. it is your meat; it is your flesh (part of your body)

33F. 1. it is shimmering, it is a glittering trinket
    2. it is (white) chalk, it is becoming chalk-colored, it is a chalk-colored thing

   3. it is becoming green, it is a green-colored thing
   4. he is becoming angry, it is slaver
   5. it is becoming dirty, it is a dirty thing ~ it is a black thing
   6. it is becoming completed, it is a good thing [*lit*, it is a completed thing]
   7. he is giving s.th. a flat surface, it is a platform
   8. it is becoming flat-surfaced, it is a flat-bottomed thing
   9. he is bending s.th., it is a bow
  10. he is excavating s.th., it is a pit
  11. it is revolving, it is a circle
  12. it is becoming narrow, it is a narrow thing
  13. he is becoming energetic, it is effort
  14. it is swirling, it is a swirl

33G. 1. His flesh is sick; i.e., He is sick.
   2. He is quickly losing his property.
   3. They are well acquainted with the essence of herbs.
   4. They know the characteristics of the stars.
   5. He is dressing him in a rich costume.
   6. Their bows are of metal.
   7. The vital blood of the ones who were dying reached all the way to there.
   8. They are setting the litter down there.
   9. Your (pl) effort is really needed.
  10. The one who is not bravehearted just runs away.
  11. There they caught their breath. They caught their breath.
  12. They went carrying wooden platforms.
  13. Their clothing was of maguey fiber.

EXERCISE 34

34A. 1. it is becoming yellow-colored; it is yellow dye, it is yellow
   2. it is swirling; it is a spiral, it is helical
   3. it is shrinking; it is a narrowed thing, it is narrow
   4. it is becoming completed; it is a completed thing, it is good
   5. it is becoming dirty; it is a dirty thing, it is dirty
   6. it is becoming chalk-colored; it is a chalk-colored thing, it is chalk-colored
   7. he is eating s.th.; it is a good thing, it is good
   8. he is tying s.th.; it is a knot, it is tied
   9. he is burning fields; it is a burnt field, it is burnt
  10. I am minding my own business; it is a private thing, it is private

34B. 1. it has become inky; it is an inky thing, it is inky
    2. it has become dirty; it is a dirty thing, it is dirty
    3. it has become like maguey fiber; it is a wiry thing, it is wiry
    4. it has become green; it is a green thing, it is green
    5. it has become large; it is a long thing, it is long
    6. he has become strong; he is a strong person, he is strong
    7. it is standing forever; it is an eternal thing, it is eternal
    8. it has become greenish; it is a greenish thing, it is green
    9. it has become close-woven; it is a thick thing (such as a blanket), it is thick
   10. *it has owned breath; it is a spiritual thing, it is spiritual

34C. 1. it has stunk, it is foul smelling
    2. it has become watery, it is watery
    3. it has become sick, it is miserable
    4. it has become new, it is new
    5. it has become cold, it is cold
    6. it has become black, it is black
    7. it has become yellow, it is yellow
    8. it has become cold, it is cold

34D. 1. it is customarily awaited, it is worthy of being awaited
    2. it is customarily counted, it is countable
    3. it is customarily wanted, it is desirable
    4. it is customarily lamented, it is lamentable
    5. it is customarily sold, it is sellable
    6. it is customarily stolen, it is susceptible to theft

34E. 1. The city is walled.
    2. The things are many.
    3. We old men are alone.
    4. Their dogs are big.
    5. They are lazy. They are lazy.
    6. Their faces are very white.
    7. The farmer is strong.
    8. Its smoke is very foul smelling.
    9. The hair of some is black.
   10. Their skirts are not long.
   11. Three are very strong.
   12. The sandals of the men are quite expensive.
   13. *My* face is bloody.
   14. The scorpion is diverse; i.e., Scorpions are of various kinds.
   15. His beard is very long.

16. This is edible. ~ These are edible.
17. He is very worthy of being feared and respected.
18. The boat is very large. ~ The boats are very large.

EXERCISE 35

35A. 1. it is bitter, it is very bitter
    2. it is sharp-pointed, it is slightly sharp-pointed
    3. it is yellow, it is quite yellow
    4. it is stiff, it is very stiff
    5. they are big, they are quite big
    6. it is cold, it is frigid
    7. it is ball-like, it is slightly ball-like
    8. it is strong, it is quite strong

35B. 1. I am white; I am white at the head, i.e., I am white-headed
    2. he is evil; he is evil at the lips, i.e., he is evil-tongued
    3. it is pointed; it is pointed at the base
    4. you are strong; you are strong at the heart, i.e., you are strong-hearted
    5. we are evil; we are evil in war
    6. I am white; I am white at the head, i.e., I am white-headed
    7. it is dry; it is dry like land, i.e., it is dry land
    8. it is dry; it is dry like land, i.e., it is dry land
    9. he is tall; he is tall as a man, i.e., he is a tall man
   10. it is foul smelling; it is foul smelling like a stewpot
   11. it is thick; it is thick at the feathers, i.e., it is thickly feathered
   12. it is thick; it is thick at the plumage, i.e., it is thickly feathered
   13. it is round; it is round at the back, i.e., it is round-backed
   14. you (pl) are black; you are black ones in the shape of gods, i.e., you are black gods

35C. 1. it is precious, it is a precious cloak
    2. it is iron, they are their iron staffs
    3. he is evil, it is an evil word (~ speech)
    4. it is maguey fiber, they are their maguey-fiber cloaks
    5. she is sick, she is your sick mother

35D. 1. His friend is not stouthearted.
    2. They were their maguey-fiber breechcloths. ~ They had maguey-fiber breechcloths.
    3. The blanket is richly finished.
    4. Their dogs are awfully large.
    5. His important property comes forth.

6. The youth is evilhearted.
7. He used to give them costly blankets.
8. They came in order to land. (. . . to come out onto dry land)
9. I am already an owner of white at the head; i.e., I am already white-headed.
10. The one summoned is sweet of speech, i.e., pleasant speaking.

EXERCISE 36

36A. 1. Their skirts are long. They are their skirts that are long.
2. The bread is honeyed. It is bread that is honeyed.
3. The smoke is foul smelling. It is smoke that is foul smelling.
4. The breeze is cold. It is a breeze that is cold.
5. The mat is good. It is a mat that is good.
6. The water is good. It is water that is good.
7. The farmer is strong. He is a farmer who is strong.
8. My slave is lazy. He is my slave who is lazy.

36B. 1. You, who are prudent, are a lord. You are a person who is prudent.
2. What we have set is a fire. It is a fire that we have set.
3. I, who am good, am your son. I am your son who is good.
4. That which they made is a house. It is a house that they made.
5. That which is dry is land. It is land that is dry.

36C. 1. The steward who is big went. The big steward went.
2. The bread that is white is needed. The white bread is needed.
3. Here a sickness that was big occurred. Here a big sickness occurred.
4. His is digging gold that is yellow. He is digging yellow gold.
5. He is selling blankets that are precious. He is selling precious blankets.

36D. 1. The food that they used to eat used to be just made communally. [*Lit*, it used to make itself as one]
2. He is selling various kinds of feathers.
3. The snake sees the seated plebeians.
4. His water is cold water.
5. They are acquainted with the stars located there.
6. The traces of the ones who built it are indeed also many.
7. He took along a few other stewards.
8. Behold [*lit*, here they are] the words that the old men go along saying.
9. The peyote that grows there is *their* discovery.
10. The tree that was standing (there) was very thick.
11. He showed them the necklace(s) that they brought.

12. The boats that they brought in were two in number.
13. Every person heard it.
14. They are giving them all the things that they carried.

EXERCISE 37

37A. 1. I am the very one who disturbed them.
　　2. The blouses that the women made were very precious.
　　3. He is indeed the one who composed the anecdote.
　　4. The shamans who killed the merchant were very frightened.
　　5. The commoners whose fields are there are lazy.
　　6. The tamales that he sells are the ones that are turkey-egg tamales;
　　　 i.e., The tamales that he sells are turkey-egg tamales.
　　7. They took everything that they saw.

37B. 1. It was a woman fetching water who saw them. [This can also be un-
　　　 derstood as a structure of supplementation: The one who saw them
　　　 was a woman who was fetching water.]
　　2. The nobles used to guard this equipment that was needed; i.e., The
　　　 nobles used to guard this necessary equipment.
　　3. He is selling various kinds of feathers that are precious; i.e., He is
　　　 selling various kinds of precious feathers.
　　4. They captured a big warrior who was very strong.
　　5. She has (*lit*, guards) a mirror that is round.

37C. 1. I am giving you everything that is wealth.
　　2. The pulque that they used to drink was very strong [*lit*, filled with
　　　 breath].
　　3. He brought many Spaniards.
　　4. Everything that is agricultural produce is there; i.e., All agricultural
　　　 produce is there.
　　5. A great many people from here died; i.e., A great many natives died.
　　6. All who were Spaniards were frightened; i.e., All the Spaniards were
　　　 frightened.
　　7. Everything that now exists was *their* discovery.
　　8. They took from them everything that was their war equipment; i.e.,
　　　 They took all their weapons from them.
　　9. He is burning the paper that is a thing splattered with (liquid) rub-
　　　 ber; i.e., He is burning the paper splattered with (liquid) rubber.
　　10. The twig that you have is very thin.

37D. 1. I gave him what he wanted.
　　2. They stab the one who wants to leave; i.e., They stab anyone who
　　　 tries to leave.

    3. I saw the one who stole.

    4. What you said is indeed true. [*lit,* . . . it is indeed truth]

    5. He saw what we would do.

    6. He can quickly learn what he studies.

37E. 1. There it is told how the first boat(s) that came, came to arrive.

    2. Every fruit is there.

    3. All these mushrooms are inedible raw.

    4. He who eats a lot (of it) sees many frightening things.

    5. All the different kinds of cotton are there.

    6. No longer did anyone who was a commoner leave; i.e., No longer did any commoner leave.

    7. He is acquainted with all the various kinds of precious stones.

    8. All the old people moved.

    9. He is selling good red peppers.

    10. He is acquainted with the medicines that are deadly.

    11. The gold that they carried was a very large amount.

    12. The salutations that they carried were very many.

    13. Perhaps one of our kinsmen is already coming.

    14. One of my older brothers (~ an older brother of mine) and I had a fight. [*lit,* we killed one another, *a hyperbolic way of saying* we fought]

EXERCISE 38

38A. 1. The priest came (H) to my home.

    2. He stood dressed in his disguise. [*lit,* he stood having entered . . .]

    3. They are staring at one another mutually; i.e., They are staring at *one another.*

    4. They came frightenedly out of their city.

    5. I just drank; i.e., I didn't do anything other than drink.

    6. It falls at their command; i.e., It fires at their command.

    7. He ruled for only eighty days.

    8. We lived like a song.

    9. He entered the young men's house.

    10. I spread my arms like a macaw (as a macaw spreads its wings).

    11. In their homeland it is very cold.

    12. They entered someone's home.

    13. It can be drunk in all three ways. [*lit,* it will drink itself well . . .]

    14. They used to cause them to enter into their insignia; i.e., They used to dress them in their insignia.

38B. 1. In truth he did see it.

    2. They carry pine straw in the bottom.

3. It will be cold day after tomorrow.
4. The box has handles on both sides [*lit,* two sides].
5. There was an earthquake in the afternoon.
6. He has been sick for a very long time.
7. In olden times he was the one who was their god.
8. They spoke strongly.

38C. 1. All go to the sun's home.
2. All the time they go around with their heads bound up.
3. He entered the large young men's house.
4. They rested there for only two days.
5. It is needed every month.

38D. 1. It was every day that they walked hither.
2. It was every night that they closed it.
3. It was just quietly that they left.
4. It is very slowly that they come going.
5. It was for one full year that it was standing forth.
6. It is thus for one full day that people enter.
7. It is far into the night that she departs.
8. It is indeed here that they will dance.

38E. 1. When it used to be seen, it was just going rolling along. [Notice that *momimilohtiuh* is translated as imperfect because of its association with *ittōya.*]
2. Popcorn grows well there in their homeland.
3. Return (pl) there from whence you came.
4. When he saw his maize, he was happy. [Notice translation of *pāqui* as a past-tense form.]
5. At this time, it was drizzling. [Notice the translation of *ahhuach-quiauhtimani* as a past-tense form.]
6. When it still lives in its homeland, it is all night long that the mockingbird sings.
7. People are very happy when all sing.
8. When our enemies saw him, they would have fled.
9. Where they eat, there they sleep.
10. When it had become thus, then the guns fired; i.e., At this point, the guns fired.

EXERCISE 39

39A. 1. He thinks that perhaps it is a child who is crying.
2. Observe well with regard to which one asserts himself first (~ which one is taken first).
3. They are going in order to take captives.

4. They thought that they would kill him there.
5. They are going to meet someone.
6. Some others came in order to help them.
7. Already he is going in order to give himself to the gods.
8. All the commoners come together in a group in order to make tamales for themselves (~ for one another). [*Lit,* they fall as one.]

39B. 1. If he is still a child, the parents still carry him.
2. If sometime it even seemed that perhaps he was drinking pulque, then they used to go locking him up.
3. Even though they were living at a distance, they arrived swiftly.
4. Today, although insignia are no longer much needed, the making just goes on being followed; i.e., they continue to be made.
5. If somewhere something is to be done, it is still quite night when all go.
6. Even though you are not strong, you will be able to carry it (on your back).
7. They are lazy, even though they are wiry.
8. If he still sees nothing that will make him tipsy, he sells his blanket.

39C. 1. Every single person went in order to meet people.
2. He used to think that it was there that they would die in battle.
3. He is going in order to bathe.
4. They knew something regarding who he was who became frightened.
5. Let's go dig for water so that we may drink there.
6. He is coming to look at people in secret [*lit,* in disguise].
7. Let's not steal lest we be stoned.
8. If your offering is nothing, you will not be able to enter.
9. Although he died at home—i.e., not in battle—he was indeed a man.
10. Do not commit adultery, lest you be pelted with stones, i.e., lest you be stoned.
11. Even though they are the ones who are the hosts, they are dancing.
12. If he is already upsetting it, when he is holding it at dawn, it says to him, "Let me go!" [*lit,* when he is causing it (i.e., the thing) to be abroad at dawn]

EXERCISE 40

40A. 1. They are becoming lords of the sun.
2. All are becoming priests.
3. Who do you know yourself to be? i.e., Who do you think you are?
4. I am eating it raw.
5. They are coming along, having become iron.
6. They are becoming butterflies.

40B. 1. He is (coming) standing alone.
2. Their child was born a woman; i.e., Their child was born a girl.
3. The hearth was covered with ashes.
4. Perhaps they were their javelines.
5. The tree is standing fat; i.e., The tree is big around.
6. You appear an old man; i.e., You look old. ~ You seem old.

40C. 1. It is full of sand. ~ It is covered with sand. It is full of sand. ~ It is covered with sand.
2. Immediately the archer begins to pierce it with arrows.
3. It is beginning to run.
4. It is filled with straw. ~ It is covered with straw. It is covered with straw.
5. It is beginning to spill out.
6. We shall stop singing.

40D. 1. You are covered with dirt. You are covered with dirt.
2. We are becoming fools.
3. He will hear it quite straight; i.e., He will hear a true report.
4. He became *his* image. ~ *He* became his image.
5. When already the rain wants to come, at that time this bird begins to sing; i.e., Just before rain comes, this bird begins to sing.
6. Who do I think I am [to act so presumptuously]?
7. Already I am looking old.
8. They will not be long in going to go to war.
9. It is beginning to drizzle.
10. The war boat does not seem to be of wood.
11. Their clothing was of maguey fiber.
12. He who becomes a priest is chosen.

EXERCISE 41

41A. 1. Ø-Ø(tōl-loh-Ø)Ø = it is an owner of many reeds; Ø-Ø(tōl-loh-Ø-cā-n)Ø = it is a place that is characterized by reeds
2. Ø-Ø(tlīl-iuh-Ø)qui = it is an inky entity; Ø-Ø(tlīl-iuh-Ø-cā-n)Ø = it is a place where an entity has become inky
3. Ø-Ø(yēc)tli = it is good; Ø-Ø(yēc-cā-n)Ø = it is a good place
4. Ø-Ø(nāhui)Ø = they are four in number; Ø-Ø(nāuh-cā-n)Ø = they are four places
5. Ø-Ø(cac-namaca-Ø)c = he is a shoe seller; Ø-Ø(cac-namaca-Ø-cā-n)Ø = it is a place where one sells shoes
6. Ø-Ø(tla-xca-l-chīuh-Ø)qui = she is a tortilla maker; Ø-Ø(tla-xca-l-chīuh-Ø-cā-n)Ø = it is a place where one makes tortillas

7. Ø-Ø(tē-chōc-tih-Ø)Ø = it is a thing that makes people cry; Ø-Ø(tē-chōc-tih-Ø-cā-n)Ø = it is a place of lamentation
8. Ø-Ø(tē-cuiltōnoh-Ø)Ø = it is a thing that enriches people; Ø-Ø(tē-cuiltōnoh-Ø-cā-n)Ø = it is a place of pleasure
9. Ø-Ø(ā-huah-Ø)Ø = he is a water owner; Ø-Ø(ā-huah-Ø-cā-n)Ø = it is a place of water owners
10. Ø-Ø(tepē-huah-Ø)Ø = he is a hill owner; Ø-Ø(tepē-huah-Ø-cā-n)Ø = it is place of hill owners
11. Ø-Ø(iz-qui)Ø = it is an equal amount; Ø-Ø(iz-qui-cā-n)Ø = they are an equal number of places

41B. 1. Ø-m(āltiā)ya-Ø = he was bathing; Ø-ī(ne-āltiā-yā-n)Ø = it is his bathing place
2. Ø(cal-ac-ohua)ya-Ø = people were entering; Ø-Ø(cal-ac-ohua-yā-n)Ø = it is a place where people customarily enter, i.e., it is an entrance
3. Ø(quīza)ya-Ø = he was leaving; Ø-ī(quīza-yā-n)Ø = it is the place where he leaves
4. Ø(tla-yohua)ya-Ø = it was getting dark; Ø-Ø(tla-yohua-yā-n)Ø = it is a dark place
5. Ø(ā-tl-i)ya-h = they were drinking water; Ø-īm(ā-tl-i-yā-n)Ø = it is their drinking place
6. Ø(cal-aqui)ya-Ø = he was entering; Ø-ī(cal-aqui-yā-n)Ø = it is the place where he enters
7. Ø(cēhui)Ø-Ø = it is becoming cool; Ø-ī(cēuh-yān)Ø = it is its resting place
8. Ø(pano-hua)ya-Ø = people were crossing the river; Ø-Ø(pano-hua-yā-n)Ø = it is a place where people cross the river, i.e., it is a bridge
9. Ø(tla-xca-l-namac-ō)ya-Ø = people were selling tortillas; Ø-Ø(tla-xca-l-namac-ō-yā-n)Ø = it is a place where tortillas are customarily sold
10. Ø-tla(pia-lō)ya-Ø = people were guarding things; Ø-Ø(tla-pia-lō-yā-n)Ø = it is a place where people customarily guard things
11. Ø(ye)ya-Ø = he was (being); Ø-ī(ye-yā-n)Ø = it is his place ~ it is his seat

41C. 1. it is a prickly pear cactus, it is a place of many prickly pear cacti
2. it is a rock, it is stony ground
3. they are flowers of various shapes and sizes, it is a flower garden
4. it is a house, it is a settlement
5. they are houses of various shapes and sizes, it is a village
6. it is water; in the midst of the water
7. you are the ones; in your (pl) midst
8. it is water, it is a place of abundant water
9. it is a sapota, it is a place of many sapotas
10. it is night; in the middle of the night

41D. 1. it is a well; at a well ~ in a well
      2. it is a bundle; in a bundle
      3. it is a long corridor; in a long corridor [*also,* in a monastery school]
      4. it is a case; in a case
      5. it is his bag; in his bag
      6. it is my stomach; in my stomach ~ inside me
      7. it is his face; on his face
      8. it is a fire; in a fire ~ at a fire
      9. it is my hand; in my hand
     10. it is a city district; in a city district

41E. 1. it is an arsenal; in an arsenal; from an arsenal ~ toward an arsenal
      2. they are five in number; five times
      3. it is straw; like straw
      4. it is a doorway; in a doorway; from out of a doorway
      5. it is my will; willingly
      6. it is a tortilla; like a tortilla
      7. it is his right hand; from his right hand
      8. in four places; from four places
      9. it is a box; in a box; from within a box ~ from the east
     10. it is his left hand; in his left hand; from within his left hand

41F. 1. I have cut it down the middle.
      2. All sleep there in the monastery school.
      3. It is divided in four parts.
      4. Its growing place is in the forest.
      5. They are coming out into the middle of the courtyard.
      6. Its home is in the crags.
      7. He sets it down in the fire there in the courtyard.
      8. He died in the interior of the desert region.
      9. No one will utter anything. It will be kept to yourselves. [*Lit,* It is only in your stomachs.]
     10. Let guard be kept everywhere along the shore.
     11. It started out from there where the sun sets [*lit,* from the sun's entering place].
     12. It is indeed for a long time that we have much desired to look upon his face.
     13. They are three places to which they go when they die.
     14. He is pouring a little water into a small bowl.
     15. He used to bathe at midnight.
     16. Did you tie it firmly [*lit,* like a rock]?

EXERCISE 42

42A. 1. Ø-ī(tloc)Ø = it is his side; at his side
2. Ø-īm(pal)Ø = it is their grace; by their grace
3. Ø-n(icam-pa)Ø = it is my rear; at my rear
4. Ø-mo(huān)Ø = it is your company; in your company; with you
5. Ø-to(pampa)Ø = it is our behalf; in our behalf
6. Ø-mo(pal-tzin-co)Ø = it is your (H) grace; by your (H) grace

42B. 1. They do not burn with the king.
2. They are always at our side.
3. What shall we do in order for us to be able to get out?
4. If only I had lived well!
5. We have come to know ourselves (~ one another) only by the grace of our lord.
6. Here is another; drink it. [*Lit,* It is indeed another; drink it.] The medicine is indeed good; by means of it your flesh (i.e., your body) will become strong.
7. In order to carry it, he stands the cup upright in his right hand. ~ He carries it in this fashion: he stands the cup upright in his right hand.
8. It is about one fathom long.
9. Live well so that you will die well.
10. How big it is!
11. I cannot go to your house, because it is already quite late.
12. He is being driven away because of some fault of his.

42C. 1. Ø-Ø(tlathui-nāhuac)Ø = it is a dawn vicinity; near dawn
2. Ø-ī(nāhuac)Ø = it is his vicinity; near him
3. Ø-Ø(cal-tzālan)Ø = it is an area between houses; between houses
4. Ø-ī(tzālan)Ø = it is an area between them; between them
5. Ø-Ø(tepē-pan)Ø = it is a mountain surface; on a mountain
6. Ø-ī(pan)Ø = it is its surface; on it
7. ah-Ø-tē(īx-pan)Ø = it is not s.o.'s face surface, i.e., it is not before people; in the absence of people
8. Ø-Ø(tlāl-lan)Ø = it is an inner part of land; beneath the earth
9. Ø-ī(tlan)Ø = it is his side; beside him ~ in his company
10. Ø-īn(huīc)Ø = it is their direction; in their direction ~ toward them
11. Ø-Ø(ilhuica-c-huīc)Ø = it is a heaven-place direction; toward heaven
12. Ø-Ø(ilhuica-pa-huīc)Ø = it is a heavenward direction; toward heaven
13. Ø-Ø(tlāl-pan)Ø = it is ground surface; on the ground
14. Ø-īm(īx-pam-pa)Ø = it is their face-surface direction; from in front of them

42D. 1. The stars are very high.
  2. It begins to call out first; then the other kinds of birds that live near the water answer it.
  3. It is growing everywhere on the mountains.
  4. The people who are near his house are gathering together; i.e., His neighbors are gathering together.
  5. Then in front of people he threw off his breechcloth.
  6. Where night comes upon them, there they seek a cave (~ caves).
  7. He will fall down from a roof terrace.
  8. It snowed upon all of them.
  9. If he was a king's son, they used to leave his necklace there in the temple.
  10. When it used to be caught, it was considered an evil omen.

42E. *The Deer* (*Florentine Codex*, XI, 15)

   The deer with antlers [*lit,* the deer that is a horn owner] is a male. Its antlers are chalk-colored [*lit,* it is chalk-colored at the horns]; its antlers are tapering and branched [*lit,* it is tapering-branched at the horns]. When its antlers have become loose [*lit,* lazy], it casts them off [*lit,* it throws itself from the horns]. It inserts its antlers in the crotch of a tree; then it tramples backwards; there it breaks its horns like a stick. In this fashion (~ by this means) it goes causing them to come out young (again).

   The deer without antlers [*lit,* the deer that is not a horn owner] is a female.

EXERCISE 43

43A. 1. Ø-Ø(nāhu-ilhui-ti-ca)Ø = on the fourth day
  2. Ø-ī(ca)Ø = by means of it ~ thanks to it
  3. Ø-Ø(tepē-t-icpac)Ø = it is the top of the mountain; on top of the mountain
  4. Ø-ī(cpac)Ø = it is the top of its head; over its head
  5. Ø-Ø(tle-ti-tlan)Ø = next to the fire; near the fire; in the fire
  6. Ø-ī(tlan)Ø = it is his side; beside him
  7. Ø-Ø(te-ti-tech)Ø = in contact with a rock; on a rock
  8. Ø-ī(tech)Ø = on it; concerning it

43B. 1. I am shooting an arrow with a spear thrower.
  2. I threw at him with a rock. I threw at him with a rock.
  3. The braves pressed themselves tightly against the wall.
  4. They went to arrive at their boat(s); i.e., They reached their boat(s).
  5. He looked a second time at the head of the bird.
  6. Let our lords arrive (H) in the land.

7. It is on the seashore in the sand that it hatches.
8. I thrashed him with a stick.

43C. 1. He came to arrive at one Cuauhtitlan; i.e., He reached a place called Cuauhtitlan.
2. He is living there at Teotlixco toward the coast.
3. Immediately thereupon they ascend to the top of Snake Mountain.
4. It is the one that is the large lake that extends around us here in Mexihco.
5. They carried them by boat across to Xicalanco.
6. They went in order to show it to the king at the monastery school at Tlillan.

43D. 1. If it is true that you are Mexihcas, what is the name of the ruler in Mexihco?
2. The Toltecs are also called Chichimecs.
3. These somewhat resemble the Cuextecs (i.e., the Huaxtecs).
4. It is said that the Toltecs considered no place distant.
5. If a Mexihca is one in number, he will be able to surpass them, even if his enemies are ten in number.
6. The Tepanec is indeed our enemy.
7. The Tlaxcaltecs and the Chololtecs formerly were clashing with one another.
8. All of the Tlaxcaltecs' Otomis [vassal warriors] died.
9. All the Tenochcas became very frightened.
10. The person from Tliliuhqui Tepec (i.e., Black Mountain) went.
11. Thereby the waterfolk know that is will rain a lot when dawn comes.
12. The Tlaxcaltecs went pressing from the rear.

43E. *A Blood-Offering Ceremony (Florentine Codex,* IX, 10)

When he has bled himself upon [the paper], immediately thereupon he comes out into the middle of the courtyard. First he performs the "throwing" ceremony [*lit,* first he throws things]. He throws his blood toward heaven. Next there toward the sun's exit, which used to be called "From within a Box" [i.e., East], it is four times that he throws his blood. Next there toward the sun's entrance, which used to be called "Toward the Abode for Women" [i.e., West], it is also four times that he throws his blood. Next there toward the land on his left hand, which used to be called "Region of the Land close to Thorns" [i.e., South], it is also four times that he throws his blood. Next there toward the land on his right hand, which used to be called "On the Land of the Cloud Snakes" [i.e., North], it is also four times that he throws his blood. Only then did [i.e., does] he stop, when he bleeds [i.e., has bled] himself to the four quarters.

43F. *The Tree Squirrel* (*Florentine Codex,* XI, 10)

A tree squirrel is the one that is a forest-dwelling squirrel [*lit,* a squirrel that lives in a forest]. It is in the tree tops that it eats. It is always only in trees that it lives, and therefore it is called "tree squirrel." It eats all pine cones. It eats the tips of new growth of trees. Also it eats tree worms. It goes around continually barking the tree; there it captures the tree worms. It whistles shrilly [*lit,* it whistles with its hands].

EXERCISE 44

44A. 1. It has hands and it has feet; i.e., It has hands and feet.
  2. He takes a steam bath three times or four times; i.e., He takes a steam bath three or four times.
  3. And then he summoned the astrologers.
  4. He will not drink wine or pulque.
  5. And the king said to them, "Rest."
  6. They quickly shout, they shrill, and they whoop.
  7. Here once again I have looked upon your (pl) faces (H) and your (pl) head tops (H); i.e., Here once again I behold your noble persons.
  8. When she has recovered, immediately thereupon she enters the steam bath, and there she drinks the white medicine.

44B. 1. The man is in one place, and [*lit,* with this] the woman is in another.
  2. All day and with it (i.e., also) all night he was just wanting (to know) where was the road that he would follow.
  3. His equipment is nothing, and his property is nothing, but he is a good person; i.e., He has no possessions or property, but he is a good person.
  4. Its eggs are four in number or perhaps five in number; i.e., It has four or five eggs.
  5. Also it is only in a miserable land that they dwell, but, nevertheless, they are also knowers of green stones.
  6. Did you buy it, or did you perhaps make it?

44C. *The Turkey Vulture* (*Florentine Codex,* XI, 42)

A turkey vulture is black, dirty black, with a bright red head [*lit,* it is chili-colored at the head] and with chalk-colored feet [*lit,* it is chalk-colored at the feet]. Its food is anything that is dead, foul smelling, and filthy [*lit,* everything that is something dead, that is foul smelling, and that is filth is its food].

44D. *The God Owner at Tecanman* (*Florentine Codex,* II, 195)

The god owner [i.e., custodian priest] at Tecanman was the one who was responsible for [*lit,* he speaks upon it] the pine wood that would be the torches. And furthermore he was the one whose job it was to collect the red ocher, the black ink, and the foam sandals, the sleeveless jacket, and the bells that were necessary to Xiuhteuctli, the Old Man God, when he used to die [when the impersonator of Xiuhteuctli was sacrificed].

44E. *Protection from Hail* (*Florentine Codex*, IV/V, 192)
When it rains and it is hailing a lot, one, whose field is there, or his chili patch, or his bean field, or his chia, scatters ashes from the fire outdoors in his courtyard. They say that thereby his field will not be hailed on; they say that thereby the hail perishes.

44F. *The Broken Grinding Stone* (*Florentine Codex, IV/V, 194*)
The people here used to consider the grinding stone an evil omen. When someone there sits (i.e., sat) grinding, if it breaks (i.e., broke), thereby it seemed, they said, that the one who had been grinding would shortly die, or else he who was the homeowner, or their children, or else someone of the people of her household would die.

EXERCISE 45

45A. 1. Its head is large; it is the full amount (i.e., the size) of the turkey cock from here; i.e., Its head is as large as that of the native turkey cock.
2. The honorableness of the merchants and of the vanguard merchants was equal [*lit,* it was one-rock].
3. That is not good, but this is good; i.e., This is better than that.
4. You are a greater drunkard than your father.
5. I am stronger than you.
6. You are more propertied and outfitted than I; i.e., You are wealthier than I.
7. Your property and your equipment are more abundant than mine.
8. The faults of you kings are greater than the faults of your subjects.
9. He is taller than I.
10. The boats of those who came later were bigger than the boats of those who came first.
11. Snow is exceedingly white; still nothing is as white; i.e., Snow is whiter than anything else.
12. If now during the summer you are dying of cold, how much colder will you be when freezing weather comes [*lit,* at the time of freezing]?

45B. *The Cuitlamiztli* (*Florentine Codex,* XI, 6)
A *cuitlamiztli* lives in a forest. It is exactly like a mountain lion [*lit,* it is indeed only already also the one that is a mountain lion]. It is called *cuitlamiztli* [*lit,* it is an excrement lion] for this reason: when it has cap-

tured a deer it begins to eat it; it eats it; it eats it energetically; it lies eating it; it really finishes it. It is for two or three days that it does not eat anything (else); it just eats it entirely; it just lies stretched out [*lit*, it lies fallen]; it lies digesting. It is called *cuitlamiztli* for this reason: because it is a glutton and because it does not hide. At night it comes to eat turkeys; it eats them up, although they are twenty in number. When it has become sated, it just kills them and along with them [*lit*, with it] the sheep.

45C. *The Ringtail* (*Florentine Codex*, XI, 6)

A ringtail [*lit*, it is a dog-eater] is just like the *cuitlamiztli* [*lit*, it is indeed only already also the one which is the *cuitlamiztli*]. It is called "dog-eater" for this reason: at night, it comes to the village. It cries. And when it has cried, then all the dogs answer it. All howl [*lit*, they shout]. All hear its cry from it; then they go toward it. And when they have sat down together near it, when they have formed a circle around it, then it captures as many as it will be able. It eats them. Dogs are its favorite food [*lit*, dogs are much its very foods].

45D. *Peyote* (*Florentine Codex*, XI, 129)

This peyote is white. And it is only there that it grows toward the north [*lit*, toward the arsenal] in the desert region, which is called Mictlan [*lit*, Toward the Abode of the Dead]. It affects [*lit*, it comes out upon him] the one who eats it or drinks it, just as mushrooms do. He also sees many things that are frightening or that are laugh-provoking [*lit*, it has made someone laugh]. It is perhaps for one day or two days that it affects him, but it finally leaves him [*lit*, but only also it leaves him]. But, it indeed damages his mind [*lit*, it damages his heart]. It causes people to lose their reason [*lit*, to destroy things]; it makes people drunk; it affects people.

EXERCISE 46

46A. 1. Ø(tōch-ti)Ø-Ø = he is becoming a rabbit [*(tōch)-tli* + verbalizing suffix *-ti*]

2. ni-tla(mahui-z-oa)Ø-Ø = I am amazed at s.th. [the deverbative noun stem *(mahui-z)-tli* + transitive verbalizing suffix *-oa*]

3. Ø-tē(iztlaca-huia)Ø-Ø = he is deceiving people [*(iztlaca)-tl*, "lie" + transitive verbalizing suffix *-huia*]

4. Ø(mazā-ti)Ø-Ø = he is becoming a deer, i.e., he is becoming a wild animal [*(mazā)-tl* + verbalizing suffix *-ti*]

5. ti-tē(mahui-z-ti-lia)Ø-Ø = you honor and respect s.o.; [the deverbative noun stem *(mahui-z)-tli* + intransitive verbalizing suffix *-ti* + causative suffix *-lia*]

6. Ø-tla(ihi-yō-huia)Ø-Ø = he is using his breath in relation to s.th., i.e., he is toiling for s.th. [*(ihi-yō)-tl* + transitive verbalizing suffix *-huia*]
7. Ø(tēl-pōch-yah-Ø-cā-ti)Ø-Ø = he is becoming a leader of youths [the compound preterit agentive noun *(tēl-pōch-yah-Ø)-qui,* "a leader of youths" + intransitive verbalizing suffix *-ti*]
8. ni-tla(mātla-huia)Ø-Ø = I am using a net on s.th. [*(mātla)-tl* + transitive verbalizing suffix *-huia*]
9. Ø(tequi-huah-Ø-cā-ti)Ø-Ø = he is becoming a tribute owner, i.e., he is becoming a warrior [the preterit agentive noun of possession *(tequi-huah-Ø)-Ø* + intransitive verbalizing suffix *-ti*]
10. Ø-tē(tētzā-huia)Ø-Ø [for *Ø-tē(tētzāuh-huia)Ø-Ø*] = it serves as an omen to people [*(tētzāhui)-tl* + transitive verbalizing suffix *-huia*]

46B. *A Rabbit in the House (Florentine Codex,* IV/V, 167)

Also the rabbit was regarded as an omen when it used to enter some-one's home. The farmers, the people in the fields, say, "Soon his house will perish on earth. Or soon someone will run away. Soon he will fol-low the path of the rabbit or the deer; soon he will become a rabbit; soon he will become a deer; soon he will cause himself to be a rabbit; soon he will cause himself to become a deer."

46C. *Panning for Gold (Florentine Codex,* XI, 233)

There where a vein of gold [*lit,* a road of gold] crops out [*lit,* it is falling] in a river, the river carries the gold, washes it along. Thereby, because of that, before the Spaniards came, the Mexihcas, the Anahua-cas, who were clever people, used not to dig out gold and silver; they just took the river sand and panned it in wooden trays. They saw the gold, wherever it came to settle [*lit,* it came to fall] with the appearance and the size of maize kernels. And then at that time they used to take that resembling sand. Later they melted it; they smelted it; they were clever with it; they formed [*lit,* they used to set them down] necklaces, bracelets, ear pendants, and labrets.

46D. *A Post-Conquest Poem (Anales del Museo Nacional,* Epoca V, vol. I, p. 469; adapted by author)

Mother, when I die
bury me beneath your hearth.
When you go to make tortillas,
there for me weep.
If someone asks you,
"Lady, why do you cry?,"
say to him, "The wood is green,
and it makes me sob
because it smokes intensely."

EXERCISE 47

47A. *The Owl* (*Florentine Codex,* XI, 42)

An owl is round, ball-like; it is round-backed [*lit,* it is round at the back]. Its eyes are circular [*lit,* it is like spindle whorls at the eyes]; it is flat-faced [*lit,* it is flat at the face]. It has horns of feathers [*lit,* it is horned with feathers]. It is roundheaded; it is mug-headed. Its feathers are dense [*lit,* it is dense at the feathers]; its plumage is dense. It is blind during the day. It is in crags or in a tree hollow that it is born. It is at night that it regularly eats, because it sees better at night [*lit,* it sees still very well]. It is deep-voiced when it calls. It says, "Tecolo, tecolo, o, o."

47B. *A Skirmish* (*Florentine Codex,* XII, 95)

"O Mexihcas, up!"

Immediately there upon there was shouting and blowing [of shell trumpets]. And the sentinel took up his shield.

Immediately thereupon they followed the Spaniards, they went knocking them down, and they went capturing them. The captured Spaniards were fifteen in number, and immediately thereupon they brought them back. And as for their boat [the Spaniards' boat], then thereupon they retired it. They stopped [*lit,* they went to place it] in the middle of the lake [*lit,* water].

And when they had taken [*lit,* they came in order to make them arrive] the eighteen who would die there to the place called Tlacochcalco, immediately afterwards they stripped them. They took from them all their war equipment and their cotton shirts and everything that was on them. They tore everything from them. Immediately thereupon they became slaves. They killed them.

And their friends remained watching them from the middle of the lake.

47C. *A Messenger from the Hereafter* (*Florentine Codex,* VIII, 3)

A noble lady, whose home was at Tenochtitlan, died from a sickness. Then she was buried in her courtyard; they paved it with stones over her. When the dead woman had been buried for four days, she revived during the night. She frightened people greatly. There where she had been buried, it opened up at the grave, and the stones with which she had been covered went severally to fall at a distance.

And this woman, after she had revived, then went in order to converse with Moteuczomah, she went in order to say to him what she had seen. She recounted it to him, she said to him, "Indeed for this purpose did I revive: I came in order to say to you, 'It is indeed already finished [*lit*, complete ~ a full amount]. Indeed with *you* the kingdom in Me-xihco is coming to an end. Indeed in *your* time the city of Mexihco will go being captured. The ones who already are coming, they are indeed the ones who are coming to subjugate the land. They shall dwell in Me-xihco.'"

And this woman who had died continued to live twenty-one years longer [*lit*, her life was twenty-one years more] and gave birth to an-other child, which was a male.

EXERCISE 48

48A. *Huitzilopochtli* (*Florentine Codex*, I, 1)

Huitzilopochtli (i.e., Left-Hand-like-a-Hummingbird) was just a com-moner, just a human being. He was a shaman. He was an apparition (~ a portent of evil). He was a demented agitator. He was a deceiver. He customarily instigated [*lit*, he customarily invents them] wars. He was a troop commander; he was a battle strategist [*lit*, a war preparer].

Indeed about him it was said, "He hurls upon people the turquoise snake [i.e., the fire snake] and the fire drill,"—which means "war" or "flood and burnt fields" [i.e., war]. And when people celebrated a holi-day, people sacrificed captives [*lit*, people used to survive captives]; people sacrificed "bathed ones" [*lit*, people used to survive "bathed ones"]. The merchants "bathed" people.

And thus was he adorned: he wore ear pendants of lovely-cotinga feathers [*lit*, he was a turquoise-bird ear-pendant owner]; he had a fire-snake mask [*lit*, he was a turquoise-snake mask owner]; he wore a tur-quoise sash [*lit*, he was a turquoise-sash owner]; he had a maniple [*lit*, he was a maniple owner]; he had jingles [*lit*, he was a jingle owner]; he had bells [*lit*, he was a bell owner].

48B. *The Laughing Falcon* (*Florentine Codex*, XI, 42)

A laughing falcon resembles a king vulture. It calls [*lit*, speaks] in this manner: at times it is as if some person is bursting out laughing, [and at times] it is as if it speaks like a human. It can pronounce these words: "yeccan, yeccan, yeccan" (i.e., "it is a propitious time," etc.). When it laughs it says "hahahahaha, hahai, hahai, hahai, ai." Especially when it sees its food, it really bursts out laughing.

48C. *Distracted Messengers* (*Florentine Codex*, VI, 219)

It is said that Quetzalcoatl was king in Tollan [now called Tula]. It is said that two women were bathing in his bathing place. When he saw them, immediately he sent some people to see who were bathing. But these messengers just remained looking at the bathing women. They did not go to report to him [*lit*, to advise him]. Quetzalcoatl later again sent off his "page" (which means "his messenger") to see who were the ones bathing. He also just did likewise; he never brought back [*lit*, he never went in order to return it] his report [*lit*, his message].

In this fashion there it began and took root that one says "an errand is being run in the manner of pages."

KEY TO THE SUPPLEMENTARY READINGS

NOTE: No attempt has been made at elegance in these translations. They try to remain as faithful as possible to Nahuatl without falsifying English. In this regard, special attention should be given to the frequent mismatch of the use of tenses in the two languages.

1. *A Nahuatl Version of a Fable by Aesop* (Collection of author)

The goat and the coyote, when they had become thirsty, jumped into a well. And when they had gotten their fill of drinking, the goat then diligently looked [*lit,* he looked and looked] everywhere, seeking a place where they would be able to get out. But the coyote said to him, "Don't worry, for I have seen what we shall do so that we shall be able to get out. If you will stand up straight and place your forefeet [*lit,* hands] against the wall, and raise your head so that your horns will lie falling well toward your rear, I shall then climb up on your back, so that I shall be able to get out of the well. And when I have gotten out, then I'll get [*lit,* take] you out.

And the goat, when he had heard the coyote's words with pleasure, then obeyed him. Thereupon the coyote got out, and after he had gotten out [*lit,* he had come in order to get out], then he walked laughing at him at the edge of the well. And the goat became very annoyed with the coyote's mockery.

And the coyote said to the goat, "My friend, if your brains [*lit,* your heart] were as extensive as your beard, you would have first sought a place where you would be able to get out before jumping into the well."

With this fable people are taught how much it is first necessary for us to think about what we want to do in order that we not later fall into imprudence and foolishness.

2. *Mushroom Visions* (*Florentine Codex,* IX, 38–39)

When the host has offered up incense [*lit,* he has warmed things], immediately thereupon the ones who will dance come out—the field marshal [*lit,* person from the place of the lord-of-men] and all the high-ranking warriors [*lit,* shaved-heads], the seasoned warriors [*lit,* Otomis], the proven warriors [*lit,* tribute owners], and the young braves. But the merchant chiefs do not dance; they only remain there, keeping aloof, because they are the ones who host the affair. And the elderly merchants are the ones who meet people with flowers and tobacco; the paper necklaces are covered with turquoise mirrors, and the maguey-fiber quetzal feathers are covered with sparkles by means of mica.

Foremost came the mushrooms which used to be served and which they used to eat at the time when it was (as they used to say) the hour of the blowing [of conch shells]. They used no longer to eat any food [*lit,* anything which was food], although they used to drink just chocolate alone during the night. And the mushrooms that they used to eat were honeyed (~ covered with honey). At the time when the mushrooms are already taking effect on them, then they dance or they cry. And some who are still in command of their senses [*lit,* they know their hearts] then get into their places and sit (leaning) against the wall. They no longer dance, they just sit there nodding.

Someone envisions that he will soon die; he is there weeping. Someone envisions that he will die in battle. Someone envisions that he will be eaten by a beast. Someone envisions that he will take captives in war. Someone envisions that he is one who will become rich, who will be prosperous. Someone envisions that he will buy slaves, that he will be a slaveowner. Someone envisions that he will commit adultery and that he will be pommeled with stones, that he will be stoned. Someone envisions that he will commit thefts, that he also will be stoned. Someone envisions that he will fracture someone's skull and that he [who? the one whose skull has been fractured?] will put him in prison [*lit,* he will go locking him up]. Someone envisions that he will drown [*lit,* he will die in water]. Someone envisions that he is one who will live calmly and peacefully until [*lit,* at the time] he dies. Someone envisions that he will fall off a roof terrace, that he will fall and die. However much will happen to people, he used to see it—that perhaps he will be drowned.

And when the mushrooms have left them, they converse with one another, they tell one another what they have envisioned. And they envision what will happen to each of those who have eaten no mushrooms and what they will go along doing. There are some who perhaps are committing thefts, or perhaps committing adulteries, or however many things of all those that have been said: that he will take captives, that he will become a proven warrior [*lit,* a tribute owner], that he will become a leader of youths, that he will die in battle, that he will become prosperous, that he will buy slaves, that he will sing on numerous occasions, that he will bathe people [ceremonially, in preparation for sacrifice], that he will commit adultery, that he will hang himself by the neck, that he will die in water, that he will be drowned. Whatever thing that will happen to them, he sees it all—that perhaps he is going to die in the coastal regions.

And when the time the night divides has arrived, when it is already in the very middle of the night, the one who is host immediately thereupon acquits himself [i.e., he performs a ritual for the gods]. He burns paper that is splattered with rubber.

3. *The Specter Called "Human Bundle of Ashes"* (*Florentine Codex,* IV/V, 177)

Also the "Human Bundle of Ashes" was an omen; it served people as an omen. Thus was it said, "It is in all the same as Tezcatlipoca's disguise, his transfiguration, his self-manifestation."

When it used to be seen, it just went rolling, went whining, went billowing. The one who saw it was forewarned that he would soon die, perhaps in battle, perhaps just at home [i.e., not in battle], or perhaps that something evil would come upon him [*lit,* it will cause itself to meet him], would fall upon him.

He who was not stronghearted, who was not bravehearted, who was just a cowardly person, if he saw it, just departed from its presence, ran away. There it appalled him; it stunned him, whereby he would quickly die, or something evil would befall him.

But he who was really bravehearted, who was called a "war hellion," set himself for it, decked himself out for it, prepared himself for it. Thereupon thus he said to himself that at night he would search for a specter. He walked everywhere; he went following every roadway; he walked at night; he went seeking it in case something might somewhere show itself to him, in order that he might request its gift, its favor, thorns.

And if it showed itself to him thus while he was seeking it, he attacked it, he seized it firmly, he hung onto it. He no longer let it go. He tried to get it to talk. He said to it, "Who are you, my buddy? Address me. It is not that you will not speak. I indeed caught you. I will not let you go." For a long time he continued trying to get it to talk.

At the time when it spoke to him, when it answered him, if he had already annoyed it, or if it perhaps was near dawn, or if he was causing it to be abroad at dawn, it said to him, "Let me go. You are already hurting me. What your heart desires, I will give to you."

"What will you give me?"

It said to him, "Behold [*lit,* here it is]. I give you one thorn."

"I am not willing. I do not receive it."

"What shall I do?"

It offered to give him [*lit,* it gives them to him] two, three, four. He did not at all let it go for that. Then, when he had answered back firmly, when he had reasserted his refusal [*lit,* when he had wiped all doubt from its mind], then it said to him, "I give you all wealth. You will be famed on earth." Then he let it go; indeed he had seen what his heart is seeking—for that he had lived sighing, he had lived in torment.

4. *The Net Landers* (*Florentine Codex,* X, 181–183)

The name of the Matlatzincas comes from their manner of working. When they shell maize, they just put it into a net and just beat it. And when they used to carry something (on their backs), they did not use a sack. They also just put shelled corn in a net, which is called a "straw-sling." They carry pine needles in the bottom, they line the base with them (~ they form a base with them).

Even more are they called "Matlatzincas" also because they are quite skilled with the sling. The young boys are forever going around carrying slings. Just as the Chichimecs always go carrying bows, they [the Matlatzincas] also always go carrying slings. They always go hurling rocks at things with them. Even more, however, are they called "Matlatzincas" because when they made an offering of a human, a commoner, they used to kill him in the presence of the devil's image; [but] they did not kill him with any instrument [*lit,* with something]; they just squeezed him in a net.

Also their name is "Cuacuatas": in the singular [*lit,* a single one], "Cuatatl," in the plural [*lit,* many], "Cuacuatas." They are named "Cuatatl" because they always go around carrying slings, always go around with a sling tied about the head. *Cua-* means "head"; *tatl* means "sling"; thus it means "head-sling owner," or it means *cuate,* or *cuatetl,* "their heads are like stone." It means "his head is of stone."

The home, the land, of these Cuacuatas, which is a place called Matlatzinco, is very cold. Therefore these Cuacuatas are also very strong, robust, hard, and sinewy. And also because they use slings that wound people [*lit,* they bite people] from afar, therefore they really also did not make things calm either in peace [*lit,* in the land] or in war. And of someone who is presumptuous or frequently disrespectful, it is said "he is called 'Cuatatl,'" and it is said "he is like a Cuata."

Good wine, good pulque, which is very strong [*lit,* it is very filled with breath] and therefore quickly potent [*lit,* it has gone out on someone], quickly inebriating [*lit,* it has made someone drunk], and quickly deranging [*lit,* it has destroyed people], also is called "Cuatatl." It is said, "This is really *cuatatl;* it tastes really *cuatatl.*"

Furthermore, the Matlatzincas are called "Tolohqueh." In the singular [*lit*, a single one] "Toloh," in the plural [*lit*, many] "Tolohqueh." It is taken from their mountain that is there. It is said its name is Tolohtzin or Toloh Tepetl. Some say—however also the Tolohqueh say—that the city is Tolohcan, and Tolohqueh the people, because reeds [*tōlin*] grow in abundance there.

These Tolohqueh, whose other name is Matlatzincas, speak a foreign tongue [*lit*, they mumble], but there are also Nahuatl speakers. But some [of these] stutter their words when they pronounce them. In their language there is the letter "R."

Nothing grows upon the land of these Cuacuatas. There is only maize, beans, and amaranth. There are no chili peppers, no salt. The main foods of these are tamales and beans. Also their main drink is fruit *atole*. Popcorn grows well there on their homeland. Their clothing, their capes were of maguey fiber. They had maguey-fiber capes [*lit*, their maguey fiber capes existed]. They had maguey-fiber breechcloths [*lit*, their maguey-fiber breechcloths existed]. These also busy themselves with, and amuse themselves with, bewitching people and casting spells on people.

The name of the god of the Tolohqueh is Coltzin (i.e., Honorable Grandfather). There were many ways whereby they used to honor him. No one else was involved. They did not advertise it among others. They celebrated the feast day with no outside participation [*lit*, apart ~ separately]. Neither the Mexihcas nor the Tepanecs helped them.

When they used to sacrifice a human being, they just squeezed the poor commoner in a net. They placed him in a net. They wrung it. His arms, the head of his haunch bones, his ribs, protruded in various places from the net. There also the blood sprinkled abundantly forth.

5. *An Omen of the Coming of the Spaniards* (*Florentine Codex*, XII, 3)

Once the waterfolk were seining for fish, or perhaps using nets. They caught a gray bird, which resembled a crane. Immediately they went to show it to Moteuczomah at the *calmecac* at Tlillan. The sun was declining, but is was still day. On its head there was something like a mirror, circular, spiral-shaped, and as if it had the illusion of depth [*lit*, it stood pierced]. There the sky appeared, the stars, the fire drill [Castor and Pollux]. And Moteuczomah was very impressed with it as an omen when he saw the stars and the fire drill. And when he looked a second time at the bird's head he now further saw what looked like some people coming trampling one another, coming spilling along, coming along decked out for war; deer were bearing them. And immediately he summoned the soothsayers and the wisemen. He said to them, "You do not know what I have seen—it is as if some people are coming trampling one another." And they were about to answer him, but when they saw it, it disappeared. They were not able to say anything.

6. *First Contact with the Spaniards* (*Florentine Codex,* XII, 5–6)

And when the ones who came to the ocean shore were seen, and when they continued to remain aboard ship, then the Cuetlaxtec, Pinotl, an important steward, went of his own free will. He carried a few other stewards: the steward at Mictlan Cuauhtlah (i.e., the forest at Mictlan), Yaotzin; the third was the steward at Teocinyohcan, whose name was Teocinyacatl; the fourth was Cuitlalpihtoc, who was just a leader living at Tetlan [*lit,* who was a dweller at Tetlan]; the fifth was Tentlil, also just a leader.

Only these were the ones who went to see them, just as if they were going in order to sell them something. In this fashion did they go in order to see them in disguise, in this fashion they went in order to consider them: they went in order to give them costly capes, which were exquisitely finished; even among them were the capes of Moteuczomah, which no other person can wear—they are strictly his private property, his very birthright.

It was in a boat that they went when they went in order to see them. When they did this thus, Pinotzin said, "Let's beware of lying to the lord Moteuczomah. It is indeed in war that you have lived [i.e., you have lived in danger before]. Let's just go; let's go in order to die, in order that he will hear it quite straight." (Moteuczomah was his name as a lord, and his regal title was Tlacateuctli.)

Then, thereafter, they went out upon the water [*lit,* to the interior of the water]. They entered the boat. They let themselves be carried by the current. The waterfolk rowed them.

When they drew near the Spaniards, then in their presence they made obeisance [*lit,* they ate earth] at the prow of the boat, since they thought that it was Quetzalcoatl Topiltzin [*lit,* Our Prince] who had come to arrive.

The Spaniards called to them, saying to them, "Who are you? Where have you come from? Where is your home?"

Immediately they said, "It is indeed from Mexihco that we have come."

They answered back, "If it is true that you are Mexihcas, what is the name of the king in Mexihco?"

They said to them, "Our lords, his name is indeed Moteuczomah."

Immediately thereafter they gave them all the things that they carried: costly capes like those that are here mentioned: the one with the sun design [*lit,* covered with suns], the turquoise knotted one, the one with the jar design, the one with the paint-decorated eagle design, the one with the snake-mask design, the one with the wind-jewel design, the one with the turkey-blood design, or perhaps the one with the water-vortex design, and the one with the mirror-smoke design.

When these were all the things which they gave them, they [the Spaniards—ambiguity of reference is avoided in the Nahuatl by the contrast of *huāl-* (referring to the Mexihcas) and *on-* (referring to the Spaniards)] gave them [jewels] in return, they gave them jewels that were green and yellow, that were as if they resembled amber.

And when they [the Spaniards] took them, when they saw them, they were amazed.

And therewith they ordered them, saying to them, "Go. We are now going again to Castile. We will not tarry in coming to arrive at Mexihco." Immediately thereafter they went.

Immediately thereafter also they [the Indians] came, they returned. And when they came out on dry land, they immediately came straight to Mexihco. Every day and every night they walked in order to come and advise Moteuczomah, they came to tell to him, they came to inform him of the true accuracy of it. Their goods that they had gone to take came being pampered.

And immediately thereafter they advised him, "Our lord, our beloved child, kill us [*lit,* hide us (H)]. Behold what we have seen. Behold what we have done. There your elders [*lit,* your grandfathers] have indeed guarded things for you along the ocean front [*lit,* at the face of the ocean]. We indeed went to see our lords, the gods, in the midst of the water. We went to give them all of your honorable capes. And behold their honorable property that they gave us. They said, 'If it is true that you have come from Mexihco, behold what you will give to the king Moteuczomah. By it he will know us.'"

They thus said to him all as they said it to them in the middle of the water.

And Moteuczomah said to them, "You have suffered hardship, you have accomplished with effort. Rest. I have indeed looked in secret. No one will say anything; no one will utter anything; no one will let a word slip; no one will let a word fall; no one will mention it. You are to keep it strictly to yourselves [*lit,* it is strictly within you]."

7. *The Destruction of Cholollan [now called Cholula] (Florentine Codex, XII, 29)*

And the Tlaxcaltecs and the Chololtecs formerly had contended against one another, had looked at one another with anger, had looked at one another with hatred, had hated one another; they used to despise one another, could nowhere get along with one another. Because of this, they [the Tlaxcaltecs] incited them [the Spaniards] so that they would do them [the Chololtecs] evil. They said to them, "The Chololtec is indeed very evil; he is indeed our enemy. He is strong like the Mexihca. He is indeed a friend of the Mexihca (~ The Mexihca is indeed his friend)."

When the Spaniards heard this, immediately thereafter they went to Cholollan. They carried the Tlaxcaltecs and the Cempohualtecs. They went girded for war. When they had arrived [*lit,* they had gone to arrive], immediately thereafter people were summoned [*lit,* people summon people], people were shouted for [*lit,* people shout for people], so that all would come—the princes, the kings, the leaders, the warriors, and the commoners. All crowded together in the temple courtyard. And when all had assembled, then they closed up the entrances, all the places where people enter.

Immediately thereafter people were speared, were killed, were beaten. The Chololtecs had suspected nothing. They met the Spaniards without arrows and without shields. It was as if they were killed treacherously; havoc was just caused to be wreaked upon people; people were just caused to be killed treacherously. The Tlaxcaltecs indeed truly just incited them against people.

And regarding everything that was happening, they used to transmit a full report [*mochi . . . in tlahtōlli: lit,* all . . . words ~ every word] to Moteuczomah, they used to tell it [a full report] to him; they used to cause him to hear it [a full report]. And the messengers—as soon as they arrived, they started off again [*lit,* all arrived, all started off], and they just continued to come back; at no time lay silent the reports [*lit,* the words] that he heard, [the reports] that he was caused to hear. And every commoner [*lit,* every person who was a commoner] just went around disturbed; it was very frequently that the people were upset. It was as if there was an earthquake, as if the earth trembled, just as if everything was reeling; all were terrified.

And when all had died in Cholollan, then they [the Spaniards] began in order to come on to Mexihco. They came bunched together, they came in a mass, they came stirring up the dust. Their metal staffs, their metal bat staffs were as if everything was glistening. And their metal swords were as if water was bobbing along; their metal shirts and their metal helmets were as if everything rattled. And some came protecting themselves encased in iron [*lit,* with quite everything of iron], they came having become iron, they came glittering. Therefore they came being much respected. Therefore they (H) came causing much terror. Therefore they were seen with much fear. Therefore they were respected greatly.

And their dogs came leading the way, they came guiding them, they came standing out in front of them, they came spread out in front of them; they came continually panting; drivel came constantly hanging [from their mouths].

8. *Sorcerers against the Spaniards* (*Florentine Codex,* XII, 21–22)

Then at that time Moteuczomah sent out messengers; the people he sent were all those who were evil persons—the seers and shamans. And therewith he sent out the chieftains, the strong ones, and the braves who would supervise all the edibles that would be necessary to the Spaniards: the turkey, the turkey eggs, and the white tortillas, and whatever they might request, and that with which their hearts could be satisfied. They were to observe them well.

He sent captives; thereby he got prepared in case they would drink their blood. And the messengers did it thus. And when they [the Spaniards] saw it, they were very disgusted, they spit again and again, they clinched their eyes shut, they blinked repeatedly, they repeatedly shook their heads. And the food which they sprinkled with blood, which they bloodied, revolted them, nauseated them, because the blood was reeking strongly.

And the reason Moteuczomah did it thus was that he thought they were gods; he considered them gods; he believed they were gods. Therefore they were called, therefore they were named "gods who come from heaven." And the black ones were called "blacks of gods" (~ "divine blacks"). . . .

And it is said that Moteuczomah sent the shamans and the seers to see of what nature they were, and if perhaps they could bring them under demonic influence, hex them, if perhaps they could cast a spell on them, bewitch them, or if perhaps they would exorcise them by means of something, or if perhaps they would conjure them by means of demoniacal words, so that perhaps they would take sick and die, or perhaps by this they would turn back.

And when they did their work and their commands upon the Spaniards, they were absolutely powerless, they were able to do nothing.

Immediately afterwards they abruptly came back, came to confer with Moteuczomah. "They are such, they are so strong, we are not equals of any [of them]. We are as nothing."

9. *The Spaniards Flee from Tenochtitlan* (*Florentine Codex,* XII, 65–67)

And when night came, when midnight arrived, immediately thereupon the Spaniards who had crowded together left, and therewith every single Tlaxcaltec. The Spanish went in the lead, and the Tlaxcaltecs went following behind, they went pressing from behind, as if they went serving as their walls [*lit,* they go having become their walls], their rearguard. They went carrying wooden platforms; they went placing them over the canals over which they went crossing.

At that time it was drizzling, it was sprinkling, it was raining slightly. The canals over which they crossed were several . . . at Tecpantzinco, Tzapotlah, and Atenchicalco. And when they went to arrive at Mixcoatechialtitlan, the fourth canal, then the ones who were departing were seen. A woman fetching water saw them. Immediately thereupon she shouted, she said, "Mexihcas, come running! Already they are leaving; already your enemies are slipping out [*lit,* they are leaving in disguise ~ in stealth]!" Immediately another person [*lit,* also one person] shouted from the top of [the pyramid of] Huitzilopochtli. His shout spread well over people. Every person heard it. He said, "Braves, Mexihcas, your enemies are already going out! Let all hasten here with war canoes and upon the roads!"

And when he was heard, immediately thereupon all made an outcry; immediately thereupon all broke forth. The owners of war canoes sped. They paddled vigorously. They collided with one another in boats. They went colliding with each other in boats. They went cautiously to Mictlantonco and Macuilcuitlapilco. And it was from both sides that the war canoes met together against them. The war canoes of the Tenochcas and the war canoes of the Tlatilolcas converged upon them. And some went on foot; they went straight to Nonoalco; they went going toward Tlacopan [now called Tacuba]; they went to head them off.

Immediately thereupon the war-canoe owners hurled barbed arrows upon the Spaniards. It was from both sides, on both sides, that the barbed arrows came falling. And the Spaniards also shot arrows at the Mexihcas; they shot them with metal arrows and guns. There was dying on both sides. The Spaniards and Tlaxcaltecs were pierced with arrows. The Mexihcas were pierced with arrows. And when the Spaniards arrived at Tlaltecayoacan, where the Toltec canal is, it was as if they plummeted down, plunged headlong down. All fell there. The Tlaxcaltecs, the Tliliuhqui Tepec people and the Spaniards and the horses and a few women scattered down. The canal became quite filled thereby; thereby it became quite filled to the brim. And the ones who went in the rear got out, crossed over right on the people, right over bodies [*lit,* flesh].

And when they went to arrive at Petlacalco, where still another canal stood, it was just quietly, calmly, softly, quite softly that they left over a wooden bridge. There they went to recuperate; there they caught their breath; there they restored their strength [*lit,* they arose as men].

And when they went to arrive at Popotlan, dawn came, it became light. Already they [the Mexihcas] came attacking; they went joining one another from afar. And immediately thereupon the Mexihcas went shouting war cries against them, they went bunching them up, they went standing against them. They went capturing Tlaxcaltecs, and the Spaniards went along dying. But also the Mexihcas and Tlatilolcas were being killed. People went dying on both sides. The ones who followed them chased them from Tlacopan. And when they went chasing them from Tliliuhcan, from

Xocotl Iihiohuihcan, it was there in Xoxocotlah that Chimalpopoca, Moteuczomah's son, died in battle. At the time when they went in order to leave, he lay struck with a barbed spear and lay beaten. Also it was right there that Tlaltecatzin died, the lord of the Tepanecs, who was leading the Spaniards, who went misleading them, who went misdirecting them, who went putting them on the wrong road, who went leading them off the track, who went leading them astray.

Immediately thereafter they crossed over the Tepzolatl, a small stream. They crossed over, they forded across there at Tepzolac. Then they climbed to Acuehco. They went to settle down at Otoncalpolco; the courtyard was surrounded with a palisade; it was walled with wood. There they rested; there each rested. And there they refreshed themselves, they caught their breath, they recovered their breath. There they recuperated. There the guide from Teocalhueyacan came to meet them.

10. *A Brief History of the Conquest* (*Florentine Codex,* VIII, 21–22)

In the year 1519, when Captain Don Hernando Cortés came to sally forth, very many were the boats which came in which the Spaniards who had sallied forth to war traveled [*lit,* they came along being]. And when Moteuczomah found out about it, immediately he sent messengers. His messengers went, and the greetings [i.e., gifts of greeting] that they carried were very many and the goods were very costly.

And they thought that indeed he was Quetzalcoatl who had come. And when they arrived [*lit,* they went to arrive], then they gave him, Captain Don Hernando Cortés, all the greetings [gifts] that they carried.

And after the Spaniards came inland [*lit,* they came entering], then the Otomis [vassal warriors] of the Tlaxcaltecs went to meet them in war. The ones who thereby fought against and made war on the Spaniards were not just few in number, they were very many. And all of the Otomis [warriors] of the Tlaxcaltecs died. The Spaniards killed them. Therefore the Tlaxcaltecs became very frightened, and they, the Tlaxcaltecs, immediately sent messages; they went to give them food and everything that was necessary to them. And therewith they went greeting them happily, therewith they carried them there to their homeland, Tlaxcallan.

And it was for just a few days that the Spaniards sat down there and rested. And they, the Spaniards, immediately went to Cholollan. There they killed many Chololtecs.

And at that time, when Moteuczomah heard about it, he became very afraid; and with him all the Tenochcas became very afraid. Therefore Moteuczomah again sent messengers. Those whom he sent, the lords and princes, went to meet Captain Don Hernando Cortés; very much was the gold which they carried. And it was there between Popoca Tepetl and Iztac Tepetl [now called Iztaccihuatl], at a place called Ithualco, that they went to meet him. There they conversed. One of Moteuczomah's elders and they gave him his words [of welcome]. Therewith they gave him all their gifts of greeting [*lit,* means of greeting people], their gifts of salutation [*lit,* their means of approaching people], the gold and some other things.

And he just came straight here to Mexihco. When he, Don Hernando Cortés, arrived [*lit,* he came to arrive], he just came outfitted for war. And as for Moteuczomah, it was there at the edge of the houses, at Xolohco, that he went to meet him. He just went to meet him happily. And he prayed to and greeted Captain Don Hernando Cortés. Then he carried him to a large palace. There all the Spaniards settled.

And several days later, the captain tied Moteuczomah up.

And when word arrived [*lit,* it came to arrive] from there on the coast that another group of Spaniards had arrived, the captain went to meet them. He carried a number of Spaniards and natives [*lit,* people from here]. And he went leaving Don Pedro Alvarado here, and with him some other Spaniards who were guarding things at the palace.

And when Huitzilopochtli's day arrived [*lit,* it went out], Don Pedro Alvarado and the Spaniards who were under him killed many of the Mexihcas who were celebrating Huitzilopochtli's festival. Because of this the war began.

And when the captain returned from there on the coast, he brought many Spaniards. The Mexihcas did not stop [*lit,* they did not cause themselves to leave things] on that account. They caused the war to quicken.

And in the year 1520, at that time Moteuczomah died. And the Spaniards left; they went to Tlaxcallan. And a great sickness happened here in Mexihco; all became sick with smallpox. And very many of the natives died.

In the year 1521, the Spaniards came again. They settled there at Tetzcohco. They fought the Mexihcas for a long time, conquered them, fought them.

In the year 1522, the Mexihcas, who had scattered, who had collapsed because of the war, came together again and settled down together.